Macmillan/McGraw-Hill Edition

McGRAW-HILL READING

McGraw-Hill
School Division

New York   Farmington

Contributors

The Princeton Review, Time Magazine

The Princeton Review is not
affiliated with Princeton
University or ETS.

McGraw-Hill School Division

A Division of The McGraw·Hill Companies

McGraw-Hill School Division
Two Penn Plaza
New York, New York 10121

Printed in the United States of America

ISBN 0-02-184745-2/K, U.5

2 3 4 5 6 7 8 9 043/073 04 03 02 01 00 99

McGraw-Hill
School Division

New York   Farmington

McGraw-Hill Reading
Authors
Make the Difference...

Dr. James Flood

Ms. Angela Shelf Medearis

Dr. Jan E. Hasbrouck

Dr. Scott Paris

Dr. James V. Hoffman

Dr. Steven Stahl

Dr. Diane Lapp

Dr. Josefina Villamil Tinajero

Dr. Karen D. Wood

Contributing
Authors

Dr. Barbara Coulter

Ms. Frankie Dungan

Dr. Joseph B. Rubin

Dr. Carl B. Smith

Dr. Shirley Wright

Part 1
START TOGETHER

Focus on Reading and Skills

All students start with the SAME:

- Read Aloud
- Pretaught Skills
  Phonics
  Comprehension
- Build Background
- Selection Vocabulary

...Never hold a child back. Never leave a child behind.

Part 2
MEET INDIVIDUAL NEEDS

Read the Literature

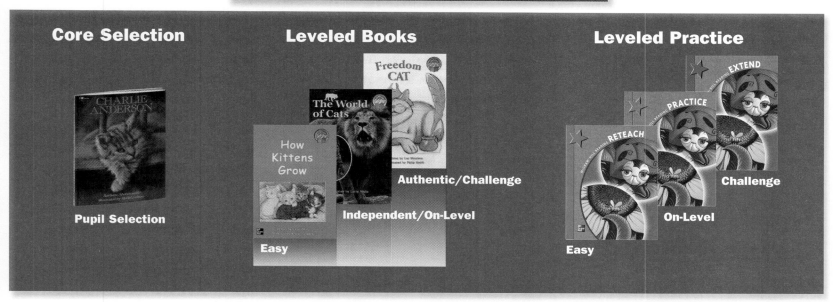

Core Selection

Pupil Selection

Leveled Books

Easy

Independent/On-Level

Authentic/Challenge

Leveled Practice

Easy

On-Level

Challenge

Examples Taken From Grade 2

Part 3
FINISH TOGETHER

Build Skills

All students finish with the SAME:

- Phonics
- Comprehension
- Vocabulary
- Study Skills
- Assessment

v

McGraw-Hill Reading Applying the Research

Phonological Awareness

Phonological awareness is the ability to hear the sounds in spoken language. It includes the ability to separate spoken words into discrete sounds as well as the ability to blend sounds together to make words. A child with good phonological awareness can identify rhyming words, hear the separate syllables in a word, separate the first sound in a word (onset) from the rest of the word (rime), and blend sounds together to make words.

Recent research findings have strongly concluded that children with good phonological awareness skills are more likely to learn to read well. These skills can be improved through systematic, explicit instruction involving auditory practice. McGraw-Hill Reading develops these key skills by providing an explicit Phonological Awareness lesson in every selection at grades K-2. Motivating activities such as blending, segmenting, and rhyming help to develop children's awareness of the sounds in our language.

Guided Instruction/ Guided Reading

Research on reading shows that guided instruction enables students to develop as independent, strategic readers. The *reciprocal-teaching model* of Anne-Marie Palincsar encourages teachers to model strategic-thinking, questioning, clarifying, and problem-solving strategies for students as students read together with the teacher. In McGraw-Hill Reading, guided instruction for all Pupil Edition selections incorporates the Palincsar model by providing interactive questioning prompts. The *guided-reading model* of Gay Su Pinnell is also incorporated into the McGraw-Hill Reading program. Through the guided-reading lessons provided for the leveled books offered with the program, teachers can work with small groups of students of different ability levels, closely observing them as they read and providing support specific to their needs.

By adapting instruction to include successful models of teaching and the appropriate materials to deliver instruction, McGraw-Hill Reading enables teachers to offer the appropriate type of instruction for all students in the classroom.

Phonics

Our language system uses an alphabetic code to communicate meaning from writing. Phonics involves learning the phonemes or sounds that letters make and the symbols or letters that represent those sounds. Children learn to blend the sounds of letters to decode unknown or unfamiliar words. The goal of good phonics instruction is to enable students to read words accurately and automatically.

Research has clearly identified the critical role of phonics in the ability of readers to read fluently and with good understanding, as well as to write and spell. Effective phonics instruction requires carefully sequenced lessons that teach the sounds of letters and how to use these sounds to read words. The McGraw-Hill program provides daily explicit and systematic phonics instruction to teach the letter sounds and blending. There are three explicit Phonics and Decoding lessons for every selection. Daily Phonics Routines are provided for quick reinforcement, in addition to activities in the Phonics Workbook and technology components. This combination of direct skills instruction and applied practice leads to reading success.

Curriculum Connections

As in the child's real-world environment, boundaries between disciplines must be dissolved. Recent research emphasizes the need to make connections between and across subject areas. McGraw-Hill Reading is committed to this approach. Each reading selection offers activities that tie in with social studies, language arts, geography, science, mathematics, art, music, health, and physical education. The program threads numerous research and inquiry activities that encourage the child to use the library and the Internet to seek out information. Reading and language skills are applied to a variety of genres, balancing fiction and nonfiction.

Integrated Language Arts

Success in developing communication skills is greatly enhanced by integrating the language arts in connected and purposeful ways. This allows students to understand the need for proper writing, grammar, and spelling. McGraw-Hill Reading sets the stage for meaningful learning. Each week a full writing-process lesson is provided. This lesson is supported by a 5-day spelling plan, emphasizing spelling patterns and spelling rules, and a 5-day grammar plan, focusing on proper grammar, mechanics, and usage.

Meeting Individual Needs

Every classroom is a microcosm of a world composed of diverse individuals with unique needs and abilities. Research points out that such needs must be addressed with frequent intensive opportunities to learn with engaging materials. McGraw-Hill Reading makes reading a successful experience for every child by providing a rich collection of leveled books for easy, independent, and challenging reading. Leveled practice is provided in Reteach, Practice, and Extend skills books. To address various learning styles and language needs, the program offers alternative teaching strategies, prevention/intervention techniques, language support activities, and ESL teaching suggestions.

Assessment

Frequent assessment in the classroom makes it easier for teachers to identify problems and to find remedies for them. McGraw-Hill Reading makes assessment an important component of instruction. Formal and informal opportunities are a part of each lesson. Minilessons, prevention/intervention strategies, and informal checklists, as well as student self-assessments, provide many informal assessment opportunities. Formal assessments, such as weekly selection tests and criterion-referenced unit tests, help to monitor students' knowledge of important skills and concepts. McGraw-Hill Reading also addresses how to adapt instruction based on student performance with resources such as the Alternate Teaching Strategies. Weekly lessons on test preparation, including test preparation practice books, help students to transfer skills to new contexts and to become better test takers.

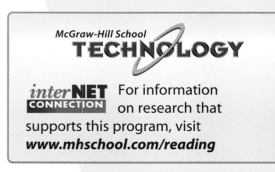

McGraw-Hill School
TECHNOLOGY

interNET CONNECTION For information on research that supports this program, visit **www.mhschool.com/reading**

McGraw-Hill Reading

Theme Chart

MULTI-AGE Classroom

Using the same global themes at each grade level facilitates the use of materials in multi-age classrooms.

GRADE LEVEL	Experience Experiences can tell us about ourselves and our world.	Connections Making connections develops new understandings.
Kindergarten	**My World** We learn a lot from all the things we see and do at home and in school.	**All Kinds of Friends** When we work and play together, we learn more about ourselves.
Subtheme 1	At Home	Working Together
Subtheme 2	School Days	Playing Together
1	**Day by Day** Each day brings new experiences.	**Together Is Better** We like to share ideas and experiences with others.
2	**What's New?** With each day, we learn something new.	**Just Between Us** Family and friends help us see the world in new ways.
3	**Great Adventures** Life is made up of big and small experiences.	**Nature Links** Nature can give us new ideas.
4	**Reflections** Stories let us share the experiences of others.	**Something in Common** Sharing ideas can lead to meaningful cooperation.
5	**Time of My Life** We sometimes find memorable experiences in unexpected places.	**Building Bridges** Knowing what we have in common helps us appreciate our differences.
6	**Pathways** Reflecting on life's experiences can lead to new understandings.	**A Common Thread** A look beneath the surface may uncover hidden connections.

Themes: Kindergarten – Grade 6

Six Units IN EVERY GRADE

Expression	Inquiry	Problem Solving	Making Decisions
There are many styles and forms for expressing ourselves.	By exploring and asking questions, we make discoveries.	Analyzing information can help us solve problems.	Using what we know helps us evaluate situations.
Time to Shine We can use our ideas and our imagination to do many wonderful things.	**I Wonder** We can make discoveries about the wonders of nature in our own backyard.	**Let's Work It Out** Working as part of a team can help me find a way to solve problems.	**Choices** We can make many good choices and decisions every day.
Great Ideas	In My Backyard	Try and Try Again	Good Choices
Let's Pretend	Wonders of Nature	Teamwork	Let's Decide
Stories to Tell Each one of us has a different story to tell.	**Let's Find Out!** Looking for answers is an adventure.	**Think About It!** It takes time to solve problems.	**Many Paths** Each decision opens the door to a new path.
Express Yourself We share our ideas in many ways.	**Look Around** There are surprises all around us.	**Figure It Out** We can solve problems by working together.	**Starting Now** Unexpected events can lead to new decisions.
Be Creative! We can all express ourselves in creative, wonderful ways.	**Tell Me More** Looking and listening closely will help us find out the facts.	**Think It Through** Solutions come in many shapes and sizes.	**Turning Points** We make new judgments based on our experiences.
Our Voices We can each use our talents to communicate ideas.	**Just Curious** We can find answers in surprising places.	**Make a Plan** Often we have to think carefully about a problem in order to solve it.	**Sorting It Out** We make decisions that can lead to new ideas and discoveries.
Imagine That The way we express our thoughts and feelings can take different forms.	**Investigate!** We never know where the search for answers might lead us.	**Bright Ideas** Some problems require unusual approaches.	**Crossroads** Decisions cause changes that can enrich our lives.
With Flying Colors Creative people help us see the world from different perspectives.	**Seek and Discover** To make new discoveries, we must observe and explore.	**Brainstorms** We can meet any challenge with determination and ingenuity.	**All Things Considered** Encountering new places and people can help us make decisions.

Let's Work It Out

Working as part of a team can help me find a way to solve problems.

Contents

"Whistling" a poem by *Jack Prelutsky*

Subtheme: Try and Try Again

SKILLS			
Phonics	**Comprehension**	**Vocabulary**	**Grammar**
• **Introduce** Initial /k/k	• **Introduce** Story Structure	• **Introduce** High-Frequency Words: *for*	• **Introduce** Naming Words
• **Introduce** Final /k/ck	• **Review** Story Structure	• **Review** *for, you, me*	
• **Review** /k/k, /k/ck; Blending with Short *a, i, o, u*			

Tom Is Sick

SKILLS			
Phonics	**Comprehension**	**Vocabulary**	**Grammar**
• **Introduce** Initial /g/g	• **Introduce** Summarize	• **Introduce** High-Frequency Words: *he*	• **Review** Naming Words
• **Introduce** Final /g/g	• **Review** Summarize	• **Review** *her, for, is*	
• **Review** /g/g; Blending with Short *a, i, o, u*			

Pug

Unit Planner

Tom Is Sick

Pug

	WEEK 1 Tom Is Sick	**WEEK 2** Pug
📖 **Leveled Books**	Patterned Book: *Just for the Duck*	Patterned Book: *Gus and His Dog*
☑ **Tested Skills**	☑ **Phonics and Decoding** Initial /k/k, 246W–246, 250C–250 Final /k/ck, 248C–248, 250C–250 Blending with Short a, i, o, u, 252C–252, 256C–256 ☑ **Comprehension** Story Structure, 249C–249, 255A–255 ☑ **Vocabulary** High-Frequency Word: *for*, 251C–251 *for, you, me*, 257C–257 ☑ **Beginning Reading Concepts** Naming Words, 247C–247	☑ **Phonics and Decoding** Initial /g/g, 258I–258, 262C–262 Final /g/g, 260C–260, 262C–262 Blending with Short a, i, o, u, 264C–264, 268C–268 ☑ **Comprehension** Summarize 261C–261, 267A–267 ☑ **Vocabulary** High-Frequency Word: *he*, 263C–263 *he, for, is*, 269C–269 ☑ **Beginning Reading Concepts** Naming Words, 259C–259
Language Arts	✏ **Writing:** Letter Formation, 246W–246, 248C–248 Interactive Writing, 258A–258B	✏ **Writing:** Letter Formation, 258I–258, 260C–260 Interactive Writing, 270A–270B

CENTER Activities

		WEEK 1	WEEK 2
Curriculum Connections	Social Studies	Language Arts: Mice In a Row, 247B	Drama: Breakfast Is Served, 265/266D
	Mathematics	Math: 249B	Language Arts: A Dog Story, 269B
	Science	Writing: Pick Up Story, 253/254D	
	Music	Science: Raindrops Are Falling, 257B	
	Art		
	Drama		
	Language Arts		
🖐 **CULTURAL PERSPECTIVES**		Races, 251A	Hats, 259B Pets, 261B Scrolls, 263A

A Pet for Ken

A Big Bug

A Pup and a Cat

WEEK 3 — A Pet for Ken

WEEK 4 — A Big Bug

WEEK 5 — A Pup and a Cat

WEEK 6 — Review, Assessment

Patterned Book: *Meg's Elephant*

Patterned Book: *Bob's Bath*

Self-Selected Reading of Patterned Books

Self-Selected Reading

Week 3

☑ **Phonics and Decoding**
Initial /e/e, 270I–270, 274C–274
Medial /e/e, 272C–272, 274C–274
Blending with Short e, u,
276C–276, 280C–280

☑ **Comprehension**
Story Structure, 273C–273,
279A–279

☑ **Vocabulary**
High-Frequency Word: *she*,
275C–275
she, he, for, is, 281C–281

☑ **Beginning Reading Concepts**
Action Words, 271C–271

Week 4

☑ **Phonics and Decoding**
Initial /b/ b, 282I–282, 288C–288
Final /b/b, 284C–284, 288C–288
Blending with Short a, e, i, o, u,
288C–288, 292C–292

☑ **Comprehension**
Summarize, 285C–285, 291A–291

☑ **Vocabulary**
High-Frequency Word: *has*,
287C–287
has, he, she, me, for, 293C–293

☑ **Beginning Reading Concepts**
Action Words, 283C–283

Week 5

☑ **Phonics and Decoding**
Initial /k/k, /g/g, /b/b, 294I–294,
298C–298
Final /k/ck, /g/g, /b/b, 296C–296,
298C–298
Blending with Short a, e, i, o, u,
300C–300, 304C–304

☑ **Comprehension**
Story Structure, 297C–297
Summarize, 303A–303

☑ **Vocabulary**
High-Frequency Words: *for, he,
she, has*, 299C–299, 305C–305

☑ **Beginning Reading Concepts**
Naming Words and Action Words,
295C–295

Week 6

☑ **Assess Skills**

Phonics and Decoding
Initial /k/k, /g/g, /e/e, /b/b
Final /k/ck, /g/g, /b/b
Medial /e/e
Blending with Short a, e, i, o, u

Comprehension
Story Structure
Summarize

Vocabulary
High-Frequency Words: *for, he, she,
has, for, you, me, is*

Beginning Reading Concepts
Naming Words
Action Words

☑ **Unit 5 Assessment**

☑ **Standardized Test Preparation**

✎ **Writing:** Letter Formation,
270I–270, 272C–272
Interactive Writing, 282A–282B

✎ **Writing:** Letter Formation,
282I–282, 284C–284
Interactive Writing, 294A–294B

✎ **Writing:** Interactive Writing,
306A–306B

Language Arts: Inside-Outside, 271B

Math: 273B

Drama: Dog Care "101," 277/278D

Science: Animals of Africa, 281B

Paper Dolls, 275A

Language Arts: What Animal Am I?
283B

Social Studies: 285B

Art: 287A

Science: Build a Bug, 289/290D

Language Arts: Step-By-Step Bath,
293B

Language Arts: Pick a Letter, 295B

Science: Habitats, 297B

Science: 299A

Social Studies: Friends, 301/302D

Social Studies: Let's Talk It Out, 305B

Unit Resources

LITERATURE

DECODABLE STORIES These four-color stories in the Pupil Edition consist of words containing the phonetic elements that have been taught, as well as the high-frequency words. The stories reinforce the comprehension and concepts of print skills.

LEVELED BOOKS These engaging stories include the high-frequency words and words with the phonetic elements that are being taught. They reinforce the comprehension skills and correlate to the unit themes.

Patterned
- *Just for the Duck*
- *Gus and His Dog*
- *Meg's Elephant*
- *Bob's Bath*

ABC BIG BOOK Children build alphabetic knowledge and letter identification as they enjoy a shared reading of this story that correlates to the theme.
- *Mice Mischief: An Alphabet Story*

LITERATURE BIG BOOKS Shared readings of the highest-quality literature reinforce comprehension skills and introduce children to a variety of genres.
- *Any Kind of Dog*
- *The Enormous Carrot*

READ ALOUDS Traditional folk tales, fables, fairy tales, and stories from around the world can be shared with children as they develop their oral comprehension skills and learn about other cultures.
- *Hare and Tortoise*
- *It Could Always Be Worse*
- *Winter Days in the Big Woods*
- *Winnie the Pooh Gets Stuck*

STUDENT LISTENING LIBRARY
Recordings of the Big Books, Patterned Books, and Unit Opener and Closer Poetry.

SKILLS

PUPIL EDITION Colorful practice pages help you to assess children's progress as they learn and review each skill, including phonics, high-frequency words, readiness, comprehension, and letter formation.

PRACTICE BOOK Practice pages in alternative formats provide additional reinforcement of each skill as well as extra handwriting practice.

BIG BOOK OF PHONICS RHYMES AND POEMS Traditional and contemporary poems emphasize phonics and rhyme and allow children to develop oral comprehension skills.

BIG BOOK OF REAL-LIFE READING This lively big book, which introduces children to important study skills, focuses on environmental print in this unit. The context for the teaching is the Read Aloud selection children have just heard.

WORD BUILDING BOOK
Letter and word cards to utilize phonics and build children's vocabulary. Includes high-frequency word cards.

LANGUAGE SUPPORT BOOK
Parallel teaching and practice activities for children needing language support.

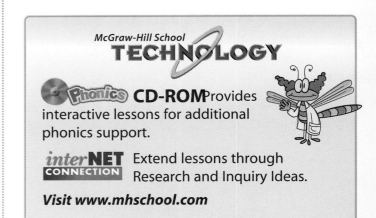

McGraw-Hill School
TECHNOLOGY

Phonics CD-ROM Provides interactive lessons for additional phonics support.

interNET CONNECTION Extend lessons through Research and Inquiry Ideas.

Visit www.mhschool.com

Resources for Meeting Individual Needs

	EASY	ON-LEVEL	CHALLENGE	LANGUAGE SUPPORT

UNIT 5

Tom Is Sick

EASY
Tom Is Sick
Teaching Strategies 246, 247, 248, 249, 250, 251, 252, 255, 256, 257
Alternate Teaching Strategy T24–T27
 **Writing** 258B
 CD-ROM

ON-LEVEL
Tom Is Sick
Teaching Strategies 246–252, 255–257
Alternate Teaching Strategy T24–T27
 **Writing** 258B
Patterned Book *Just for the Duck*
 CD-ROM

CHALLENGE
Patterned Book *Just for the Duck*
Teaching Strategies 246, 247, 248, 249, 250, 251, 252, 255, 256, 257
 **Writing** 258B
 CD-ROM

LANGUAGE SUPPORT
Teaching Strategies 246, 247, 248, 249, 250, 251, 252, 255, 256, 257
Alternate Teaching Strategy T24–T27
 Writing 258B
 CD-ROM

Pug

EASY
Pug
Teaching Strategies 258, 259, 260, 261, 262, 263, 264, 267, 268, 269
Alternate Teaching Strategy T25, T27–T29
Writing 270B
CD-ROM

ON-LEVEL
Pug
Teaching Strategies 258–264, 267–269
Alternate Teaching Strategy T25, T27–T29
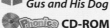 **Writing** 270B
Patterned Book *Gus and His Dog*
CD-ROM

CHALLENGE
Patterned Book *Gus and His Dog*
Teaching Strategies 258, 259, 260, 261, 262, 263, 264, 267, 268, 269
Writing 270B
CD-ROM

LANGUAGE SUPPORT
Teaching Strategies 258, 259, 260, 261, 262, 263, 264, 267, 268, 269
Alternate Teaching Strategy T25, T27–T29
Writing 270B
CD-ROM

A Pet for Ken

EASY
A Pet for Ken
Teaching Strategies 270, 271, 272, 273, 274, 275, 276, 279, 280, 281
Alternate Teaching Strategy T26, T27, T30, T31
Writing 282B
CD-ROM

ON-LEVEL
A Pet for Ken
Teaching Strategies 270–276, 279–281
Alternate Teaching Strategy T26, T27, T30, T31
Writing 282B
Patterned Book *Meg's Elephant*
 CD-ROM

CHALLENGE
Patterned Book *Meg's Elephant*
Teaching Strategies 270, 271, 272, 273, 274, 275, 276, 279, 280, 281
 **Writing** 282B
 CD-ROM

LANGUAGE SUPPORT
Teaching Strategies 270, 271, 272, 273, 274, 275, 276, 279, 280, 281
Alternate Teaching Strategy T26, T27, T30, T31
Writing 282B
 CD-ROM

A Big Bug

EASY
A Big Bug
Teaching Strategies 282, 283, 284, 285, 286, 287, 288, 291, 292, 293
Alternate Teaching Strategy T27, T29, T31, T32
Writing 294B
CD-ROM

ON-LEVEL
A Big Bug
Teaching Strategies 282–288, 291–293
Alternate Teaching Strategy T27, T29, T31, T32
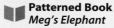 **Writing** 294B
Patterned Book *Bob's Bath*
 CD-ROM

CHALLENGE
Patterned Book *Bob's Bath*
Teaching Strategies 282, 283, 284, 285, 286, 287, 288, 291, 292, 293
 **Writing** 294B
 CD-ROM

LANGUAGE SUPPORT
Teaching Strategies 282, 283, 284, 285, 286, 287, 288, 291, 292, 293
Alternate Teaching Strategy T27, T29, T31, T32
 Writing 294B
CD-ROM

A Pup and a Cat

EASY
A Pup and a Cat
Teaching Strategies 294, 295, 296, 297, 298, 299, 300, 303, 304, 305
Alternate Teaching Strategy T24–T32
Writing 306B
CD-ROM

ON-LEVEL
A Pup and a Cat
Teaching Strategies 294–300, 303–305
Alternate Teaching Strategy T24–T32
Writing 306B
Patterned Book *Patterned Book Choice*
CD-ROM

CHALLENGE
Patterned Book *Patterned Book Choice*
Teaching Strategies 294, 295, 296, 297, 298, 299, 300, 303, 304, 305
 **Writing** 306B
 CD-ROM

LANGUAGE SUPPORT
Teaching Strategies 294, 295, 296, 297, 298, 299, 300, 303, 304, 305
Alternate Teaching Strategy T24–T32
Writing 306B
 CD-ROM

INFORMAL

Informal Assessment

- Phonics and Decoding, 246W, 248C, 250C, 252C, 256C, 258I, 260C, 262C, 264C, 268C, 270I, 272C, 274C, 276C, 280C, 282I, 284C, 286C, 288C, 292C, 294I, 296C, 298C, 300C, 304C
- Comprehension, 247B, 249B, 249C, 255A, 257A, 259B, 261B, 261C, 267A, 269A, 271B, 273B, 273C, 279A, 281A, 283B, 285B, 285C, 291A, 293A, 295B, 297B, 297C, 303A, 305A
- High-Frequency Words, 251C, 257C, 263C, 269C, 275C, 281C, 287C, 293C, 299C, 305C
- Beginning Reading Concepts, 247C, 259C, 271C, 283C, 295C

Performance Assessment

- Research and Inquiry Project, 246O, 306C
- Interactive Writing, 258A–258B, 270A–270B, 282A–282B, 294A–294B, 306A–306B
- Listening, Speaking, Viewing Activities, 246U, 248A, 250A, 252A, 256A, 258B, 258G, 260A, 262A, 264A, 268A, 270B, 270G, 272A, 274A, 276A, 280A, 282B, 282G, 284A, 286A, 288A, 292A, 294B, 294G, 296A, 298A, 300A, 304A, 306B
- Portfolio
  Writing, 258A, 270A, 282A, 294A, 306A
  Cross-Curricular Activities, 247B, 249B, 251B, 253/254D, 257B, 259B, 261B, 263B, 265/266D, 269B, 271B, 273B, 275B, 277/278D, 281B, 283B, 285B, 287B, 289/290D, 293B, 295B, 297B, 299B, 301/302D, 305B

Practice

- **Phonics and Decoding**
  /k/k, 246, 250, 294, 298
  /k/ck, 248, 250, 296, 298
  /g/g, 258, 260, 262, 294, 296, 298
  /e/e, 270, 272, 274
  /b/b, 282, 284, 286, 294, 296, 298
  Blending with Short a, e, i, o, u, 252, 256, 264, 268, 276, 280, 288, 292, 300, 304
- **Comprehension**
  Story Structure, 249, 255, 273, 279, 297
  Summarize, 261, 267, 285, 291, 303
- **High-Frequency Words** for, he, she, has, 251, 257, 263, 269, 275, 281, 287, 293, 299, 305
- **Beginning Reading Concepts**
  247, 259, 271, 283, 295

FORMAL

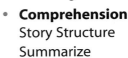

Unit 5 Assessment

- **Phonics and Decoding**
  Initial /k/k
  Final /k/ck
  Initial and Final /g/g
  Initial and Medial /e/e
  Initial and Final /b/b
  Blending with Short a, e, i, o, u
- **Comprehension**
  Story Structure
  Summarize
- **High-Frequency Words**
  for, he, she, has
- **Beginning Reading Concepts**
  Naming Words
  Action Words

Diagnostic/Placement Evaluation

- Individual Reading Inventory
- Running Record
- Phonics and Decoding Inventory
- Grade K Diagnostic/Evaluation
- Grade 1 Diagnostic/Evaluation
- Grade 2 Diagnostic/Evaluation
- Grade 3 Diagnostic/Evaluation

Test Preparation

- Standardized Test Preparation Practice Book

Assessment Checklist

Student .... Grade ....

Teacher ....

	Tom Is Sick	Pug	A Pet for Ken	A Big Bug	A Pup and a Cat	Assessment Summary
LISTENING/SPEAKING						
Participates in oral language experiences						
Listens and speaks to gain knowledge of culture						
Speaks appropriately to audiences for different purposes						
Communicates clearly (gains increasing control of grammar)						
READING						
Demonstrates knowledge of concepts of print						
Uses phonological awareness strategies, including						
• Identifying, segmenting, and combining syllables						
• Producing rhyming words						
• Identifying and isolating initial and final sounds						
Uses letter/sound knowledge, including						
• Applying letter-sound correspondences to begin to read						
• Phonics and Decoding: initial /k/ *K,k;* final /k/ *ck*						
• Phonics and Decoding: initial, final /g/ *G,g*						
• Phonics and Decoding: initial, medial /e/ *E,e*						
• Phonics and Decoding: initial, final /b/ *B,b*						
• Blending with *a, i, o, u, e*						
Develops an extensive vocabulary, including						
• High-frequency words: *for, he, she, has*						
Uses a variety of strategies to comprehend selections						
• Story Structure						
• Summarize Story Events						
Responds to various texts						
Recognizes characteristics of various types of texts						
Conducts research using various sources						
Reads to increase knowledge						
WRITING						
Writes his/her own name						
Writes each letter of the alphabet						
Uses phonological knowledge to write messages						
Gains increasing control of penmanship						
Composes original texts						
Uses writing as a tool for learning and research						

+ Observed   − Not Observed

Unit Opener

Introducing the Theme

Let's Work It Out
Working as part of a team can help me find a way to solve problems.

PRESENT THE THEME Read the theme statement to children. Remind children of a problem that was recently solved by a group. Discuss ways in which the children worked together to find the solution.

READ THE POEM Read the poem "Whistling" aloud. Ask children to identify the problem in the poem.

WHISTLING

Oh, I can laugh and I can
   sing
and I can scream and
   shout,
but when I try to whistle,
the whistle won't come
   out.

I shape my lips the
   proper way,
I make them small and
   round,
but when I blow, just air
   comes out,
there is no whistling
   sound.

But I'll keep trying very
   hard
to whistle loud and clear,
and someday soon I'll
   whistle tunes
for everyone to hear.

Jack Prelutsky

AUDIO Student Listening Library

DISCUSS THE POEM Ask children to tell some of the things the person is doing to solve the problem of being unable to whistle. Invite children to offer more suggestions.

THEME SUMMARY Each lesson relates to the unit theme *Let's Work It Out* as well as to the global theme *Problem Solving*. These thematic links will help children to make connections from their experiences with solving problems as a group to the literature of the unit.

Literature selections presented within the first two lessons are also related to the subtheme *Try and Try Again*. Lead children to see that we often need to try more than once before we solve a problem.

Selections for the third and fourth lessons are more closely tied to the subtheme *Teamwork*. These stories provide examples of friends working together to solve problems.

The fifth lesson gives children the opportunity to reread their favorite literature selections and discuss the main theme of *Let's Work It Out*.

Research *and* Inquiry

Theme Project: "How To Care for a Pet" Book

Have the class choose a pet that they would like to learn how to care for. Have children brainstorm things to do to care for the pet. Then ask each group to choose one thing from the list as a basis for their project.

List What They Know Ask children to talk about the particular aspect of care the group selected. List the facts they provide.

Ask Questions and Identify Resources Have children identify questions they have and create a list of resources, such as veterinarians.

Create a Presentation Have children make a drawing that depicts both the information they already knew and the information they discovered.
inter NET CONNECTION To help children learn more about pet care, visit **www.mhschool.com/reading**.

Center Activities

Setting Up the Centers

Independent Learning Centers will help to reinforce children's skills across all areas of the curriculum. Here's what you will need to help you set up the centers in this unit.

Reading/Language Arts Center

- cut-outs of mice
- drawing paper, pencils
- letter cards, animal cards, alphabet cards
- pictures of inside and outside activities
- teacher-made picture/word cards
- letter grid, counters
- audiocassette player
- Student Listening Library Audiocassette

For suggested activities, see pages 247B, 253/254D, 269B, 271B, 283B, 293B, 295B.

Math Center

- animal cards
- cut-outs of carrots

For suggested activities, see pages 249B, 273B.

Science Center

- cookie sheet, spray bottle
- picture books
- chart paper, markers, paste, scissors
- insect diagram
- cotton balls, egg cartons, pipe cleaners

For suggested activities, see pages 257B, 281B, 289/290D, 297B, 299A.

Social Studies/ Cultural Perspectives Center

- chart paper, markers
- paint, paintbrushes
- magazines, scissors, paste
- string, cardboard, tape
- felt, beads, butcher paper

For suggested activities, see pages 251B, 259B, 261B, 263B, 275B, 285B, 301/302D, 305B.

Art/Drama Center

- cooking props
- stuffed animal (dog), dog-grooming equipment
- construction paper, markers, scissors, paste

For suggested activities, see pages 265/266D, 277/278D, 287B.

Managing the Centers

MANAGEMENT TIP Have a list of a few things children can do when they finish their work at the center. These should be simple activities that do not require a lot of preparation, explanation, or clean-up.

INSTRUCTIONAL TIP As you work with small groups for direct instruction, assign the rest of the class to the various centers to complete work independently.

ASSESSMENT TIP Have children write notes in a "Center Journal" after each center activity they complete. Review journals periodically, asking children to recall center activities.

CLEAN-UP TIP Assign each child a specific clean-up task. Rotate the tasks frequently to allow children to experience a variety of different tasks.

Tom Is Sick

Children will read and listen to a variety of stories about trying more than one solution in order to best solve a problem.

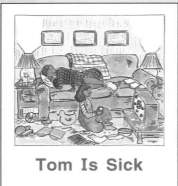

Tom Is Sick

Decodable Story,
pages 253–254 of the
Pupil Edition

Listening
Library
Audiocassette

Patterned Book,
page 257B

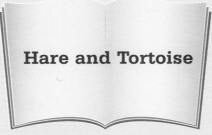

Hare and Tortoise

Teacher Read Aloud,
page 251A

ABC Big Book,
pages 247A–247B

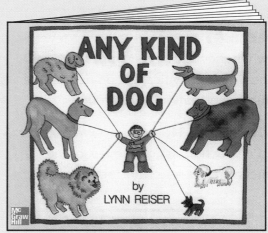

Listening
Library
Audiocassette

Literature Big Book,
pages 249A–249B

**Pupil Edition,
pages 246–257**

**Big Book of Real-Life Reading,
page 32**

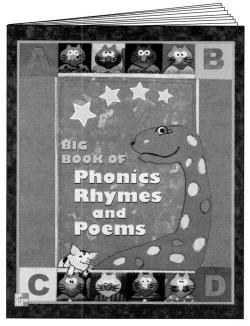

**Big Book of Phonics Rhymes and
Poems, pages 29, 30**

 **Listening
Library
Audiocassette**

ADDITIONAL RESOURCES

**Practice Book,
pages 246–257**

- **Phonics Kit**
- **Language Support Book**
- **Alternate Teaching Strategies,** pp T24–T27

McGraw-Hill School
TECHNOLOGY

Phonics CD-ROM Provides
extra phonics support.

interNET CONNECTION Research & Inquiry Ideas.

Visit www.mhschool.com

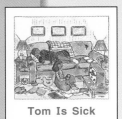

Tom Is Sick

READING AND LANGUAGE ARTS

- **Phonological Awareness**
- **Phonics** *initial /k/k; final /k/ck*
- **Comprehension**
- **Vocabulary**
- **Beginning Reading Concepts**
- **Listening, Speaking, Viewing, Representing**

DAY 1

Focus on Reading Skills

Develop Phonological Awareness, 246U-246V

"Katie's Kangaroo" *Big Book of Phonics Rhymes and Poems*, 29

 **Introduce Initial /k/k**, 246W-246
Practice Book, 246
Phonics/Phonemic Awareness Practice Book

 **CD-ROM**

Read the Literature

Read *Mice Mischief: An Alphabet Story* **Big Book,** 247A-247B
Shared Reading

Build Skills

☑ Naming Words, 247C-247
Practice Book, 247

DAY 2

Focus on Reading Skills

Develop Phonological Awareness, 248A-248B

"Miss Mary Mack" *Big Book of Phonics Rhymes and Poems*, 30

Introduce Initial /k/ck, 248C-248
Practice Book, 248
Phonics/Phonemic Awareness Practice Book

Phonics **CD-ROM**

Read the Literature

Read *Any Kind of Dog* Big Book, 249A-249B
Shared Reading

Build Skills

☑ Story Structure, 249C-249
Practice Book, 249

- **Cross Curriculum**

 Language Arts, 247B

 Math, 249B

- **Writing**

 Writing Prompt: Which mouse did you like best? Tell why.

 Journal Writing, 247B
Letter Formation, 246W

 Writing Prompt: What kind of pet would you like to have? Write about it.

 Journal Writing, 249B
Letter Formation, 248C

DAY 3

Hare and Tortoise

Focus on Reading Skills

Develop Phonological Awareness, 250A–250B

"Katie's Kangaroo" and "Miss Mary Mack" *Big Book of Phonics Rhymes and Poems*, 29-30

Review /k/k,/k/ck, 250C-250
Practice Book, 250
Phonics/Phonemic Awareness Practice Book

 Phonics CD-ROM

Read the Literature

Read "Hare and Tortoise" Teacher Read Aloud, 251A-251B
Shared Reading

Read the Big Book of Real-Life Reading, 32-33
 Maps

Build Skills

 High-Frequency Words: *for*, 251C-251
Practice Book, 251

 Activity Cultural Perspectives, 251A

 Writing Prompt: Have you ever been in a race? Write about how it felt. If you have not been in a race, write about what you think it would be like.

DAY 4

Tom Is Sick

Focus on Reading Skills

Develop Phonological Awareness, 252A–252B

"Pam the Pup"

 Review Blending with Short *a, i, o, u*, 252C-252
Practice Book, 252
Phonics/Phonemic Awareness Practice Book

 Phonics CD-ROM

 Read the Literature

Read "Tom Is Sick" Decodable Story, 253/A-253/254D

 Initial /k/k, Final /k/ck; Blending
 Story Structure
 High--Frequency Words: *for*
 Concepts of Print

Build Skills

 Story Structure, 255A-255
Practice Book, 255

 Activity Writing, 253/254D

 Writing Prompt: Write about a time you helped someone who was sick.

Letter Formation,
Practice Book, 253-254

DAY 5

Tom Is Sick

Just For the Duck

by Anne Miranda
illustrated by Kristen Goeters

Focus on Reading Skills

Develop Phonological Awareness, 256A–256B

"Pam the Pup"

 Review Blending with Short *a, i, o, u*, 256C-256
Practice Book, 256
Phonics/Phonemic Awareness Practice Book

 Phonics CD-ROM

 **Read the Literature**

Reread "Tom Is Sick" Decodable Story, 257A

Read "Just for the Duck" Patterned Book, 257B
Guided Reading
 Initial /k/k, Final /k/ck; Blending
 Story Structure
 High-Frequency Words: *for*
 Concepts of Print

Build Skills

 High-Frequency Words: *for, you, me*, 257C-257
Practice Book, 257

 **Activity** Science, 257B

 Writing Prompt: Write about a time when you had to keep trying to do something before you could get it right.

Interactive Writing, 258A-258B

Develop Phonological Awareness

Listen

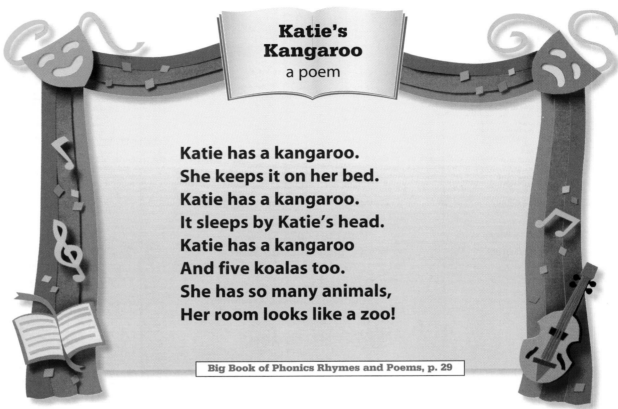

Katie's Kangaroo
a poem

Katie has a kangaroo.
She keeps it on her bed.
Katie has a kangaroo.
It sleeps by Katie's head.
Katie has a kangaroo
And five koalas too.
She has so many animals,
Her room looks like a zoo!

Big Book of Phonics Rhymes and Poems, p. 29

Objective: Hearing and Saying Sentences

LISTEN TO THE POEM FOR INFORMATION

- Read the poem "Katie's Kangaroo" aloud.

- Remind children that a sentence gives a complete thought. Read lines from the poem and ask questions, such as:

  (Line 2) Where does Katie keep her kangaroo?
  (Line 4) Where does the kangaroo sleep?
  (Line 6) How many koalas does Katie have?
  (Line 8) What does Katie's room look like?

- Have children answer the questions using complete sentences.

ASK QUESTIONS

- Have children ask each other questions about the poem. Help them to answer in sentences.

WORDS IN SENTENCES

- Reread line 1 of the poem. Clap and count the words as you read it again.

- Have four children stand up and tell each child to say one word from the line, "Katie has a kangaroo." Point out that there are four children and four words.

- Then repeat the activity for line 2 of the poem.

Objective: Listen for Initial /k/

LISTEN FOR SOUND

- Say the word *Katie*. Emphasize the /k/ sound, and have children say it with you.
- Then say the word *kangaroo* and ask if the words begin with the same sound.

SEGMENTING

- Segment the initial sound of the word *Katie* (K-atie). Have children repeat the segmented word with you.
- Then segment the word *kangaroo*.
- Have children think of other words with the initial /k/ sound and then segment the initial sound of each word.

> k-oala   k-ey   k-eep

PLAY "PASS THE KEY"

- Have children sit in a circle. Give a key to a child and say the word, emphasizing the /k/ sound.
- Explain that you will complete the sentence: *Katie has a ___.* If the word you say begins with /k/, the child passes the key to the next person.

> kite   kettle   kitten   koala

Read Together

From Phonemic Awareness to Phonics

Objective: Identify /k/ K,k

IDENTIFY THE LETTER FOR THE SOUND

- Explain that the letters *K* and *k* stand for the sound /k/. Say the sound, and have children say it with you.

- Display the *Big Book of Phonics Rhymes and Poems*, page 29. Point to the letters in the corner as you identify them. Say the sound with the children.

REREAD THE POEM

- Reread the poem, pointing to each word. Have children join in on the parts that repeat. Say the

words that begin with /k/ in a louder voice.

KEEP A K

- Write the letter *k* on slips of paper and give one to each child. Say words from the poem. If the word begins with /k/, children place the letter face up in front of them.

- If it does not begin with the /k/ sound, have children put the paper face down in front of them.

Katie's Kangaroo

Katie has a kangaroo
She keeps it on her bed.
Katie has a kangaroo.
It sleeps by Katie's head.

Katie has a kangaroo
And five koalas, too.
She has so many animals,
Her room looks like a zoo!

Big Book of Phonics Rhymes and Poems, page 29

246V

OBJECTIVES

Children will:

- identify the letters *K, k*
- identify /k/ *K, k*
- form the letters *K, k*

MATERIALS

- letter cards from the Word Play Book

TEACHING TIP

INSTRUCTIONAL Show children pictures of a *kite* and a *can*. Say both words, and write them on the chalkboard. Hold each picture under its initial word, and have children repeat the word after you. Point out that both words have the same beginning sound but do not begin with the same letter. Say each letter's name as you point to it, and ask children to repeat it.

ALTERNATE TEACHING STRATEGY

INITIAL /k/*k*

For a different approach to teaching this skill, see page T24.

▶ **Visual/Auditory/ Kinesthetic**

Introduce Initial /k/ k

TEACH

Identify /k/ *K, k* Tell children they will learn to write the sound /k/ with the letters *K, k*. Have children say the /k/ sound and write the letters on the chalkboard. Ask if children know any first names that begin with *k*. Write the following names and read them aloud, emphasizing the initial /k/ and underlining the *K: Kim, Ken, Kate, Kevin, Kelly, Kurt*.

Form *K, k* Display letters *K,k* and, with your back to the children, trace large letters *K,k* in the air. Ask children to do the same, pointing out how the forms are similar and how they are different. Have children trace the forms on their letter cards. Give children diamond-shaped paper cutouts, and ask them to color their *kites*. Then have them turn the cutout over and write the letters *K, k* on the reverse side.

PRACTICE

Complete the Pupil Edition Page Read the directions to the children on page 246, and make sure they clearly understand what they are being asked to do. Identify each picture, and complete the first item together. Work through the page with children, or have them complete the page independently.

ASSESS/CLOSE

Identify and Use *K,k* Say the following list of words, and have children wave their *kites* when they hear a word that begins with the sound /k/: *kite, sit, kit, lap, key, king*.

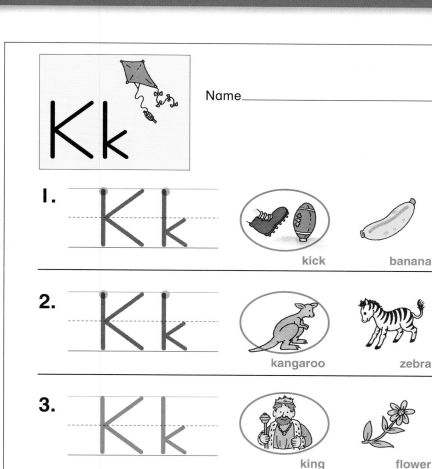

Name

1. Kk

kick   banana   king

2. Kk

kangaroo   zebra   kitten

3. Kk

king   flower   key

4. Kk

kitchen   bread   kite

Write the letters *Kk.* • Say the word that names each picture. • Listen for the sound at the beginning of each word. • Draw a circle around each picture whose name begins with the same sound as *kite.*

McGraw-Hill School Division

246   Unit 5   Introduce Initial /k/k

Pupil Edition, page 246

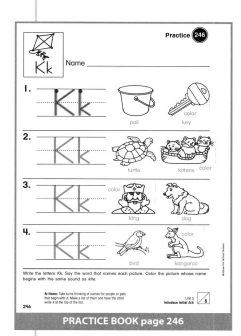

PRACTICE BOOK page 246

Meeting Individual Needs for Phonics

EASY	ON-LEVEL	CHALLENGE	LANGUAGE SUPPORT
Write on the chalkboard the following words that begin with *K,k: Kim, kite, kid, kindergarten.* Read each word to children several times. Then ask children to make up sentences using each word.	**Have** children make rhymes with words that begin with *k*; for example, you say: *Someone who is always late is my older sister____,* or *Have you seen my new blue mittens? They are fuzzy, just like ____.* Ask children to write a *k* for every rhyme they complete.	**Have** children draw a picture of a scene that contains at least two objects that begin with the letter *k.* (Suggestions: kitten, king, kick, kettle, key, kangaroo)	**Invite** children to chant the following initial *k* words: *Key, kit, kangaroo. Kite, kid, koala too.* List the *k* words on the chalkboard, and ask volunteers to underline the letter *k.*

OBJECTIVES

Children will:

- recognize the ABC story strucure
- recognize words with initial *k*

SUSAN BLACKABY lives with her husband in Portland, Oregon. They are both writers. Mrs. Blackaby says, "If you just poke your nose out the front door, there is a story out there to write about."

JOE BODDY lives on the side of a mountain in Missoula, Montana. He began to draw when he was just 4 years old. He loves being an illustrator and working at home.

TEACHING TIP

You may wish to use a pointer or a pencil to track print as you read. A pointer will help draw children's attention to the appropriate point in the text, and may be easier than using your hand or finger.

Read the Big Book

Before Reading

Build Background

EVALUATE PRIOR KNOWLEDGE Hold up a picture of a mouse. Ask children to identify the animal, and ask where they have seen mice. Talk about places where mice usually live, and what animals are enemies of mice. Ask children to name other books they have read about mice.

Preview and Predict

DISCUSS AUTHOR AND ILLUSTRATOR Display the Big Book cover and read the title. Ask children to name the color of each mouse. Identify the author and the illustrator, and make sure children understand that they wrote the words and drew the pictures.

TAKE A PICTURE WALK Take a picture walk through several spreads of the book. Ask if the book is a real life story, or a fantasy. Discuss what children see, and how the alphabet is a part of the story.

MAKE PREDICTIONS Ask children to predict what the story might be about.

Set Purposes

Ask children what they want to find out about the mice. Explain how they can name the letter on each page, and use the picture and the letter to say the words.

"Look at the **bed**," said Dee.

Mice Mischief, an Alphabet Story, pages 4-5

During Reading

Read Together

- Before you begin to read, point to the first word in the first sentence. Explain that this is where you will begin to read. Continue to track print as you read the story. *Tracking Print*

- Point out the key word on each page, and relate it to the letters at the top of the page. Make sure that children understand that the word apple begins with the /a/ sound. *Concepts of Print*

- Ask children which mouse might be younger and why. (Bink is probably younger because he is smaller.) *Make Inferences*

- Make the /k/ sound and have children say it with you. After you read page 15, have children say the word with that sound. *(king)* *Phonics*

Bink gets stuck on the **edge**.

9

Mice Mischief, an Alphabet Story, page 9

After Reading

Return to Predictions and Purposes

Ask children if they found out what they wanted to know about Dee and Bink. See if their predictions were correct.

Literary Response

JOURNAL WRITING Ask children to draw and write about an exciting part of the story.

ORAL RESPONSE Ask questions such as:

- *Did you think the cat would catch the mice?*

- *Did you think the rug was a good hiding place?*

ABC Activity

Ask children to sit in a circle. Hold up a letter card and ask a child to say the name of the letter and the sound that it makes. Continue around the circle.

INFORMAL ASSESSMENT

ABC ORDER

HOW TO ASSESS

Give children five capitals and five corresponding lowercase letter cards. Ask children to match the cards and put them in ABC order.

FOLLOW-UP

Help children who experience difficulty by reviewing ABC order with letter cards.

CENTER Activity

Cross Curricular: Language Arts

MICE IN A ROW Cut out 26 mice shapes, and write an uppercase letter of the alphabet on one side, and a lowercase letter of the alphabet on the other side. Children put the mice in ABC order.

▶ **Mathematical/Logical**

OBJECTIVES

Children will:
- identify naming words

MATERIALS
- *Mice Mischief:* An Alphabet Story

TEACHING TIP

INSTRUCTIONAL As children are introduced to the concept of nouns, focus on examples that are clear to the children. For example, some children may have difficulty determining whether the apple tree in the story is a place or a thing.

Introduce Naming Words

PREPARE

Discuss Words that Name

Ask children to name people whom they know at school. List some of the names. Then have children say the name of your school, and point out that the school is a particular place. Let volunteers point to some things in the classroom and name them.

TEACH

Recognize Words that Name

Explain to children that you are going to look for words that name persons, places, or things. Display the Big Book, *Mice Mischief: An Alphabet Story*, and have children recall the story. Have children find the following examples of naming words: Persons: king, man; Places: palace, yard; Things: desk, fan, ladder, jar. Then invite children to find examples in the classroom to add to each category.

PRACTICE

Find the Person, Place, Thing

Read the directions on page 247 to the children, and make sure they clearly understand what they are asked to do. Identify each picture, and complete the first item. Then work through the page with children, or have them complete the page independently.

ASSESS/CLOSE

Review the Page

Check children's work on the Pupil Edition page. Note areas where children need extra help.

Name_____

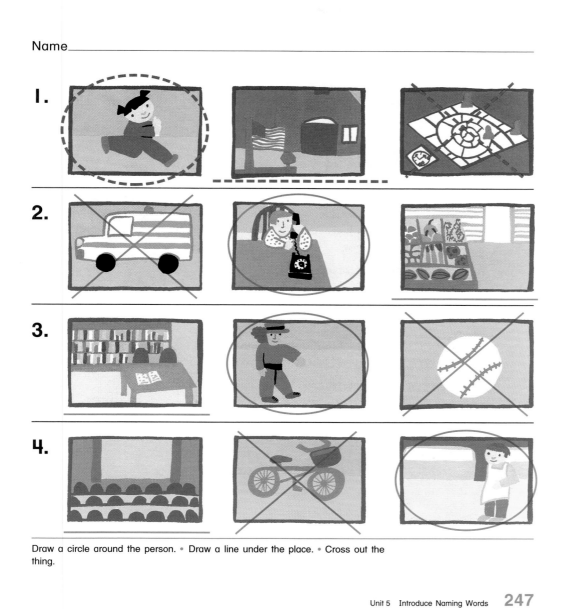

1.

2.

3.

4.

Draw a circle around the person. • Draw a line under the place. • Cross out the thing.

Pupil Edition, page 247

PRACTICE BOOK, page 247

Meeting Individual Needs for Beginning Reading Concepts

EASY	ON-LEVEL	CHALLENGE	LANGUAGE SUPPORT
Sing the familiar song, "The People on the Bus." Ask children to name people, places, and things in the song. Encourage children to make up their own verses, and do the same.	**Label** three small boxes with words or pictures: Persons, Places, Things. Children sort picture cards that show examples of each.	**Divide** children into two teams to play "Name the Word." Give a category, such as "person at school." Each person on the team has the opportunity to say a noun and scores a point for each.	**Have** children name the people in their families. Then ask where they live, and point out that it is a place. Then ask them to name things in their homes.

Develop Phonological Awareness

Listen

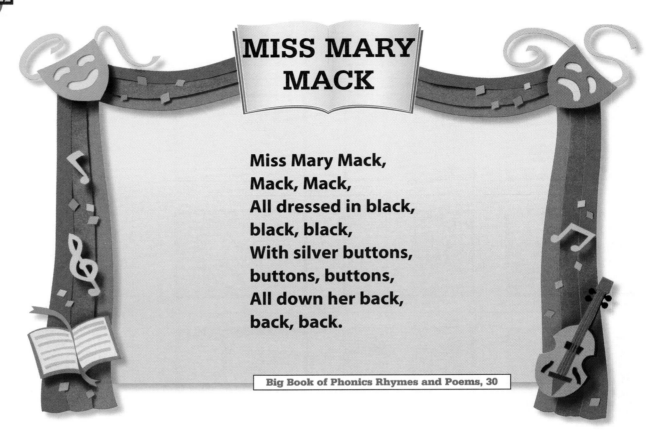

MISS MARY MACK

Miss Mary Mack,
Mack, Mack,
All dressed in black,
black, black,
With silver buttons,
buttons, buttons,
All down her back,
back, back.

Big Book of Phonics Rhymes and Poems, 30

Objective: Listen for Repeating Words

LISTEN TO THE POEM

- Read the poem "Miss Mary Mack" aloud.
- Point out that some of the words in the poem repeat. Invite children to join in on the repeating words as you reread the poem.

CLAP FOR REPEATING WORDS

- Tell children that you will read the poem again. When children hear repeating words, have them clap each time they hear the word.

TRY A NEW RHYME

- Invite children to think of words that rhyme with other colors, such as *moo* and *blue*. Substitute the new words and repeat the poem together.

> **Miss Mary Moo, Moo, Moo,**
> **All dressed in blue, blue, blue...**

Objective: Listen for Final Digraph *ck*

SEGMENTING

- Say the word *back*. Emphasize the final /k/ sound and have children say it with you.

PLAY A GAME

- Have children sit in a circle to play "Pass the Button." Give a button to a child and say the word *Mack*. The child repeats the word and then says a rhyming word.

> **Mack   back**

- He or she passes the button to the next child, who says the previous word and another rhyming word.

> **back   sack**

EXTEND THE GAME

- Continue having children find other words that rhyme.
- Say the word *tick*. Emphasize the final /k/ sound and have the children say it with you. Have children play the game again beginning with the word *tick*.

Read Together

From Phonemic Awareness to Phonics

Objective: Identify *ck* as Letters for /k/

IDENTIFY THE LETTERS FOR THE SOUND

- Explain that the letters *ck* sound like /k/. Have children say the sound with you.
- Display the Big Book of Phonics Rhymes and Poems, page 30. Say the word *Mack* and frame the *ck*. Have children repeat the sound after you.

REREAD THE POEM

- Reread the poem, having children join in on the repeating words. Point to each word and emphasize the /k/ sound.

FIND WORDS WITH CK

- Write the letters *ck* on an index card. Invite volunteers to match the letters to words in the poem that end with *ck*. Say the words together.

Mm

Miss Mary Mack

Miss Mary Mack,
   Mack, Mack,
All dressed in black,
   black, black,
With silver buttons,
   buttons, buttons,
All down her back,
   back, back.

30

Big Book of Phonics Rhymes and Poems, 30

 **OBJECTIVES**

Children will:

- identify the letters *ck*
- identify /k/*ck*
- form the letters *ck*

MATERIALS

- letter cards from the Word Play Book

TEACHING **TIP**

INSTRUCTIONAL If you have a recording of the song "This Old Man," play it for the children; otherwise, sing it to them, and have them join in the chorus, singing *Knick knack paddywack, give a dog a bone; this old man came rolling home.* Explain that the words *knick knack paddywack* do not mean anything in the song, but are fun words to sing.

ALTERNATE TEACHING STRATEGY

FINAL /k/*ck*

For a different approach to teaching this skill, see page T24.

▶ **Visual/Auditory/ Kinesthetic**

Introduce Final /k/ck

TEACH

Identify /k/*ck*   Tell children they will learn to write the sound /k/ at the end of a word with the letters *ck*. Explain that in English *k* does not usually end a word unless it has a partner, the letter *c*, before it. Ask children to repeat after you: *Did Rick see the duck?* Have them raise their hands when they say a word that ends in /k/.

Form *ck*   Display letters *ck* and trace them with your finger. With your back to the children, trace large letters *ck* in the air. Ask children to write *ck* four or more times on letter strips.

PRACTICE

Complete the Pupil Edition Page   Read the directions on page 248 to the children, and make sure they clearly understand what they are being asked to do. Identify each picture, and complete the first item. Work through the page with children, or have them complete the page independently.

ASSESS/CLOSE

Identify and Use *ck*   Say the following list of words, and have children quack like a *duck* if they hear final /k/: *pack, luck, rock, lick, sun, sick.* Write the words, and ask children to hold up their ck letter strips when the word has the *ck* ending.

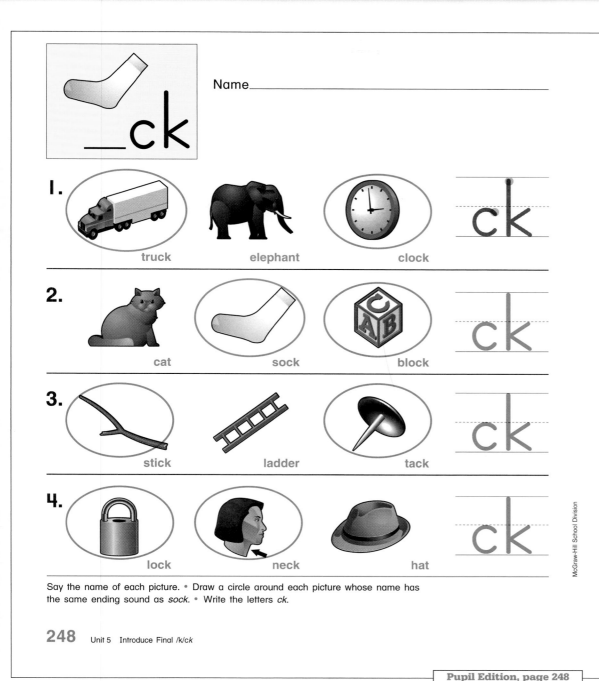

Name_____

1.
truck   elephant   clock   ck

2.
cat   sock   block   ck

3.
stick   ladder   tack   ck

4.
lock   neck   hat   ck

Say the name of each picture. • Draw a circle around each picture whose name has the same ending sound as *sock*. • Write the letters *ck*.

248   Unit 5   Introduce Final /k/ck

McGraw-Hill School Division

Pupil Edition, page 248

ADDITIONAL PHONICS RESOURCES

Practice Book *page 248*
Phonics Workbook

McGraw-Hill School
TECHNOLOGY

Phonics CD-ROM
Activities for practice with Initial Letters

PRACTICE BOOK page 248

Meeting Individual Needs for Phonics

EASY	ON-LEVEL	CHALLENGE	LANGUAGE SUPPORT
Give children fingerpaint and have them paint a picture of an object that ends in *ck*. Ask children to paint the letters *ck* under the picture.	**Show** children pictures and ask them to write *ck* on letter strips for every picture of something whose name ends with the sound /k/, for example: *sock, hat, lock, duck, mat, sick.*	**Hand** one child a "magic" *sack*. Ask the child to pretend to put in something that ends in /k/ and name the item. Items can include those that might or might not actually fit in a sack: *chick, tack, brick, stick, truck, sock.* Children write *ck* in the air for each item.	**Say** the word *sack*, and write *ck* as children say the /k/ sound. Then have them say rhyming words: *back, Zack, Jack, quack, knack, pack, rack, tack,* and so on. Continue with *pick.*

* understand story structure

LYNN REISER practices psychiatry in Connecticut and also teaches at the Yale University School of Medicine. She began to create children's books when a songwriter asked her to illustrate his book of songs. She has gone on to write and illustrate many books for children. She wrote this story when her family wanted to get a dog.

Read the Big Book

Before Reading

Build Background

EVALUATE PRIOR KNOWLEDGE Ask how many children have a dog as a pet. Talk about how they care for a dog. Then ask children to name other pets that they have and to talk about how they care for them.

WHAT DOES A DOG NEED? Make a picture and a word chart that shows how to care for a dog. Children may draw pictures or cut pictures from magazines. Include feeding, walking, exercising, brushing, and taking a dog to the vet.

Preview and Predict

DISCUSS AUTHOR AND ILLUSTRATOR Show the Big Book cover and read the title. Have children name the animals that the boy is holding. Say the name of the author, and explain that Ms. Reiser both wrote and illustrated the book. Share some background information.

TAKE A PICTURE WALK Then take a picture walk through the first few spreads of the book. Have children describe what is happening.

MAKE PREDICTIONS Ask them to predict if the boy will get a dog.

Set Purposes

Ask children what they want to find out as they read the story. Make a list of their ideas.

Richard wanted a dog, any kind of dog.

But his mother said a dog was too much trouble,

Any Kind of Dog, pages 4-5

During Reading

Read Together

• Before you begin to read, point to the first word in the first sentence. Explain that this is where you will begin to read. Continue to track print as you read the story. *Tracking Print*

• Ask children: *Why, do you think, might Richard's mother think that a dog is too much trouble? Make inferences*

• After you read page 4, ask children: *How does the caterpillar look similar to the dog in the book?* Continue to ask children to compare the animals and dogs in the story as you continue to read. *Use Illustrations*

• Ask children: *In the beginning and middle of the story, what did Richard's mother do whenever he asked if he could have a dog?* Point out what happened at the end of the story. (She gave him a different animal.) *Understand Story Structure*

The caterpillar was very nice.
It looked a little like a dog,

Lhasa Apso

but it was not a dog.
Richard wanted a dog.
His mother said
a dog was too much trouble,

7

Any Kind of Dog, page 7

After Reading

Return to Predictions and Purposes

• Ask children if their predictions were correct. Then return to the list of ideas that children wanted to find out as they read the story. Confirm that their questions were answered. Then ask if the book tells a real-life story or a fantasy.

Literary Response

JOURNAL WRITING Invite children to draw a picture of a dog that they would like to have. Ask them to write a name for the dog.

ORAL RESPONSE Engage children in a discussion about their pictures by asking the following questions:

• *What does your dog look like?*

• *Do you think it would be too much trouble to have a dog? Why or why not?*

CENTER Activity

Cross Curricular: Math

ANIMALS IN ORDER Point out that in the story, Richard's mother gave him a small animal. Then each animal grew bigger and bigger. Provide animal cards that show different wild and domestic animals. Begin by having children arrange pictures of animals by size from the smallest to largest. Continue to add other animals.

▶ **Logical/Mathematical**

OBJECTIVES

Children will:

- recognize and understand story structure—beginning, middle, end

....

MATERIALS

- *Any Kind of Dog,* Big Book

TEACHING TIP

INSTRUCTIONAL It may be helpful to review the concept of top, *middle, and bottom* with concrete items, such as connecting blocks. Help children make the connection *between top, middle, bottom* and *beginning, middle, end.*

Introduce Story Structure

PREPARE

Review the Beginning and End of the Story

Ask children to think about the story, *Any Kind of Dog*. Ask a volunteer to tell what happened at the very beginning of the story (Richard wanted a dog). Then have a volunteer tell what happened at the very end of the story (Richard got a dog).

TEACH

Create a Beginning, Middle, and End Chart

Provide each child with a sheet of drawing paper divided into three parts. Discuss again the beginning and end of the story. Ask children to draw a picture at the top of the paper of Richard at the beginning of the story (a boy with a sad face). At the bottom of the paper, have children draw a picture of the end of the story (a happy boy with a dog). Then discuss what happened in the middle of the story. Elicit from children one or two statements that succinctly tell the middle part of the story. (Richard's mother gave Richard lots of stuffed animals instead of a dog. She thought a dog would be too much trouble.) Then have children draw a picture in the middle of the paper to represent the middle part of the story.

PRACTICE

Complete the Pupil Edition Page

Read the directions on page 249 to the children, and make sure they clearly understand what they are asked to do. Identify each picture, and complete the first item together. Then work through the page with children or have them complete the page independently.

ASSESS/CLOSE

Review the Page

Review children's work, and note children who are experiencing difficulty. Have children explain their answers to you to help you pinpoint their misunderstanding.

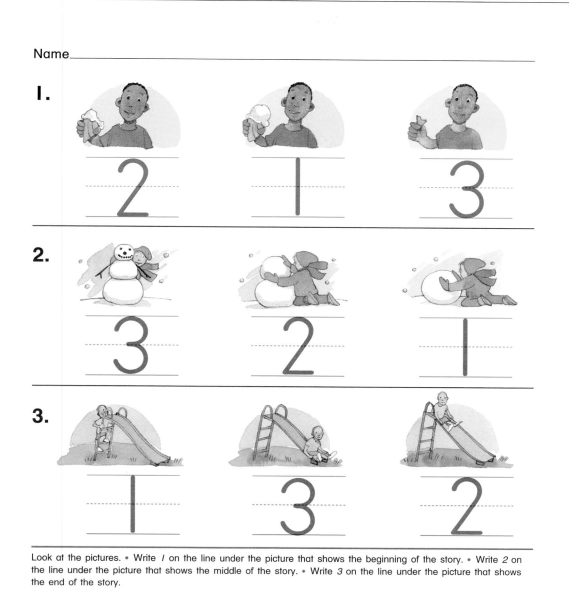

Name_____

1.

2   1   3

2.

3   2   1

3.

1   3   2

Look at the pictures. • Write *1* on the line under the picture that shows the beginning of the story. • Write *2* on the line under the picture that shows the middle of the story. • Write *3* on the line under the picture that shows the end of the story.

Unit 5   Introduce Story Structure   **249**

Pupil Edition, page 249

ALTERNATE TEACHING STRATEGY

STORY STRUCTURE
For a different approach to teaching this skill, see page T26.

▶ **Visual/Auditory/ Kinesthetic**

Look at the pictures. Write *1* on the line under the picture that shows the beginning of the story. Write *2* on the line that shows the middle of the story. Write *3* on the line that shows the end of the story.

Unit 5   Introduce Story Structure

At Home: Read a story with the child. Afterwards, have the child tell what happened in the beginning, middle, and end of the story.

PRACTICE BOOK page 249

Meeting Individual Needs for Comprehension

EASY	ON-LEVEL	CHALLENGE	LANGUAGE SUPPORT
Have children use the Story Structure charts to retell the story. You may wish to have children cut their charts into 3 parts (beginning, middle, and end). After children shuffle the parts, ask them to put the parts back in order.	**Read** or tell the familiar story of "The Three Little Pigs." Have children create their own Story Structure charts to represent the beginning, middle, and end of the story. Children can then use their Story Structure charts to retell the story.	**Have** children work in pairs. Ask each child to think of a simple story line and create a Story Structure chart with pictures to represent the beginning, middle, and end of the story. Children can trade charts and take turns telling the story using their partner's charts.	Ask three children to stand in line as they might form a line leaving the classroom. Identify the first child as the beginning of the line, the next as the middle, and the third as the end of the line. Then ask volunteers to replace the child at the beginning, middle, or end of the line.

Develop Phonological Awareness

Listen

Katie's Kangaroo
a poem

Miss Mary Mack
a poem

Katie has a kangaroo.
She keeps it on her bed.
Katie has a kangaroo.
It sleeps by Katie's head.
Katie has a kangaroo
And five koalas, too.
She has so many animals,
Her room looks like a zoo!

Miss Mary Mack,
Mack, Mack,
All dressed in black,
black, black,
With silver buttons,
buttons, buttons
All down her back,
back, back.

Big Book of Phonics Rhymes and Poems, pages 29,30

Objective: Listen for Animal Names

READ THE POEM Read the poem "Katie's Kangaroo" aloud. Invite children to name the animals that Katie keeps on her bed. (kangaroo, koalas)

TRY DIFFERENT ANIMAL NAMES Suggest children name other animals that Katie might keep on her bed.

kitty   cat   bear   duck   snake

Reread the poem aloud, substituting animal names suggested by the children. Have children clap each time they hear an animal name.

USE ANIMAL SOUNDS Read the poem again, substituting animal sounds associated with the animal names children suggested. Have children identify the animals associated with the sounds.

Objective: Listen for /k/

LISTEN FOR INITIAL AND FINAL /k/ Read the titles of the poems, emphasizing the words with initial and final /k/. Have children repeat the /k/ sound with you.

RECOGNIZE /k/ Say words from the poems or other words that have an initial or final /k/ sound. Have children meow like a kitten if the word begins with the /k/ sound. Have children quack like a duck if the word ends with the /k/ sound.

SUBSTITUTE NEW WORDS Say these model sentences, emphasizing the /k/ sound: *Katie's kangaroo can carry a kite. Can you?* Have children repeat the sentences with you. Then have children name other objects beginning or ending with the /k/ sound that Katie's kangaroo can carry. Use children's suggestions in the model sentences.

| Katie | kangaroo | koalas | king | Ken | kind, |
| Mack | black | back | lock | deck | pick | duck |

Read Together

From Phonemic Awareness to Phonics

Objective: Identify /k/K,k,ck

IDENTIFY THE LETTER Tell children that the letters *K*, *k*, and *ck* stand for the sound /k/. Display pages 29 and 30 in the Big Book of Phonics Rhymes and Poems. Point to the letters and identify them.

REREAD THE POEMS Reread the poems. Point to each word, emphasizing those with /k/.

FIND WORDS WITH *K, k, ck* Have children point to the words in the poems that begin or end with *K*, *k*, or *ck*.

Katie's Kangaroo Kk

Katie has a kangaroo
She keeps it on her bed.
Katie has a kangaroo.
It sleeps by Katie's head.

Katie has a kangaroo
And five koalas, too.
She has so many animals,
Her room looks like a zoo!

Mm **Miss Mary Mack**

Miss Mary Mack,
  Mack, Mack,
All dressed in black,
  black, black,
With silver buttons,
  buttons, buttons,
All down her back,
  back, back.

29   30

Big Book of Phonics Rhymes and Poems, pages 29,30

250B

OBJECTIVES

Children will:

- identify /k/*K,k* and /k/*ck*
- write and use letters *K,k,* and *ck*

MATERIALS

- letter cards from the *Word Building Book*

TEACHING TIP

MANAGEMENT During the year, children will be at different levels of fine motor skill development. Continue to provide tracing letters, lined handwriting paper, and different media to practice writing letters.

ALTERNATE TEACHING STRATEGY

LETTER /k/*k, ck*

For a different approach to teaching this skill, see page T24.

▶ **Visual/Auditory/ Kinesthetic**

Review /k/k, /k/ck

TEACH

Identify /k/*K,k* and /k/*ck* Tell children they will review the sound /k/ at the beginning and at the end of words and write the letters *K, k,* and *ck*. Write the three forms on the chalkboard in three distinct places. Make the /k/ sound for each. Then write the following sentence, and read it aloud, one word at a time, as you track print with your hand: *Kim's koala is sick with a cold.* Ask children to point to one of the three forms that matches each word that begins or ends in /k/.

Form *K,k, ck* Continue the above silly story about Kim, writing these sentences under the first one: *Kim's duck is also sick with a cold. What bad luck!* Ask children to write *K, k,* or *ck* on a letter strip to show every initial or final /k/ sound.

PRACTICE

Complete the Pupil Edition Page Read the directions on page 250 to the children, and make sure they clearly understand what they are being asked to do. Identify each picture, and complete the first item together. Then work through the page with children, or have them complete the page independently.

ASSESS/CLOSE

Write and Use *K,k, ck* Place the following word cards on the chalkboard ledge, and have children write *K, k* or *ck* on a letter strip to show the same arrangement: *kid, pack, Kim, kit, tuck, rock.*

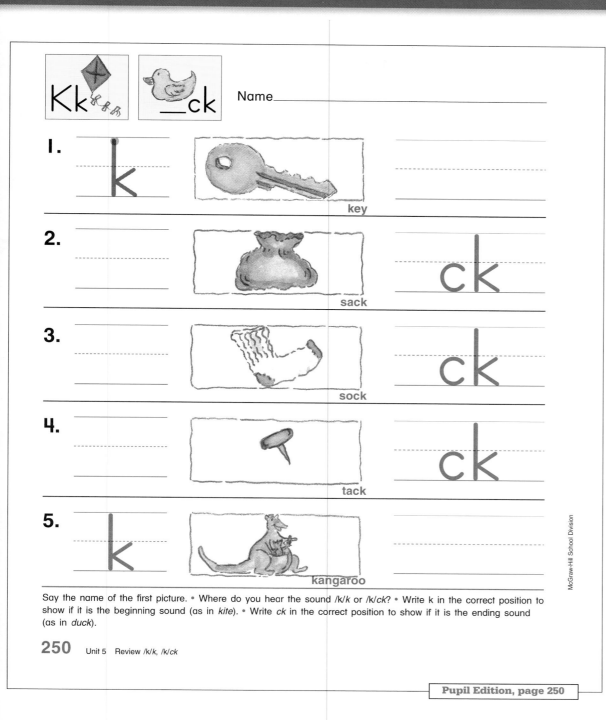

Kk _ck Name_____

1. k [key] key

2. [sack] ck sack

3. [sock] ck sock

4. [tack] ck tack

5. k [kangaroo] kangaroo

Say the name of the first picture. • Where do you hear the sound /k/k or /k/ck? • Write k in the correct position to show if it is the beginning sound (as in *kite*). • Write *ck* in the correct position to show if it is the ending sound (as in *duck*).

250 Unit 5 Review /k/k, /k/ck

McGraw-Hill School Division

Pupil Edition, page 250

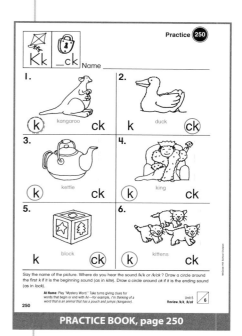

ADDITIONAL PHONICS RESOURCES

Practice Book, *page 250*
Phonics Workbook

McGraw-Hill School
TECHNOLOGY

Phonics CD-ROM
Activities for practice with Initial and Final Letters

Practice 250

Kk _ck Name_____

1. [kangaroo] k kangaroo ck
2. [duck] k duck ck
3. [kettle] k kettle ck
4. [king] k king ck
5. [block] k block ck
6. [kittens] k kittens ck

Say the name of the picture. Where do you hear the sound /k/k or /k/ck? Draw a circle around the first k if it is the beginning sound (as in *kite*). Draw a circle around *ck* if it is the ending sound (as in *lock*).

At Home: Play "Mystery Word." Take turns giving clues for words that begin or end with /k/—for example, I'm thinking of a word that is an animal that has a pouch and jumps (*kangaroo*).

250 Unit 5 Review /k/k, /k/ck 6

PRACTICE BOOK, page 250

Meeting Individual Needs for Phonics

EASY	ON-LEVEL	CHALLENGE	LANGUAGE SUPPORT
Give children word cards for initial and final /k/ words, such as: *kid, luck, pick, tack, kit, sock, Kim*. Read the cards together. Have children sort for the three forms. Write the three forms *K, k* and *ck* on the chalkboard as a guide.	**Ask** children to say the word that rhymes with each of the following words and begins with /k/: *bite, sit, lid, ring, peep*. Each time they say a word, have them write *k*. Continue by asking children to rhyme words that end in -ack, -ick, or -ock and to write *ck*.	**Have** children form a circle. Pass around a *sack* into which you have placed slips of paper with *k___* and *___ck* printed on them. Children take a slip of paper and say a word that begins or ends in /k/.	**Help** ESL children learn verb meanings of initial and final /k/ words by asking them to repeat each word as they act it out. Model gestures for the words *tuck, duck, lock, rock, pick, kick*.

250

Teacher
Read Aloud

Listen

The Hare and the Tortoise

There once was a hare who was always boasting about how fast he could run. One day he said to the other animals, "I'm so fast that no one can beat me. I dare anyone here to a race."

The tortoise said quietly, "I will race you."

"You!" laughed the hare. "That's a joke! Why, I could run circles around you all the way."

"Save your boasting until you've won," said the tortoise. "Shall we race?"

So the race began. The hare darted almost out of sight at once, and very soon he was far ahead of the tortoise, who moved along at a steady, even pace.

The hare knew he was far ahead, so he stopped and said, "I think I'll take a little nap. When I wake up, I can zip ahead of the tortoise without even trying."

So the hare settled into a nice sleep. And he was still asleep when the tortoise passed by. And when the hare finally woke up, he looked ahead, and what did he see? The tortoise was just then crossing the finish line to win the race!

Oral Comprehension

LISTENING AND SPEAKING Ask children if they have ever run in a race or watched a race. Have them share their experiences. Tell children that they will hear a fable about a race between a hare and a tortoise. Explain that a fable is a story, often about animals, that teaches a lesson. If necessary, show pictures of a hare and a tortoise and talk about how they move. Also discuss what it means to boast.

Invite children to summarize the story. Ask them to tell how the story began, what happened, and how the story ended. Then ask, *What lesson did the hare learn?*

Activity Ask children to think of a variation of the fable by choosing two different animals to run in the race. Encourage children to think about how animals move as they choose their new characters. Then have them write, dictate, or draw pictures to tell their new story.

▶ Linguistic

Real-Life Reading

Can you help the families read the street signs?

33

Big Book of Real-Life Reading, pages 32–33

Objective: Maps

READ THE PAGE Ask children which rules they need to follow when they cross the street and which signs help them. Have volunteers retell the story of "The Hare and the Tortoise." Then explain that the hare and the tortoise are on their way to the store with their parents. Show the picture and discuss the signs.

ANSWER THE QUESTION Point to each sign and ask children what they should do at each sign. Ask: *Where is it safe for the animals to walk? What does the yellow color mean on a traffic light?* Provide a simple outline of a traffic light, and have children cut out red, yellow, and green circles. Children glue the circles in the correct order to make a traffic light. Then have them use the traffic lights to act out how to cross the street.

CULTURAL PERSPECTIVES

RACES Share that people love to race against each other, whether it is running, swimming, or any other sport all over the world. In Spain, people even race against bulls. People from all over the world compete in races at the Olympics.

Activity Have children take turns acting out the story of the hare and the tortoise. Suggest they try out different endings.

▶ **Interpersonal/Linguistic**

Children will:

- **identify and read the high-frequency word** *for*

MATERIALS

- **word cards from the Word Play Book**

TECHNOLOGY TIP

INSTRUCTIONAL Write the words *for* and *four* on the chalkboard. Point out that some words sound the same, but have different spellings. Relate the word *four* and the numeral *4*.

Introduce High-Frequency Words: *for*

PREPARE

Listen to Words

Explain to the children that they will be learning a new word: *for*. Say the following sentence: *The hare ran for the line.* Say the sentence again, and ask children to raise a finger when they hear the word *for*. Repeat with the sentence: *Let's have ham for lunch.*

TEACH

Model Reading the Word in Context

Give a word card to each child, and read the word. Reread the sentences, and have children raise their hands when they hear the word.

Identify the Word

Write the sentences above on the chalkboard. Track print and read each sentence. Children hold up their word card when they hear the word *for*. Then ask volunteers to point to and underline the word *for* in the sentences.

Write the Word

Review how to write the letters *f*, *o*, and *r*. Have children practice tracing the word.

PRACTICE

Complete the Pupil Edition Page

Read the directions on page 251 to the children, and make sure they clearly understand what they are asked to do. Complete the first item together. Then work through the page with children or have them complete the page independently.

ASSESS/CLOSE

Review the Page

Review children's work, and note children who are experiencing difficulty or need additional practice.

Name

I.

The pup is <u>for</u> me.

2.

The cat is <u>for</u> you.

3.

The duck is <u>for</u> Kim.

4.

The cap is <u>for</u> Dad.

Read the sentence. • Then draw a line under the word *for* in the sentence.

Unit 5   Introduce High-Frequency Words: *for*   **251**

Pupil Edition, page 251

ALTERNATE TEACHING
STRATEGY
....
**HIGH-FREQUENCY
WORDS:** *for*

**For a different teaching
approach to this skill, see
page T27.**

Practice **251**

Name

I. "Is the cap <u>for</u> me?"
said Tom.

2. "The cap is <u>for</u> you,"
said Kim.

3. "Is the pup <u>for</u> me?"
said Pam.

4. "The pup is <u>for</u> you,"
said Mom.

Read the sentence. Draw a line under the word *for* in the sentence.

At Home: Help the child find the word *for* in a magazine
or newspaper article.

Unit 5
Introduce High-Frequency Words: *for*   251

PRACTICE BOOK page 251

Meeting Individual Needs for Vocabulary

EASY	ON-LEVEL	CHALLENGE	LANGUAGE SUPPORT
Give children a letter card with *f, o,* or *r*. Mix the cards up. Children use word cards to form the word *for*. Then each child uses the word in a sentence. Mix up the cards and repeat until all children have had a chance.	**Give** children newspapers or magazines and have them find and cut out the letters *f, o,* and *r*. Have them glue the letters to form *for*. Then write the word *for* under it. Then have them use the word in a sentence.	**Make** a stack of letter cards, including the letters *f* (2), *o* (2), *r* (2), *p, s, t, a, b, s, l, b, v, k, m, n, c, u, d*. Mix the cards and have partners take turns turning over cards, trying to collect *f, o,* and *r*. The first child to spell *for* uses the word in a sentence and scores a point. Children can play several rounds.	**Show** children the position of the mouth when pronouncing the word: *for*. Run your finger under the word card and say it slowly. Have children say the word.

251

Develop Phonological Awareness

Listen

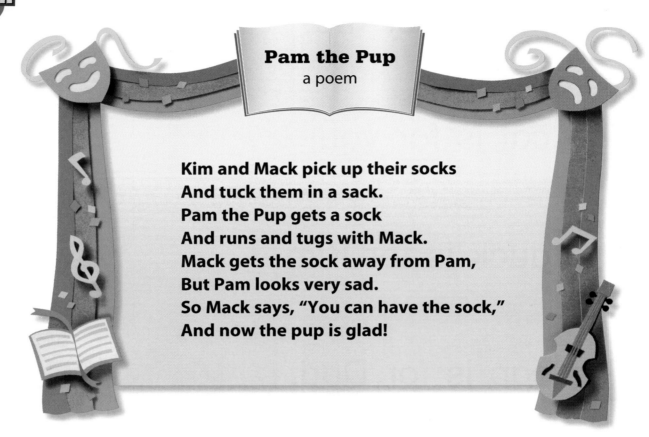

Pam the Pup
a poem

Kim and Mack pick up their socks
And tuck them in a sack.
Pam the Pup gets a sock
And runs and tugs with Mack.
Mack gets the sock away from Pam,
But Pam looks very sad.
So Mack says, "You can have the sock,"
And now the pup is glad!

Objective: Develop Listening Skills

READ THE POEM Read the poem "Pam the Pup" aloud. Ask children, *What does Mack pick up? Where does he put the things he picks up?*

> sock   sack

ACT OUT THE POEM Provide socks and a paper sack. Ask volunteers to be Kim, Mack, and Pam. Reread the poem, line by line, as the volunteers act out the poem. Repeat with other volunteers.

REVISE THE POEM Ask children what other objects Kim and Mack might pick up and put in their sack. Encourage children to think of words that rhyme.

> block   clock   rock   lock

SUBSTITUTE WORD Reread the poem several times, substituting an object children suggested each time. Invite children to clap each time they hear the substitute word in the poem.

Objective: Listen for Blending Short *a, i, o, u*

LISTEN FOR BLENDING Read the first line of the poem. As you say *up,* emphasize each sound individually by saying: /u/-/p/. Then blend the sounds to say *up.* Repeat with *pup.*

BLENDING WITH SHORT *i* Have children hold up one finger for each sound they hear as you say /p/-/i/-/k/. Tell them to hold three fingers apart. Discuss how many sounds they hear. Then have the children bring their fingers together as they blend each sound. Repeat with other short *i* words.

> kick   lick   lip

WHAT'S MY WORD? Continue blending other words with short vowel sounds, such as *lap.* Assign the sounds /a/, /o/, /u/, /l/, /k/, and /p/ to volunteers. Say: /l/-/a/-/p/. Ask children assigned those sounds to stand at the front of the room and say the sounds aloud.

Have the class say the sounds as the volunteers move closer together. Tell children to raise their hands when they think they know the word. Continue until the sounds blend into *lap.* Repeat with other volunteers and words.

> lack   lock   luck   pack   puck

From Phonemic Awareness to Phonics

Read Together

Objective: Relate *a, i, o, u* to Short Vowel Sounds

LISTEN FOR SOUNDS Read the poem, emphasizing *pup* each time you say it.

IDENTIFY THE LETTERS Say /p/-/u/-/p/. Ask: *How many sounds do you hear?* (three) Write *pup* on the board as children say each sound. Identify the letters. Invite children to say the sounds the letters stand for as you point to each letter.

Repeat with other words from the poem that contain short vowel sounds and *k,ck,l* or *p.*

MAKING RHYMING WORDS Point to the Word "pup" on the board, and ask: *What rhymes with* pup?

> up, cup

Write the words in a list under pup. Have volunteers underline *up* in each word. Guide children to see that the words have the same endings. Write these key words on the chalkboard: *pack, kick,* and *lock.* Repeat the activity.

Review **Blending with short a, i, o, u**

MATERIALS

- letter cards from the *Word Play Book*

TEACHING TIP

INSTRUCTIONAL

Remind children that they have learned two ways of showing the sound /k/ at the beginning of a word: *k* or *c*, as in *kid* and *cat*; they have learned one way of showing the /k/ sound at the end of a word: *ck*.

ALTERNATE TEACHING STRATEGY

BLENDING SHORT
a, i, o, u

For a different approach to teaching this skill, see Unit 1, page T32; Unit 2, page T32; Unit 3, page T30; Unit 4, page T32.

▶ **Visual/Auditory/ Kinesthetic**

TEACH

Identify a, i, o, u as Symbols for /a/, /i/, /o/, /u/

Tell children they will continue to read short *a, i, o, u* words.

- Display the *a, i, o, u* letter cards and say /a/, /i/, /o/, /u/. Have children repeat the sounds /a/, /i/, /o/, /u/ as you point to the cards.

BLENDING Model and Guide Practice

- Place a *ck* card to the right of the *i* card. Blend the sounds together and have children repeat after you: _*ick*.

- Place an *t* letter card before the _*ick* cards. Blend the sounds in the word to read *tick*. Have children repeat after you.

Use the Word in Context

- Invite children to use *tick* in a sentence, perhaps talking about the sound a clock makes.

Repeat the Procedure

- Use the following words to continue modeling and for guided practice with short *a, i, o, u*: *lick, pack, pup, Kim, pick, kid, luck*.

PRACTICE

Complete the Pupil Edition Page

Read the directions on page 252 to children, and make sure they clearly understand what they are being asked to do. Identify each picture, and complete the first item together. Then work through the page with children, or have them complete the page independently.

ASSESS/CLOSE

Write Short a, i, o, u Words

Observe children as they complete page 252. Then display letter cards *l, p, k, d* and have children use them to write words with short *a, i, o, u* in the middle and *ck* at the end.

Name_____

1. l o ck   lock

2. p a ck   pack

3. l i ck   lick

4. k i ck   kick

Blend the sounds and say the word. • Write the word. • Draw a circle around the picture that goes with the word.

252   Unit 5   Review Blending with Short *a, i, o, u*

Pupil Edition, page 252

McGraw-Hill School Division

ADDITIONAL PHONICS RESOURCES

Practice Book, *page 252*
Phonics Workbook

McGraw-Hill School
TECHNOLOGY

Phonics CD-ROM
Activities for Practice with Blending and Segmenting

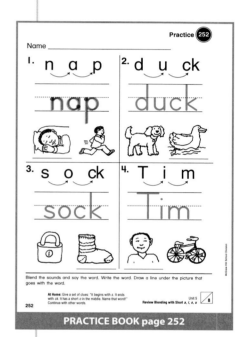

Practice 252
Name_____

1. n a p   nap

2. d u ck   duck

3. s o ck   sock

4. T i m   Tim

Blend the sounds and say the word. Write the word. Draw a line under the picture that goes with the word.

At Home: Give a set of clues: "It begins with *s*, it ends with *ck*, it has a short *o* in the middle. Name that word?" Continue with other words.

252   Review Blending with Short *a, i, o, u*   Unit 5

PRACTICE BOOK page 252

Meeting Individual Needs for Phonics

EASY	ON-LEVEL	CHALLENGE	LANGUAGE SUPPORT
Write the words *pack, duck, lock,* pick on the chalkboard. Ask children to repeat after you as you blend sounds to read the words aloud. Ask children to say the word that has the sound /a/ in the middle, then repeat the question for /i/, /o/, and /u/.	**Say** *ick* and write it on the chalkboard. Ask children to say an initial letter sound that could make a word. Repeat for *ack, ock,* and *uck,* asking children to choose a first letter sound from *l, p, r, c, t, m, s, d, n.* Write the words and ask children to read them aloud.	**Ask** children to think of a word list that ends with *-ck* to answer clues, such as the following: *goes with a shoe (sock); an animal that quacks (duck); another word for bag (sack).* Invite children to make up their own word clues.	**Give** children additional opportunities to blend short *a, i, o, u* words that begin in *k, d, s,* or *p* and end in *ck.* Label pictures of objects such as *sack, duck, pack, lock, sock, kick,* and ask children to repeat as you blend sounds to read the words aloud.

Guided Instruction

BEFORE READING

PREVIEW AND PREDICT Take a brief **picture walk** through the book, focusing on the illustrations.

- Who are the characters in the story? Where is the story taking place?

- What do you think Tom and Kim will do?

- Do you think the story will be realistic or make-believe? Why?

SET PURPOSES Ask children what they would like to find out about as they read. Suggest a question about what Kim and Tom will do.

TEACHING TIP

To put book together:

1. Tear out the story page.

2. Cut along dotted line.

3. Fold each section on fold line.

4. Assemble book.

INSTRUCTIONAL Ask children what types of care they need when they are sick. Make a picture or word list of their suggestions.

Tom Is Sick

"I can pick up for Tom," said Kim.

3

McGraw-Hill School Division

"Tom is sick," said Kim.

2

McGraw-Hill School Division

"I can pick up the sock," said Kim.

4

Guided Instruction

DURING READING

☑ **Concepts of Print**

☑ **Initial *K*, *k*, final *ck***

☑ **High-Frequency Word: *for***

☑ **Blending with Short *u***

1 **CONCEPTS OF PRINT** Focus children's attention on the title page. Read the title and ask children to look at the illustration. Ask children what information they get from the title page.

2 **PHONICS** After you read page 2, make the /k/ sound and have children make it with you. Ask them to find the word that ends with *ck*. (sick) Read the word together. Ask children to find the word that begins with *k*. (Kim)

3 **HIGH-FREQUENCY WORDS** Have children point to the word on page 3 that begins with *f*. (for) Read the word as you track print. Then have children do the same.

4 **PHONICS** After you read page 4, ask children to find other words that end with *ck*. (pick, sock)

LANGUAGE SUPPORT

ESL Demonstrate *picking up* objects. Have children pantomime the action of *picking up*. Emphasize the ending /k/ sound as you repeat and have the children repeat the word *pick*.

Guided Instruction

DURING READING

(5) **BLENDING WITH SHORT _u_** Read page 5 together. Ask children to point to the word that begins with _d_. Remind them that _ck_ sounds like /k/. Blend the sounds together to read the word. _(duck)_

(6) **STORY STRUCTURE** After you read page 6, ask children how the story began. Ask what Kim has been doing on each page of the story. (Kim picks up something else.)

(7) **CONCEPTS OF PRINT** Ask children to point to the quotation marks and the question mark on page 7. Ask who is speaking. (Tom) Ask if Tom is telling or asking. (asking)

(8) **MAKE INFERENCES** After you finish the story on page 8, ask children how Tom and Kim are feeling. Ask why they think that.

ASSESSMENT

INITIAL _k_, _k_, FINAL _ck_.
HOW TO ASSESS Show children word cards having initial _k_ and final _ck_. Ask them to read the words as they track the print.

FOLLOW UP Guide children through the pages of the story, pointing out the words with the initial _k_ and final _ck_.

"I can pick up the duck," said Kim.

5

"Kim, did you pick up for me?" said Tom.

7

"I can pick up the cap," said Kim.

6

"I did," said Kim.

8

Guided Instruction

RETURN TO PREDICTIONS AND PURPOSES
Ask children if their predictions about the story were correct. Ask if they found out what Kim did. Revisit the story if necessary.

RETELL THE STORY Have children retell the story. Children take turns and may use their books as needed.

LITERARY RESPONSE To help children respond to the story, ask:

How did Kim help Tom?

Invite children to draw and write about a time when they felt sick and someone helped them feel better. Then invite children to act out the story.

Activity

Cross Curricular: Language Arts
PICK-UP STORY Invite children to add to the story "Tom Is Sick." Make pages by writing: *"I can pick up the _____," said Kim.* Children fill in the blank, and illustrate their page. Combine the pages to make a class book.

▶ Linguistic

OBJECTIVES

Children will:

- use story structure to understand a story

MATERIALS

- *Tom Is Sick*

TEACHING TIP

INSTRUCTIONAL

Gather some items from the school nurse's office, such as a thermometer, heating pad, and bandages. Ask children what each item is used for.

Introduce Story Structure

PREPARE

Recall the Story — Ask children to recall the story *Tom Is Sick*. Ask them how the story begins, and how it ends.

TEACH

Identifying Story Structure — Reread the story together. As you read, point out that on each page of the story Kim picks up something else for Tom. Relate the story structure to a pattern by asking: *What will Kim do next?* Then continue reading to check children's responses.

PRACTICE

Complete the Pupil Edition Page — Read the directions on page 255 to the children, and make sure they clearly understand what they are being asked to do. Identify each picture, and complete the first item together. Then work through the page with children or have them complete the page independently.

ASSESS/CLOSE

Review the Page — Review children's work, and note children who are experiencing difficulty.

Name_____

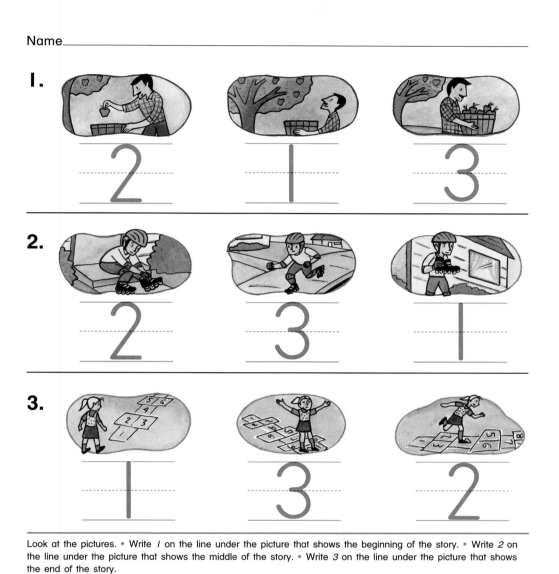

Look at the pictures. • Write *1* on the line under the picture that shows the beginning of the story. • Write *2* on the line under the picture that shows the middle of the story. • Write *3* on the line under the picture that shows the end of the story.

Unit 5 Review Story Structure   255

Pupil Edition, page 255

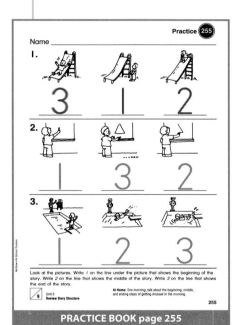

PRACTICE BOOK page 255

Meeting Individual Needs for Comprehension

EASY	ON-LEVEL	CHALLENGE	LANGUAGE SUPPORT
Use classrom props, and have children act out the story as you read it aloud. Point out the structure after you read.	**Read** an alphabet book, or "Chicka Chicka Boom Boom" by Bill Martin. Have children explain the structure of the story by describing the pattern of following the alphabet.	**Invite** children to make a counting book for the numbers 1–5 by choosing a theme and drawing items for each number or writing a short text. Talk about the structure of the stories.	**Explain** that many stories follow a pattern. Read a short rhyming story, and talk about the structure of the story.

Develop Phonological Awareness

Listen

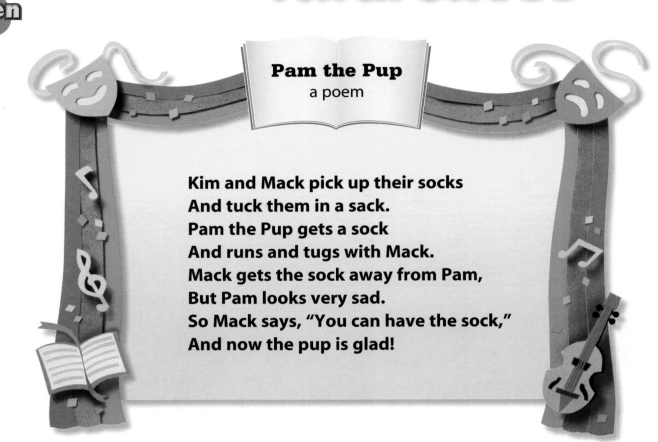

Pam the Pup
a poem

Kim and Mack pick up their socks
And tuck them in a sack.
Pam the Pup gets a sock
And runs and tugs with Mack.
Mack gets the sock away from Pam,
But Pam looks very sad.
So Mack says, "You can have the sock,"
And now the pup is glad!

Objective: Listen for Sense

READ THE POEM Read the poem "Pam the Pup" aloud. Reread the last two lines of the poem. Ask: *Why is the pup glad?* (It got the sock.) *Does that make sense?* (Yes.) Reread the poem and pause after *So Mack says.* Invite volunteers to fill in what Mack says.

> **Let's go for a walk.**
> **I will share with you.**

After each response finish reading the poem. Then ask: *Does this make sense?*

SUBSTITUTE NONSENSE WORDS Invite children to close their eyes and listen carefully. Tell them you are going to reread the poem, but this time you are going to substitute nonsense words.

Read the first line of the poem as follows: "Kim and Mack sick up their pocks." Ask children to identify the nonsense words. Repeat with other combinations of nonsense words.

> **Pam the Pup sets a gock**
> **And tuns and rugs with Mack.**

"And Mack says..."

Objective: Listen for Blending Short *a, i, o, u*

LISTEN FOR BLENDING Read the first line of the poem. Emphasize each sound in *Mack* by saying /m/-/a/-/k/. Ask children to set a connecting cube for each sound they hear. Have children touch each cube and say /m/-/a/-/k/. Then have children push the cubes together as they blend the sounds to say *Mack*. Repeat with other words in the poem that contain short vowel sounds.

> **Kim runs sad tuck**
> **Pam can sock**

CLEAN-UP TIME Tell children you are thinking of an item that Kim and Mack are putting in their sack. Give children a clue by segmenting the sounds in the item name. Have children blend the sounds to guess the item.

Say: *Kim and Mack are cleaning up.*
They will put a toy /l/-/o/-/k/ in their sack.
Pause for children to say *lock*.
Repeat with other items.

> | fan | kid | duck | pin |
> |-----|-----|------|-----|
> | ran | cot | mat | sun |

Read Together

From Phonemic Awareness to Phonics

Objective: Relate *a, i, o, u* to Short Vowel Sounds

LISTEN FOR RHYMING WORDS Read the poem. Ask children to name words that rhyme.

> | sack | Mack |
> |------|------|
> | sad | glad |

IDENTIFY THE LETTERS Say the sounds /m/-/a/-/k/. Ask: *How many sounds do you hear?* (three) Write *Mack* on the board as children say each sound. Identify the letters. Invite volunteers to say the sound the letters stand for as you point to them. Repeat with *sack*. Continue with other words in the poem.

MAKE RHYMING WORDS Point to the name *Mack* on the board and ask: *What rhymes with* Mack?

> | sack | back | lack |
> |------|------|------|
> | pack | rack | tack |

As children say the words, write them in a list under *Mack*. Use a long strip of paper to cover the first letter in each word. Circle *ack* in each word. Remove the paper, and have children read the list. Repeat the activity by helping children brainstorm lists of rhyming words for other words in the poem.

OBJECTIVES

Children will:

- identify /a/*a*, /i/*i*, /o/*o*, /u/*u*
- blend and read short *a, i, o, u* words
- write short *a, i, o, u* words
- review /k/*k*, *ck*, /l/*l*, /p/*p*, /r/*r*, /f/*f*, /k/*c*, /t/*t*, /m/*m*, /s/*s*, /d/*d*, and /n/*n*

MATERIALS

- letter cards from the *Word Play Book*

TEACHING TIP

INSTRUCTIONAL

Remind children that the letters *ck* at the end of a word make only one sound. Ask them to say the sound /k/ as you point to the *ck* in several word cards, *such as pick, sack, lock, duck.*

ALTERNATE TEACHING STRATEGY
....

BLENDING SHORT
a, i, o, u

For a different approach to teaching this skill, see Unit 1, page T32; Unit 2, page T32; Unit 3, page T30; Unit 4, page T32.

▶ **Visual/Auditory/ Kinesthetic**

Review Blending with short *a, i, o, u*

TEACH

Identify a, i, o, u as Symbols for /a/, /i/, /o/, /u/

Tell children they will continue to read short *a, i, o, u* words.

- Display the *a, i, o, u* letter cards and say /a/, /i/, /o/, /u/. Have children repeat the sounds /a/, /i/, /o/, /u/ as you point to the cards.

BLENDING Model and Guide Practice

- Place a *ck* card to the right of the *i* card. Blend the sounds together and have children repeat after you: _ick.

- Place an *s* letter card before the *ick* cards. Blend the sounds in the word to read *sick*. Have children repeat after you.

Use the Word in Context

- Invite children to use *sick* in a sentence. Ask them to share what they know about how to avoid getting a cold.

Repeat the Procedure

- Use the following words to continue modeling and for guided practice with short *a, i, o, u: sock, lock, pick, tack, duck, tick, tock.*

PRACTICE

Complete the Pupil Edition Page

Read aloud the directions on page 256. Make sure children understand what they are asked to do. Identify the pictures, and complete the first item together. Work through the page with children, or have them complete the page independently.

ASSESS/CLOSE

Build Short a, i, o, u Words

Observe children as they complete page 256. Distribute letter cards *l, p, r, f, c, t, m, s, d, n*, and ask children to build four words with short *a, i, o,* or *u* in the middle and *ck* at the end. Write the words on a chart.

Name_____

1. can ⸨cat⸩

cat

2. ⟨run⟩ rat

run

3. ⟨rip⟩ lip

rip

4. ⟨lock⟩ sock

lock

Draw a circle around the word that names the picture. • Say the word. • Then write the word.

256   Unit 5   Review Blending with Short *a, i, o, u*

McGraw-Hill School Division

Pupil Edition, page 256

ADDITIONAL PHONICS RESOURCES

Practice Book, *page 256*
Phonics Workbook

McGraw-Hill School
TECHNOLOGY

 Phonics CD-ROM
Activities for Practice with Blending and Segmenting

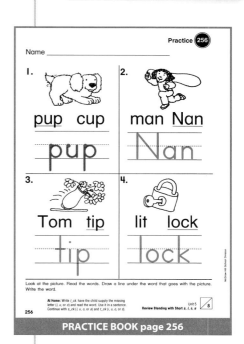

Practice 256

Name_____

1. pup cup
pup

2. man Nan
Nan

3. Tom tip
tip

4. lit lock
lock

Look at the picture. Read the words. Draw a line under the word that goes with the picture. Write the word.

At Home: Write *l_ck* have the child supply the missing letter (*i, a, o, or u*) and read the word. Use it in a sentence. Continue with *s_ck* (*i, u, a, or o*) and *t_ck* (*i, u, a, or o*).

256   Review Blending with Short *a, i, o, u*   Unit 5   8

PRACTICE BOOK page 256

Meeting Individual Needs for Phonics

EASY	ON-LEVEL	CHALLENGE	LANGUAGE SUPPORT
Give children word cards such as *Mack, Kim, dock, kid, sack, luck.* Ask children to repeat after you as you blend sounds to read the words aloud. Ask them to identify where the /k/ sound is in each word. Then have them sort words for short *a, i, o, u.*	**Ask** children to answer riddles such as the following with words from the chart they made in the Assess/Close activity: *something you can carry things in (sack, pack); a sound some clocks make (tick, tock); an animal that swims (duck).*	**Ask** children to choose four or more words from the chart they made in the Assess/Close activity, and make up a story using the words. Children may wish to do this activity with a partner or in a small group, and recite or act out the story for the rest of the class.	**Help** children distinguish short *a, i, o, u,* words that end in *ck* by having them repeat the short vowel sound they hear in *tick, pack, rock, luck.* Use each word in a simple sentence (*Hear the clock tick. Help me pack my bag.*) and have children repeat it.

Reread the Decodable Story

Tom Is Sick

 Initial *k*/final ck

 Use Illustrations

 High-Frequency Word: *for*

 Concepts of Print

Tom Is Sick

Guided Reading

SET PURPOSES Tell children that when they read the story again, they can find out more about what happened. Explain that you also want them to look for and read the words that begin with *k* and that end with *ck*. Remind them that they know the word *for* and will see it again in this story.

REREAD THE BOOK As you guide children through the story, address specific problems they may have had during the first read. Use the following prompts to guide the lesson:

• **CONCEPTS OF PRINT** Model how to run your finger from left to right as you read. Show how you track the print to the end of the line and then use the return sweep to read the first word in the second line.

• **USE ILLUSTRATIONS** Have children find the illustrations that show what Kim did for Tom. (pages 4, 5, and 6)

RETURN TO PURPOSES Ask children if they found out more about what happened in the story. Ask if they found any words that begin with *k*, or end with *ck*. Ask if anyone found the word *for*.

LITERARY RESPONSE Write three sentences from the story on the board. Have children choose one to illustrate.

Then ask children to do the following:

• describe their illustrations.

• describe what they could do to help Tom while he is sick.

INFORMAL ASSESSMENT

USE ILLUSTRATIONS
HOW TO ASSESS Ask children to draw a picture of Kim picking up something else for Tom. Point out that the page continues the pattern of the book.

FOLLOW UP If children have difficulty, take a picture walk through the book with them, pointing out the pattern.

Read the Patterned Book

Just for the Duck

- ✓ Initial /k/ k; final digraph ck
- ✓ Story Structure
- ✓ Concepts of Print
- ✓ High-Frequency Word: *for*

Just For the Duck

by Anne Miranda
illustrated by Kristen Goeters

Guided Reading

PREVIEW AND PREDICT Read the title and the author's and the illustrator's names. Take a **picture walk** through pages 2-4, noting the setting of the story and the characters. Ask whether the story seems to be real or a fantasy. Have children make predictions about what will happen in the story.

SET PURPOSES Have children decide what they want to find out from the story and predict what might happen to the little duck. Tell them that the story contains words with initial /k/ k; final ck.

READ THE BOOK Use the following prompts while the children are reading or after they have read independently. Remind them to run their fingers under each word as they read.

Pages 2-3: Point to the word that begins with f. Let's read it together: *for. High-Frequency Words*

Pages 4-5: Model: *I can use what I know about short u to read the word that begins with d. The ck makes the /k/ sound. Let's blend these sounds together, d u ck. What word in the sentence rhymes with duck?* (truck) *Phonics and Decoding*

Pages 6-7: *What has happened in the story so far? What does the mother do on each page?* (She gives the duck something else to wear or play with.) *Story Structure*

Page 8: *Let's count how many words are on this page.* (6) *Which are the longest words?* (rain, duck) *Which is the shortest word?* (is) *Concepts of Print*

RETURN TO PREDICTIONS AND PURPOSES Ask children if they found out what they needed to know from the story. See if their predictions were correct.

LITERARY RESPONSE The following questions will help focus children's responses:

- Could this story really happen? How do you know?

- What would you like to do in the rain? Draw a picture and write about it in your journal.

LANGUAGE SUPPORT

 **ESL** Read the story again, and encourage children to repeat the repetitive phrases. Then have children reread the story in pairs. Encourage children to point to the words and say the initial sound of the word.

CENTER Activity

Science

RAINDROPS ARE FALLING Have children experiment to see what happens inside a cloud to make rain fall. Provide a cookie sheet and a small spray bottle filled with water. Invite one child to hold the cookie sheet up. Another child sprays the cookie sheet a few times. Ask children to look closely and describe what happens. Children will see that some drops join together and run down, making bigger drops.

▶ **Logical/Mathematical**

OBJECTIVES

Children will:

- identify and read the high-frequency word *for*

MATERIALS

- word cards from the Word Play Book
- *Tom Is Sick*

TECHNOLOGY TIP

INSTRUCTIONAL

Write the word *four* and the numeral *4*. Remind children that the words *for* and *four* sound exactly the same, but are spelled differently and have very different meanings.

Review *for, you, me*

PREPARE

Listen to Words

Explain to the children that they will review the word *for*.

Ask children to raise their hands when they hear the word *for* in a sentence: *The cup is for you. Is the clay for you and me?*

TEACH

Model Reading the Word in Context

Have children reread the decodable book "Tom Is Sick". Ask children to listen for the word *for*.

Identify the Word

Ask children to look at their word cards, and then ask them to look for the word in sentences. Have children point to the word *for* on each page as you read the story together. Have volunteers put a self-stick note below the word. (Have children move the self-stick note from page to page.)

Write the Word

Review how to write the letters *f*, *o*, and *r*. Then children practice writing the word.

Review High-Frequency Words

Hold up word cards for the following words: *the, a, my, that, I, and, said, we, are, is, have, to, go, do, you, me.* Have children say the words.

PRACTICE

Complete the Pupil Edition Page

Read the directions on page 257 to the children, and make sure they clearly understand what they are asked to do. Complete the first item together. Then work through the page with children or have them complete the page independently.

ASSESS/CLOSE

Review the Page

Review children's work, and note children who are experiencing difficulty or need additional practice.

Name_____

1.

The duck is for you.

_____

2.

The cat is for me.

_____

3.

The pup is for you and me.

_____

Read each sentence. **1.** Draw a line under the word *for*. **2.** Draw a line under the word *me*. **3.** Draw a line under the word *you*.

Unit 5   Review *for, you, me*   **257**

Pupil Edition, page 257

Practice **257**

Name_____

1.
I have a cap (for) you.

2.
I have a cap (for) me.

3.
I have a cap (for) Dad.

4.
I have a cap (for) Mom.

Read each sentence. **1.** Draw a circle around the word *for*. Draw a line under the word *you*. **2.** Draw a circle around the word *for*. Draw a line under the word *me*. **3-4.** Draw a circle around the word *for*.

At Home: Both of you draw pictures as gifts. Write *for you* on the pictures and exchange them.

6 Unit 5
Review *for, you, me*

257

PRACTICE BOOK page 257

Meeting Individual Needs for Vocabulary

EASY	ON-LEVEL	CHALLENGE	LANGUAGE SUPPORT
Give each child a word card *for*. Then go through the alphabet, asking children to name a word that begins with that sound: *A* is for apple, *B* is for boat, *C* is for cat, and so on. Have children hold up their word card when they say the word.	**Write** the following sentences on chart paper, and have volunteers write the word *for*: The book is ___ you. The hat is ___ me. Read the sentences as you track print, and continue with other sentences.	**Have** children look for the letters *f*, *o*, and *r* in newspapers and magazines. Have them cut out letters and glue them on paper to make the word *for*. Invite them to count how many times they can make the word.	**Children** sit in a circle and hold a word card. Go around the circle and have them complete the phrase: I would like to eat ___ for lunch. Children hold up their word card when they say *for*.

257

Interactive Writing

Write a Book

Prewrite

LOOK AT THE STORY PATTERN Reread the story *Any Kind of Dog*. Emphasize the pattern of the story: Richard wants a dog. His mother gives him a different animal. Then have children help you brainstorm all of the things that are needed to take care of a dog.

Draft

WRITE A CLASS BOOK Explain that children are going to write a book titled "How to Take Care of a Dog."

- Begin by using the list that children made earlier. Have children help you complete this sentence: *A dog needs ____.* Continue until children feel that they have covered all aspects of dog care.

Write their responses on chart paper.

- Have children choose sentences that they would like to write and illustrate.

Publish

CREATE THE BOOK Compile the pages and put the book together. Read the book together.

Presentation Ideas

MAKE A COSTUME Help children to make a simple dog costume, using paper bags or paper plates for masks.

(GROUP)

▶ **Representing/Viewing**

ROLE PLAY Have children role play the text in the story. Children can use simple props and role play dog care as you read the story aloud.

(GROUP)

▶ **Representing/Viewing**

COMMUNICATION TIPS

• **Representing** When children role play, explain that in this situation they cannot use words or sounds. You will read aloud as they role play.

TECHNOLOGY TIP

Find reference webs on the Internet to answer questions about dog care.

LANGUAGE SUPPORT

ESL Invite children to bring in photos of their dogs. Have them describe the dogs, and talk about how they care for them.

Meeting Individual Needs for Writing

EASY	ON-LEVEL	CHALLENGE
Draw a Picture Invite children to draw a picture of a dog they would like to have. Help them label parts of the dog: tail, legs, head, and so on.	**Write a Description** Have children look at the book and describe Richard's dog. Work together to make a word web. Then make another word web to describe a different animal.	**Write Questions** Help children to write questions they have about dog care. Remind children to sound out words as they write. Use books or people in the community to find the answers to the questions.

Pug

The variety of literature in this lesson will offer children many opportunities to read and listen to stories about solving problems.

Pug

Listening Library Audiocassette

Decodable Story, pages 265–266 of the Pupil Edition

Gus and His Dog

by Jose Caparoz
illustrated by Don Madden

Patterned Book, page 269B

It Could Always Be Worse

A Yiddish folktale
retold by Margot Zemach

Teacher Read Aloud, page 263A

Mice Mischief
An Alphabet Story

Written by Susan Blackaby   Illustrated by Joe Boddy

Listening Library Audiocassette

ABC Big Book, pages 259A–259B

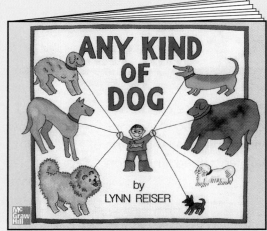

ANY KIND OF DOG

by LYNN REISER

Listening Library Audiocassette

Literature Big Book, pages 261A–261B

**Pupil Edition,
pages 258–269**

**Big Book of Real-Life Reading,
page 34**

**Big Book of Phonics Rhymes and
Poems, pages 21, 22**

 Listening
Library
Audiocassette

ADDITIONAL RESOURCES

**Practice Book,
pages 258–269**

- **Phonics Kit**
- **Language Support Book**
- **Alternate Teaching Strategies,** pp T28–T29

McGraw-Hill School
TECHNOLOGY

Phonics **CD-ROM** Provides
extra phonics support.

inter**NET**
CONNECTION Research & Inquiry Ideas.
Visit www.mhschool.com

Pug

READING AND LANGUAGE ARTS

- Phonological Awareness
- Phonics *initial /g/g*
- Comprehension
- Vocabulary
- Beginning Reading Concepts
- Listening, Speaking, Viewing, Representing

DAY 1

Focus on Reading Skills

Develop Phonological Awareness, 258G-258H
"Gobble, Gobble" *Big Book of Phonics Rhymes and Poems,* 21

 **Introduce Initial /g/g,** 258I-258
Practice Book, 258
Phonics/Phonemic Awareness
Practice Book

Phonics CD-ROM

Read the Literature

Read *Mice Mischief: An Alphabet Story*
Big Book, 259A-259B
Shared Reading

Build Skills

☑ Naming Words, 259C-259
Practice Book, 259

DAY 2

Focus on Reading Skills

Develop Phonological Awareness, 260A-260B
"Little Pig" *Big Book of Phonics Rhymes and Poems,* 22

 **Introduce Final /g/g,** 260C-260
Practice Book, 260
Phonics/Phonemic Awareness
Practice Book

Phonics CD-ROM

Read the Literature

Read *Any Kind of Dog* Big Book,
261A-261B
Shared Reading

Build Skills

☑ Summarize, 261C-261
Practice Book, 261

Cross Curriculum

 Cultural Perspectives, 259B

 Cultural Perspective, 261B

Writing

 Writing Prompt: Write another ending to the story.

 Journal Writing, 259B
Letter Formation, 258I

 Writing Prompt: What kind of dog would you like to have? Draw a picture of it.

 Journal Writing, 261B
Letter Formation, 260C

DAY 3

It Could Always Be Worse

Focus on Reading Skills

Develop Phonological Awareness, 262A-262B
"Gobble, Gobble" and "Little Pig" *Big Book of Phonics Rhymes and Poems, 21-22*
 **Review /g/g/, 262C-262**
Practice Book, 262
Phonics/Phonemic Awareness Practice Book

Phonics CD-ROM

Read the Literature

Read "It Could Always Be Worse" Teacher Read Aloud, 263A-263B
Shared Reading
Read the Big Book of Real-Life Reading, 34-35
☑ Maps

Build Skills

☑ High-Frequency Words: *he,* 263C-263
Practice Book, 263

 Activity Cultural Perspectives, 263A

 Writing Prompt: What would your bedroom look like if you could have anything you wanted in it? Write about it and draw pictures.

DAY 4

Pug

Focus on Reading Skills

Develop Phonological Awareness, 264A-264B
"Ron and His Pig"
Review Blending with Short *a, i, o, u,* 264C-264
Practice Book, 264
Phonics/Phonemic Awareness Practice Book

Phonics CD-ROM

Read the Literature

Read "Pug" Decodable Story, 265/266A-265/266D

☑ Initial and Final /g/g: Blending
☑ Summarize
☑ High-Frequency Words: *he*
☑ Concepts of Print

Build Skills

☑ Summarize, 267A-267
Practice Book, 267

 Activity Drama, 265/266D

 Writing Prompt: Write about what you like best to eat at breakfast.

Letter Formation,
Practice Book, 265-266

DAY 5

Pug

Gus and His Dog
by Jose Caporoz
illustrated by Don Madden

Focus on Reading Skills

Develop Phonological Awareness, 268A-268B
"Ron and His Pig"
Review Blending with Short *a, i, o, u,* 268C-268
Practice Book, 268
Phonics/Phonemic Awareness Practice Book

Phonics CD-ROM

Read the Literature

Reread "Pug" Decodable Story, 269A
Read "Gus and His Dog" Patterned Book, 269B
Guided Reading
☑ Initial and Final /g/g: Blending
☑ Summarize
☑ High-Frequency Words: *he*
☑ Concepts of Print

Build Skills

☑ High-Frequency Words: *he, for, is,* 269C-269
Practice Book, 269

 Activity Language Arts, 269B

 Writing Prompt: Has someone ever helped you learn something that was difficult? Write about that person.

Interactive Writing, 270A-270B

Develop Phonological Awareness

Listen

Gobble, Gobble

A turkey is a funny bird,
His head goes wobble, wobble,
And he knows just one word,
Gobble, Gobble, Gobble.

Big Book of Phonics Rhymes and Poems, p. 21

Objective: Develop an Awareness of Everyday Sounds

LISTEN TO THE POEM

- Read the poem, "Gobble, Gobble." Then reread the poem, asking children to join you on *gobble, gobble, gobble.*
- Read the last line slowly, and then read it quickly. Ask which way sounds more like a turkey would sound.
- Name another animal that children are familiar with, such as a dog. Ask children to say a word that describes how that animal sounds, such as *woof.*

THINK OF ANIMAL SOUNDS

- Continue with other animals, such as cat (*meow*), pig (*oink*), horse (*neigh*), bird (*cheep*). Encourage children to experiment with their voices as they say the sound words.
- Then reverse the activity, saying the word that names the animal sound and asking children to identify the animal.

Objective: Listen for Initial /g/

LISTEN TO THE POEM

- Read the title of the poem, and emphasize the initial /g/ sound. Have children repeat the sound with you.
- Then say the word *gobble* four times. Ask children to hold up fingers to tell how many times they heard the /g/ sound. Repeat the activity a few times. Have children place blocks in front of them to help them count.

GOBBLE FOR /G/

- Say the following list of words. Children pretend to gobble like turkeys if the word begins with /g/: *girl, have, get, dog, go, table, give.*

DIFFERENTIATE BETWEEN INITIAL SOUNDS

- Say the following pairs of words. Children choose the word that begins with /g/. Have children repeat the word if it begins with /g/.

> **go no   note goat**
> **set get   gate late**

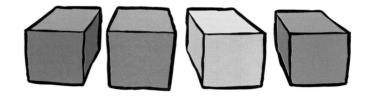

Read Together

From Phonemic Awareness to Phonics

Identify Initial /g/ G,g

IDENTIFY THE LETTER FOR THE SOUND

- Explain to children that the letters *G, g* stand for the sound /g/. Display page 21 in the Big Book of Phonics Rhymes and Poems and point to the letters in the corner. Identify the letters and have children repeat the sound.
- Read the poem again, stopping at each word that begins with /g/. Children say the last line with you.

FIND WORDS WITH G

- Point out that only uppercase *G* is used in the poem.

- Have children place stick-on notes over the uppercase *G*'s in the poem.
- Count how many *G*'s are in the poem.

SUBSTITUTE FUNNY SOUNDS

- Tell children you will reread the poem. Then substitute the word *gibble* for *gobble* throughout. Ask children to identify the "silly word."
- Then ask children to come up with a new silly sound that begins with g. Read the poem with each new sound.

> **gubble   goobble   gippy**

Gg

Gobble, Gobble
A turkey is a funny bird,
His head goes wobble, wobble,
And he knows just one word,
Gobble, Gobble, Gobble.

Big Book of Phonics Rhymes and Poems, p. 21

258H

Introduce Initial /g/g

OBJECTIVES

Children will:

- identify the letters *G, g*
- identify /g/ *G, g*
- form the letters *G, g*

....

MATERIALS

- letter cards from the Word Play Book

TEACHING TIP

INSTRUCTIONAL Show children how to write *G* and *g* by writing *C* and *c* first. Start at the top of the *C* and continue to form the *G*. Start at the top of the *c* and continue to form the *g*. Talk about curved and straight lines as you write the letters.

ALTERNATE TEACHING STRATEGY

....

INITIAL /g/g

For a different approach to teaching this skill, see page T28.

▶ **Visual/Auditory/ Kinesthetic**

TEACH

Identify /g/ *G, g* Tell children they will learn to write the letters that stand for the sound /g/-the letters *G, g*. Ask them to repeat the /g/ sound after you. Say, "Very good." Write the phrase and read it, tracking the print with your hand. Ask children to identify the word that begins with the sound /g/. Then ask them to clap their hands when they hear a word that begins with /g/ and say: Is *that Gus? Give Gus the gift. Let's go to the gate.*

Form *G, g* Display letters *G, g* and, with your back to the children trace the letters in the air. Ask children to trace the letters on their palms, then have them trace their *G, g* letter cards. Give them each an index card on which they can color a goldfish on the front and write the letters *G, g* on the back.

PRACTICE

Complete the Pupil Edition Page Read the directions on page 258 to the children, and make sure they clearly understand what they are being asked to do. Identify each picture, and complete the first item together. Then work through the page with children, or have them complete the page independently.

ASSESS/CLOSE

Identify and Use *G, g* Write the following list of words on the chalkboard. Point to each one as you say it aloud, and have children hold up their index cards with a goldfish and say *Go!* when they recognize a word that begins with the sound /g/: *get, red, goat, got, cap, gather.*

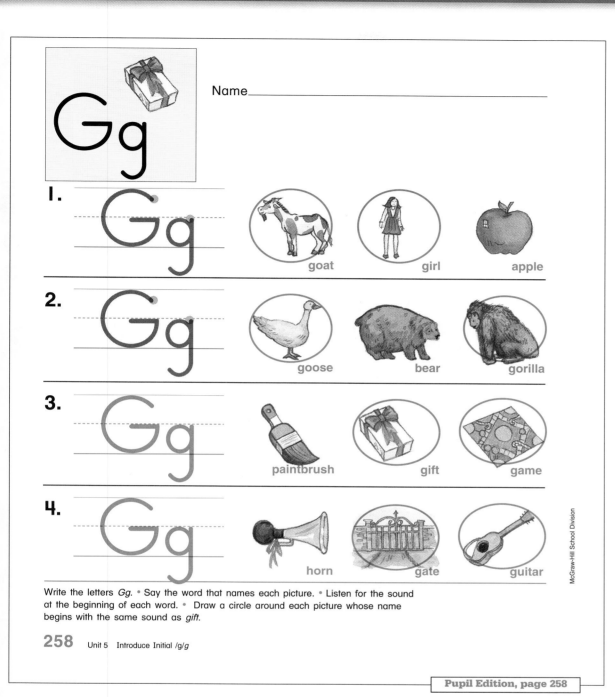

Gg

Name_____

1. G g — goat · girl · apple

2. G g — goose · bear · gorilla

3. G g — paintbrush · gift · game

4. G g — horn · gate · guitar

Write the letters *Gg*. • Say the word that names each picture. • Listen for the sound at the beginning of each word. • Draw a circle around each picture whose name begins with the same sound as *gift*.

258   Unit 5   Introduce Initial /g/g

McGraw-Hill School Division

Pupil Edition, page 258

ADDITIONAL PHONICS RESOURCES

Practice Book *page 258*
Phonics Workbook

McGraw-Hill School
TECHNOLOGY

Phonics CD-ROM
Activities for practice with
Initial Letters

PRACTICE BOOK page 258

Meeting Individual Needs for Phonics

EASY	ON-LEVEL	CHALLENGE	LANGUAGE SUPPORT
Say this riddle. Ask children to clap when they hear a word that begins with the sound /g/: *Something in my garden is good to eat. I give some to Gus, my pet pig. Part of it has a yellowish gold color. Can you guess what is in my garden?* (corn) Have children practice writing the letters.	**Show** children pictures of animals, and say their names aloud. Ask children to write a *g* for every animal whose name begins with /g/, such as: *goat, goldfish, horse, gorilla, cow, goose.* Invite children to draw their own *g* animal pictures and to label them.	**Invite** children to contribute items to an imaginary *garage* sale. The items must begin with *g*, whether they are silly or serious. Guide them to recall items such as: *games, gold, goat, gate, garbage can.* Children write *G* or *g* for each item.	**Give** directions to one child at a time, and have all the children raise their hands when they hear a word that begins with /g/, for example: *Get a book. Give the book to me. Go find a book about goats. Put it next to the book about geese. Feed the goldfish.*

258

OBJECTIVES

Children will:

- use story details
- recognize words with initial *g*

Read the Big Book

Before Reading

Develop Oral Language Sing "The Alphabet Song" together. The song is on page 2 of the Big Book of Phonics Rhymes and Poems. Then distribute letter cards. Ask children to hold up the appropriate card, and slowly sing the song again.

Remind children that they read a story about two mice. Ask them to recall some of the adventures that the mice had.

Set Purposes *Model: We read a story about two mice who got themselves into trouble. When we read the story today, let's find out more about the palace. Let's also look for the words on each page that begin with the same letter on the page.*

The mice run past the **king**.

14

15

Mice Mischief, an Alphabet Story, pages 14-15

During Reading

Read Together

- Before you begin to read, point to the first word in the first sentence. Explain that this is where you will begin to read. Continue to track print as you read the story. *Tracking Print*

- Before you read page 2, ask a volunteer to locate the letter on the page and identify it. Then have him or her find the word on the page that begins with the same letter. Continue through the story. *Phonics*

- After you read page 5, ask children to describe the room, and ask how it is the same and different from their bedrooms. Ask who might sleep in this bed. Continue to have children describe the palace throughout the story. *Use Story Details*

- Make the /g/ sound and have children say the sound with you. Read page 11, and ask what word begins with that sound. *(get)* After you read pages 12-13, have them identify the word again. *Phonics*

They tiptoe **quietly** past the dog.

Mice Mischief, an Alphabet Story, p.22

After Reading

Return to Purposes

Ask children to think about the palace in the story. Have volunteers recall specific details about scenes from the palace.

Retell the Story

Invite children to retell the story, using illustrations from the book as necessary.

Literary Response

JOURNAL WRITING Ask children to draw and write about life in a palace.

ORAL RESPONSE Ask questions such as:

- *Who might live in this palace?*

- *Would you like to live there? Why or why not?*

ABC Activity

Hold up letter cards. Ask children to remember a word in the story that begins with the sound that letter makes.

Cultural Perspective

HATS Share that people all over the world wear hats. In Mexico, the sombrero is used to keep off the sun. In Russia, people wear warm hats to stay warm in freezing weather. People sometimes wear fancy hats when they go to a party.

ACTIVITY: Use string to measure the heads of the children. Measure the string against thin cardboard. Cut the thin cardboard and tape the sides together. Provide felt, beads, glue, and markers to decorate the hat. Have a hat parade.

▶ **Intrapersonal/Kinesthetic**

TECHNOLOGY TIP

INSTRUCTIONAL

Remind children that names of people and particular places begin with capital letters. Look for examples in the classroom.

Introduce Naming Words

PREPARE

Discuss Words that Name

Ask children to name a particular place in the classroom, such as the reading corner. Make a picture or a word list of things that are found there. Then ask some children to visit that place. Point out the place, people and things.

TEACH

Identify Words that Name

Display the Big Book *Any Kind of Dog*, and recall the story. Ask children to name the people in the story. Then ask where the story takes place. Next take a picture walk through the book, and have children name things that they see.

PRACTICE

Find Persons, Places, Things

Read the directions on page 259 to the children, and make sure they clearly understand what they are asked to do. Identify each picture, and complete the first item. Then work through the page with children, or have them complete the page independently.

ASSESS/CLOSE

Review the Page

Check children's work on the Pupil Edition page. Note areas where children need extra help.

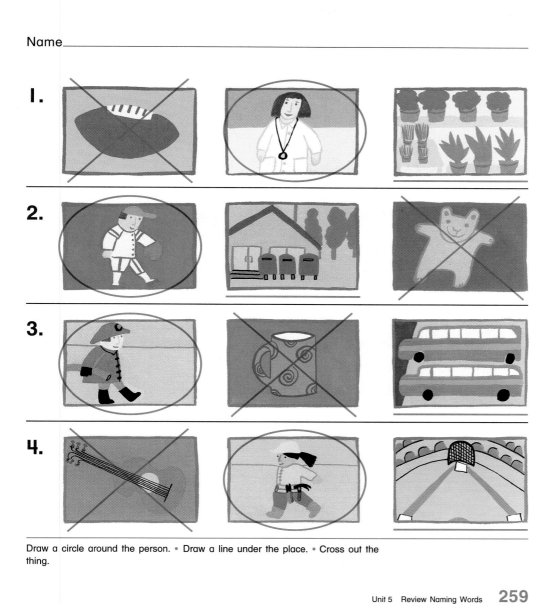

Name_____

Draw a circle around the person. • Draw a line under the place. • Cross out the thing.

Pupil Edition, page 259

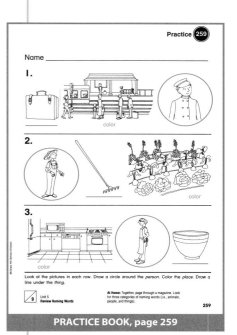

PRACTICE BOOK, page 259

Meeting Individual Needs for Grammar

EASY	ON-LEVEL	CHALLENGE	LANGUAGE SUPPORT
Visit various places in your school. Help children to make a picture/word list of the people and things that they see.	**Play** a guessing game by giving clues about a person in the classroom, such as, *I'm thinking of a girl wearing a blue sweater.* Continue with places and things. Then ask volunteers to give clues to you.	**Help** children to fold a sheet of drawing paper in thirds. Have them draw and label a picture that shows a person, a place, or a thing in each section. Discuss their choices.	**Use** a picture from a magazine, and ask questions such as: *What people are in the pictures? Where are the people? What things do you see?*

Develop Phonological Awareness

Listen

Little Pig

Little Pig had lost his way
In a fog so thick and gray.
First Pig bumped into a log.
Next, he sat upon a frog.
"Oh," Pig said in a ho-hum way,
"I guess this just is not my day!"

Big Book of Phonics Rhymes and Poems, p. 22

Objective: Become Aware of Sounds in Speech

LISTEN TO THE POEM

- Read the poem "Little Pig" to the children. Have them retell the story of the poem.
- Reread the last line of the poem. Talk about what a "ho-hum" voice might sound like. Invite volunteers to say the line of the poem using that type of voice.

USE DIFFERENT VOICES

- Discuss different voices children use when they are talking. Then reread the last two lines of the poem, substituting the word *angry* for *ho-hum*. Have volunteers say the line using an angry voice.
- Continue the activity, using *happy*, *sad*, *whispering*, and *tired* voices.

Objective: Listen for Final /g/

LISTEN TO THE POEM

- Read the title of the poem, identifying the final /g/ sound in *pig*. Have children make the sound with you.
- Say the phrase *big pig*. Emphasize the final /g/ sound, and have children repeat the phrase with you.
- Then have children complete the phrase with a word that rhymes with *pig*: *The big pig is wearing a ___. The silly pig danced a___.*

> **wig, jig**

CONTINUE WITH OTHER RHYMES

- Continue the activity using other rhymes. Emphasize the final /g/ sound.

> **The bug is on the ___.**
> **The frog is on the ___.**

- Point out the words that end with /g/.

BRAINSTORM RHYMING WORDS

- Have children brainstorm a list of words that rhyme with *pig*.
- Then have the children think of a silly sentence that rhymes.
- Have children repeat each silly sentence, emphasizing the final /g/ sound.

> **wig jig big fig**

Read Together

From Phonemic Awareness to Phonics

Objective: Identify Final /g/

IDENTIFY THE LETTER FOR THE SOUND

- Explain to children that the letter *g* stands for the /g/ sound.
- Display the Big Book of Phonics Rhymes and Poems, page 22. Point to the letters and identify them. Have children repeat the /g/ sound as you point to the letters.

REREAD THE POEM

- Reread the poem, pointing to each word as you read.

- Then tell children there is a line in the poem that has two words that end with the /g/ sound. Read the poem again, stopping at the end of each line. Have children identify the third line in the poem.

FIND THE LETTERS

- Invite children to find words in the poem that end with *g*. Read the words.
- Then ask children to count the number of letters in each word that ends with *g*.

Gg

Little Pig

Little Pig had lost his way
In a fog so thick and gray.

First Pig bumped into a log.
Next, he sat upon a frog.

"Oh," Pig said in a ho-hum way.
"I guess this just is not my day!"

22

Big Book of Phonics Rhymes and Poems, p. 22

OBJECTIVES

Children will:
- identify /g/ *g*
- write the letter *g*

....

MATERIALS

- letter cards from the *Word Building Book*

TEACHING TIP

INSTRUCTIONAL

Children may have trouble remembering the direction that the letter *g* faces. Write *dog, pig, dig* on the chalkboard. Have children trace the letter *g*, describing their movements.

ALTERNATE TEACHING STRATEGY

....

FINAL /G/g

For a different approach to teaching this skill, see page T28.

▶ **Visual/Auditory/Kinesthetic**

Introduce Final /g/ g

TEACH

Identify /g/ g

Tell children they will learn to write the sound /g/ at the end of words with the letter *g*. Write the letter on the chalkboard, have children identify it, and say the sound. Ask them to say the sound /g/ and write ___*g* on the chalkboard. Ask children to hold up their *g* letter cards when they recognize a word ending in /g/ and say: *Is the dog on the rug?*

Write and Use g

Have children trace their *g* letter cards, and then write the letter *g* four times on a letter strip. Ask them to circle a *g* every time they hear /g/ at the end of a word, and repeat the above sentence. Then follow the same procedure with this sentence: *Did Meg take the big dog for a walk?*

PRACTICE

Complete the Pupil Edition Page

Read the directions on page 260 to the children, and make sure they clearly understand what they are being asked to do. Identify each picture, and complete the first item together. Then work through the page with children, or have them complete the page independently.

ASSESS/CLOSE

Identify and Use g

Write the following list of words on the chalkboard: *tug, dig, log, rag, fog, mug*. Read each word as you point to it, and ask children to make up sentences using the words. Have them write another *g* on their letter strips for each final /g/ word they use in a sentence.

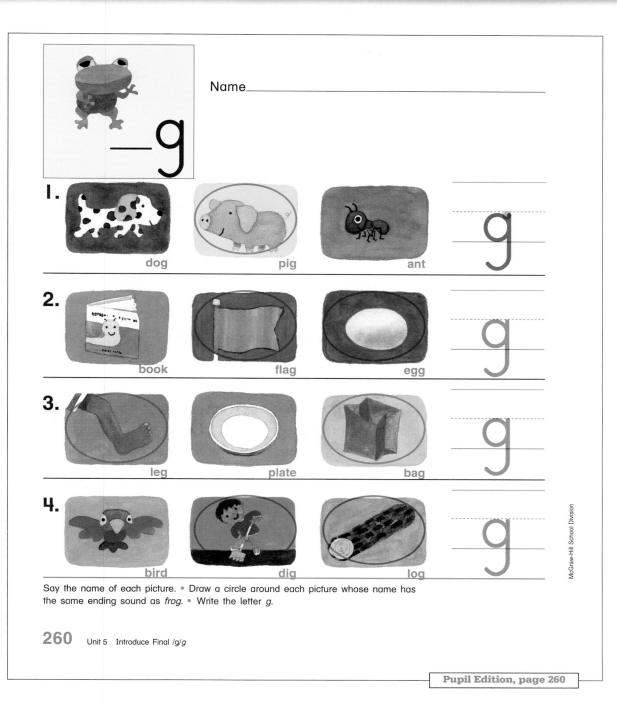

Name

_g

1. dog   pig   ant   g

2. book   flag   egg   g

3. leg   plate   bag   g

4. bird   dig   log   g

Say the name of each picture. • Draw a circle around each picture whose name has the same ending sound as *frog*. • Write the letter *g*.

McGraw-Hill School Division

260   Unit 5   Introduce Final /g/g

Pupil Edition, page 260

ADDITIONAL PHONICS RESOURCES

Practice Book, *page 260*
Phonics Workbook

McGraw-Hill School
TECHNOLOGY

Phonics CD-ROM
Activities for practice with Final Letters

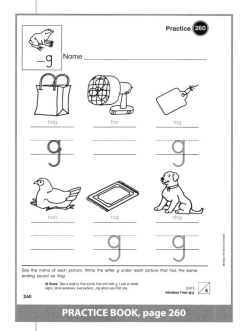

PRACTICE BOOK, page 260

Meeting Individual Needs for Phonics

EASY	ON-LEVEL	CHALLENGE	LANGUAGE SUPPORT
Give children several colors of paint and ask them to paint a picture of an object that ends in *p*. Ask children to paint the letter *p* under the picture.	**Ask** children to name objects on picture cards, such as: *log, leg, pig, rug, tag*. Have them write a *g* on their letter strips for every word that ends in /g/. Invite children to think of other words that end with /g/.	**Have** children form a circle and say a word that ends in -ag, such as *tag*. Ask each child to say a rhyming word or pass. For example: *rag, wag, bag, flag*. When no one can think of another rhyming word, change to -og or -ug and continue around the circle.	**Reinforce** children's recognition of final /g/ by having children hold up their *g* letter cards each time they hear a word that ends with the sound /g/: *Our dog lies on the rug. He can dig. We give him a hug.*

260

OBJECTIVES

- recognize words with final /g/*g*
- summarize a story

Read the Big Book

Before Reading

Develop Oral Language Sing with children the following familiar song:

Bingo

There was a farmer
Who had a dog,
And Bingo was his name-o.
B-I-N-G-O, B-I-N-G-O, B-I-N-G-O,
and Bingo was his name-o.

Demonstrate how to do the clapping pattern. Then remind children of the dog that Richard received in the story. Ask children what a good name might be for his dog.

Set Purposes *Model: When we read the story "Any Kind of Dog," we learned about a boy who wanted a dog. His mother gave him many different animals until he finally was given a dog. Let's read the story again, and find out more about the animals in the story.*

All of the animals were very nice,

but Richard still wanted a dog.

20   21

Any Kind of Dog, pages 20-21

During Reading

Read Together

- Before you begin to read, point to the first word in the first sentence. Explain that this is where you will begin to read. Continue to track print as you read the story. *Tracking Print*

- After you read page 3, ask children: *What do you know about caterpillars? Where do they live? What do they look like? Can you move like a caterpillar? Use Illustrations/Story Details*

- After you read the story, ask children the following questions to help them to summarize the story: *How did the story begin? What pets did Richard receive? How did the story end? Summarize the Story*

- Say the /g/ sound, and have children repeat it. Then read the sentence on page 1 and ask which word ends with that sound. Ask how many times they hear that word in the sentence. (dog, two) *Phonics and Decoding*

so she gave him a baby alligator.

Any Kind of Dog, p. 10

After Reading

Retell the Story

- Have children sit in a circle. Ask a child to say what the first animal was that Richard received. Continue with each succeeding animal, using illustrations from the story as necessary.

Literary Response

JOURNAL WRITING Ask children to draw a picture of a different animal that Richard's mother might have given him. Help them to write about the animal.

ORAL RESPONSE Engage children in a discussion about their pictures by asking the following questions:

- *What does your animal look like? Does it look at all like a dog?*

- *Would you like to have this animal as a pet? Why or why not?*

INFORMAL ASSESSMENT

SUMMARIZE THE STORY

HOW TO ASSESS Have children brainstorm a list of the main points of the story.

FOLLOW UP If children are having difficulty summarizing, help them to focus on the main problem in the story and how it is solved.

CULTURAL PERSPECTIVES

PETS Share that there is a wide variety of pets throughout the world. In South America, pet birds are common. In Japan, a child might choose an iguana for a pet. In outer Mongolia, children have pet horses. In Italy, a child might have a pet pigeon.

Activity Provide markers, finger paints, and paper. Ask children to make a portrait of a pet they either have or would like to have. Encourage them to use their imagination.

▶ Intrapersonal

Introduce Summarize

TECHNOLOGY TIP

INSTRUCTIONAL Reread a classroom picture book. Then ask children to explain how the story began and how it ended.

PREPARE

Revisit the Story

Ask children to recall the story *Any Kind of Dog*.

Take a picture walk through the first few pages of the book, and ask children to describe how the story begins and what the problem is.

TEACH

Understand the Story Events to Summarize

Continue reading through the story, and ask how the problem is solved and how the story ends. Then ask them to briefly explain what the story is about, and write down their ideas. Explain to children that they can remember and understand a story by *summarizing*—briefly stating what happens at the beginning, the middle, and the end of a story.

PRACTICE

Complete the Pupil Edition Page

Read the directions on page 261 to the children, and make sure they clearly understand what they are being asked to do. Identify each picture, and complete the first item together. Then work through the page with children, or have them complete the page independently.

ASSESS/CLOSE

Review the Page

Review children's work, and guide children who are experiencing difficulty.

Name_____

X | ② |

[empty drawing box]

Listen as I read two sentences. • One sentence will tell what the story "Any Kind of Dog," is about. • Circle the number of the sentence that tells what the story is about. • Cross out the number of the sentence that does not tell what the story is about.
  1. A boy goes to visit his grandma.
  2. A boy really wants a dog and in the end gets one.
On the bottom, draw a picture of what the story "Any Kind of Dog" is about.

Unit 5 Introduce Summarize **261**

Pupil Edition, page 261

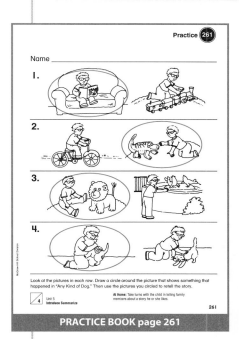

PRACTICE BOOK page 261

Meeting Individual Needs for Comprehension

EASY	ON-LEVEL	CHALLENGE	LANGUAGE SUPPORT
Guide children to fold a sheet of drawing paper in half. On one half, have them draw a picture of what happens at the beginning of the story, and on the other half, what happens at the end. Have children verbally recount the beginning and the end of the story.	**Ask** children to choose a picture book from the classroom library. Have children reread the story with you and summarize by explaining the beginning, the middle, and the end of the story.	**Choose** a part of your school day, and help children summarize the events. Help by giving an example, such as: Library Time: We listen to a story. We choose a book. We check the book out.	**Reread** classroom picture books, and begin by asking children to describe how the story begins. Then have them recount the story line, and how the story ends. Continue with several books.

261

Develop Phonological Awareness

Listen

Gobble, Gobble
a poem

Little Pig
a poem

A turkey is a funny bird,
His head goes wobble, wobble,
And he knows just one word,
Gobble, Gobble, Gobble.

Little Pig had lost his way
In a fog so thick and gray.
First, Pig bumped into a log.
Next, he sat upon a frog.
"Oh," Pig said in a ho-hum way.
"I guess this just is not my day!"

Big Book of Phonics Rhymes and Poems, pages 21–22

Objective: Develop Listening Skills

READ THE POEM As you read the poem "Little Pig" aloud, encourage children to close their eyes and picture what is happening. Then ask children questions about the poem: *What did Little Pig lose? What did he bump into? What did he sit on?*

SUBSTITUTE WORDS Create nonsense sentences by replacing words in the first two lines of the poem.

> **Little Pig had lost his head**
> **In a fog so thick and red.**

MAKE NONSENSE SENTENCES Ask: *What do fish do?* (For example, *Fish swim.*) Challenge children to make a nonsense sentence by changing one of the words. (For example, *Fish walk. Trees swim.*) Continue the activity using other simple sentences.

Objective: Listen for /g/

LISTEN FOR INITIAL AND FINAL /g/ Make the /g/ sound and ask children to repeat it with you. Then read the titles of the poems, emphasizing the initial /g/ sound in the word *gobble* and the final /g/ sound in the word *pig*. Have children repeat the words with you, stressing the initial and final /g/ sound. Read both poems aloud line by line. Stop at the end of each line and have children repeat the words that begin or end with /g/.

RECOGNIZE /g/ Say words from the poem or other words that begin or end with the /g/ sound. Invite children to gobble like a turkey if the /g/ sound is at the beginning of a word, and oink like a pig if the /g/ sound is at the end of a word.

go	get	game	gobble	gone	gas	guess
pig	fog	log	frog	dig	bag	rag	snug

IDENTIFY WORDS WITH INITIAL AND FINAL /g/ Say the following sentence: *First, Pig bumped into a log.* Invite children to repeat the sentence with you. Then encourage children to substitute other words that begin or end with /g/ for the word *log*.

bag	flag	leg	twig	wig	dog	hog	bug
jug	slug	goat	game	gate	girl	goose

From Phonemic Awareness to Phonics

Read Together

Objective: Identify /g/ G, g

IDENTIFY THE LETTERS Explain to children that the letters *G* and *g* stand for the sound /g/. Have children repeat the sound after you.

Display page 22 in the Big Book of Phonics Rhymes and Poems. Point to the letters and identify them as *G* and *g*. Say the /g/ sound and have children say the sound with you.

REREAD THE POEM Read the poem again as you point to each word. Emphasize words with the initial or final /g/. Have children repeat the words after you.

FIND WORDS WITH G, g Have children use their fingers to frame each *G* and *g* in the poem.

Gg

Little Pig

Little Pig had lost his way
In a fog so thick and gray.

First Pig bumped into a log.
Next, he sat upon a frog.

"Oh," Pig said in a ho-hum way.
"I guess this just is not my day!"

22

Big Book of Phonics Rhymes and Poems, p. 22

Review /g/ g

Children will:

- identify and discriminate between initial and final /g/ *G,g*
- write the letters *G,g*

MATERIALS

- picture cards from the *Word Building Book*

TECHNOLOGY TIP

INSTRUCTIONAL Invite children to say any first names of people that begin or end in /g/, such as: *Gail, Gus, Doug, Gilbert, Meg.* Ask children to make the sound /g/.

ALTERNATE TEACHING STRATEGY

LETTER /G/G

For a different approach to teaching this skill, see page T28.

▶ **Visual/Auditory/ Kinesthetic**

TEACH

Identify and Differentiate Between Initial and Final /g/ G,g

Tell children they will review the sound /g/ at the beginning and at the end of words and write the letters *G,g*. Write both forms of the letter on the chalkboard some distance apart, say the sound with children, and underline each form as you say *Gus* and *pig* in this sentence: *Gus has a pet pig.*

Write and Use G,g

Write *G__* and *g___* on one part of the chalkboard and *__g* on another part. Explain that these models show words that begin with /g/ and words that end in /g/. Write the above sentence on the chalkboard. Read it as you track print, and ask children to point to the model on the chalkboard that shows whether the word begins or ends in /g/. Then have them write *g* and *G* on two sides of an index card; ask them to hold up the card when they recognize a word that begins with *g*. Say the following words: *got, Nan, sad, give, get, rod, Gus.* Do the same for words that end with *g*: *pig, mad, rag, fog, fan, dig, lot, log.*

PRACTICE

Complete the Pupil Edition Page

Read the directions on page 262 to the children, and make sure they clearly understand what they are being asked to do. Identify each picture, and complete the first item together. Then work through the page with children, or have them complete the page independently.

ASSESS/CLOSE

Identify and Use G, g

Ask children to sort pictures into groups of objects whose names begin with *g* and those whose names end with *g*, such as: *pig, gift, mug, log, gate, goat.* Have them write *g* and *G*.

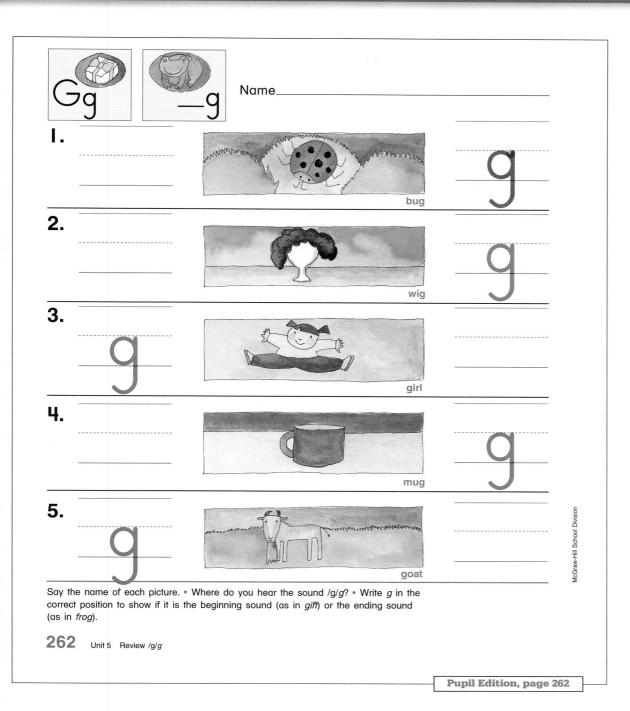

Gg _g   Name_____

1. _____ [bug] _____ g

2. _____ [wig] _____ g

3. g _____ [girl] _____

4. _____ [mug] _____ g

5. g _____ [goat] _____

Say the name of each picture. • Where do you hear the sound /g/g? • Write *g* in the correct position to show if it is the beginning sound (as in *gift*) or the ending sound (as in *frog*).

McGraw-Hill School Division

Pupil Edition, page 262

ADDITIONAL PHONICS RESOURCES

Practice Book, *page 262*
Phonics Workbook

McGraw-Hill School
TECHNOLOGY

Phonics CD-ROM
Activities for practice with Initial and Final Letters

Practice 262

Gg _g Name_____

1. g [goose] g **2.** g [dig] (g)

3. g [log] (g) **4.** (g) [gate] g

5. g [pig] (g) **6.** (g) [goat] g

Say the name of the picture. Where do you hear the sound /g/g? Draw a circle around the first *g* if it is the beginning sound (as in *gift*). Draw a circle around the second *g* if it is the ending sound (as in *frog*).

At Home: Have the child say "good" every time you say a word that begins with the same sound as *gift*.

262   Unit 5 / Review /g/g   6

PRACTICE BOOK page 262

Meeting Individual Needs for Phonics

EASY	ON-LEVEL	CHALLENGE	LANGUAGE SUPPORT
Have children trace large letters *G,g* onto sheets of white paper. Show them how to use the lines as guides as you spread white glue with your finger. Help them shake glitter over the glue, and set it aside to dry. Ask children to say words that begin and end with *g*.	**Make** word cards for the following: *got, get, rug, log, pig, gum, tag*. Provide children with letter cards to match the letters in each word. Have children work together to match the individual letter cards with the letters on the word cards, beginning at the left and proceeding to the right.	**Ask** children to hold up their *G,g* cards when they hear a word that begins or ends in /g/, and say: *Gus got the pig a tag.* Invite them to think of other things, sensible or silly, that Gus might have gotten the pig, that begin or end in *g*, such as *garden, gift, log, bug.*	**Help** ESL children reinforce fluency with initial and final /g/ words by having them say the following sentences: *Get the dog a bone. Did Meg go to the garden? The dog got through the gate.*

Teacher Read Aloud

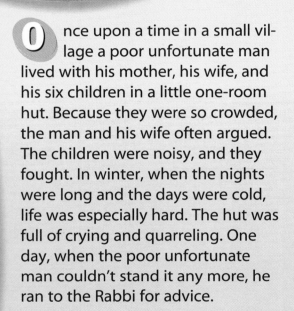

Listen

It Could Always Be Worse

a Yiddish folktale retold by
Margot Zemach

Once upon a time in a small village a poor unfortunate man lived with his mother, his wife, and his six children in a little one-room hut. Because they were so crowded, the man and his wife often argued. The children were noisy, and they fought. In winter, when the nights were long and the days were cold, life was especially hard. The hut was full of crying and quarreling. One day, when the poor unfortunate man couldn't stand it any more, he ran to the Rabbi for advice.

"Holy Rabbi," he cried, "things are in a bad way with me, and getting worse. We are so poor that my mother, my wife, my six children, and I all live together in one small hut. We are too crowded, and there's so much noise. Help me, Rabbi. I'll do whatever you say."

The Rabbi thought and pulled on his beard. At last he said, "Tell me, my poor man, do you have any animals, perhaps a chicken or two?"

"Yes," said the man. "I do have a few chickens, also a rooster and a goose."

"Ah, fine," said the Rabbi. "Now go home and take the chickens, the rooster, and the goose into your hut to live with you."

Continued on page T2

Oral Comprehension

LISTENING AND SPEAKING Ask children to list some ways life was different long ago. Explain to children that they will hear a Yiddish folktale. A folktale is a story parents have shared with their children for a very long time. After you read the story, ask: *What actions in the story keep repeating?*

Determine with the children that the rabbi kept telling the man to bring another animal into the house. Remind children that at the end of the story, the man still had the same people living in his hut. Discuss why the man was happy at the end of the story even though nothing had changed.

Activity Have children make finger puppets of the characters in the story using felt, a stapler, and markers. Encourage children to act out the story with their finger puppets.

▶ **Kinesthetic**

Real-Life Reading

Big Book of Real-Life Reading, pages 34–35

Objective: Read Environmental Print

READ THE PAGE Ask children to describe signs that they see often. Remind children of the folktale they heard, "It Could Always Be Worse," and ask them to retell the story. Explain that they will see a picture of the man's house with some familiar signs. Discuss the picture and the signs that children see.

ANSWER THE QUESTION Point to each sign and read it. Ask: *What does an exit sign mean? Where have you seen an exit sign? What does a danger sign tell us? What does each sign look like?*

Provide paper and markers. Ask children to copy the word *Exit* and decorate their EXIT sign. Suggest they hang it up in their bedrooms at home.

CULTURAL PERSPECTIVES

SCROLLS Share with children that some pictures require more space than others to draw. For very wide or long drawings, the Chinese people invented the scroll. The scroll is a clever way of rolling up a long or wide drawing so it does not take up a lot of space.

Activity Provide groups of children with two paper towel tubes, five sheets of white paper, tape, and markers. Tape the sheets of paper together to make one wide page. Attach the ends to the tubes. Have children draw a picture that makes good use of the space. Roll up the scrolls.

▶ **Spatial/Interpersonal**

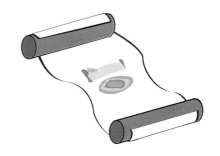

OBJECTIVES

Children will:

- **identify and read the high-frequency word** *he*

MATERIALS

- **word cards from the Word Play Book**

TECHNOLOGY TIP

INSTRUCTIONAL Point out that the word *he* takes the place of a boy's name or a man's name. Provide examples that illustrate the relationship: *Bob is here. He is here.*

He
he

Introduce High-Frequency Words: *he*

PREPARE

Listen to Words Explain to the children that they will be learning a new word, *he*. Say the following sentence: *He is at the park.* Say the sentence again, and ask children to raise a finger when they hear the word *he*. Repeat with the sentence: *Where is he?*

TEACH

Model Reading the Word in Context Give a word card to each child, and read the word. Reread the sentences, and have children raise their hands when they hear the word.

Identify the Word Write the sentences above on the chalkboard. Track print and read each sentence. Children hold up their word card when they hear the word *he*. Then ask volunteers to point to and underline the word *he* in the sentences.

PRACTICE

Complete the Pupil Edition Page Read the directions on page 263 to the children, and make sure they clearly understand what they are asked to do. Complete the first item together. Then work through the page with children, or have them complete the page independently.

ASSESS/CLOSE

Review the Page Review children's work, and note children who are experiencing difficulty or need additional practice.

Name_____

he

1.

Is he mad at Kim?

2.

He is not mad at Kim.

3.

Did he sit on the log?

4.

He sat on the log.

Read the sentence. • Then draw a line under the word *he* in the sentence.

Unit 5   Introduce High-Frequency Words: *he*   **263**

Pupil Edition, page 263

ALTERNATE TEACHING STRATEGY

HIGH-FREQUENCY WORDS: *he*

For a different approach to teaching this skill, see page T27.

▶ **Visual/Auditory/ Kinesthetic**

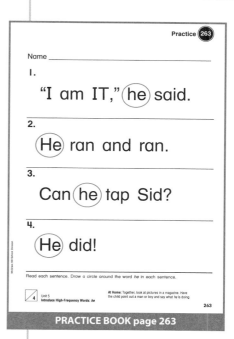

Practice 263

Name_____

1.
"I am IT," he said.

2.
He ran and ran.

3.
Can he tap Sid?

4.
He did!

Read each sentence. Draw a circle around the word *he* in each sentence.

Unit 5
Introduce High-Frequency Words: *he*

At Home: Together, look at pictures in a magazine. Have the child point out a man or boy and say what *he* is doing.

263

PRACTICE BOOK page 263

Meeting Individual Needs for Vocabulary

EASY	ON-LEVEL	CHALLENGE	LANGUAGE SUPPORT
Give each child a word card for *he*. Say a sentence that describes a child in the classroom: *Jack has brown hair*. A volunteer substitutes the word *he*: *He has brown hair*. The volunteer holds up the word card.	**Give** each child a letter card for *h* or *e*. Children look for a partner and form the word *he*. Then partners use the word in a sentence.	**Provide** copies of your local newspaper. Give each child a page, and invite them to look for and ring the word *he*. Have them count the number of words that they find.	**Ask** each child to name a special man in their lives. Children use the word *he* to describe the person: *I love Grandpa. He takes me on walks.* Write the word *he* on the chalkboard and have children point to it.

263

Develop Phonological Awareness

Listen

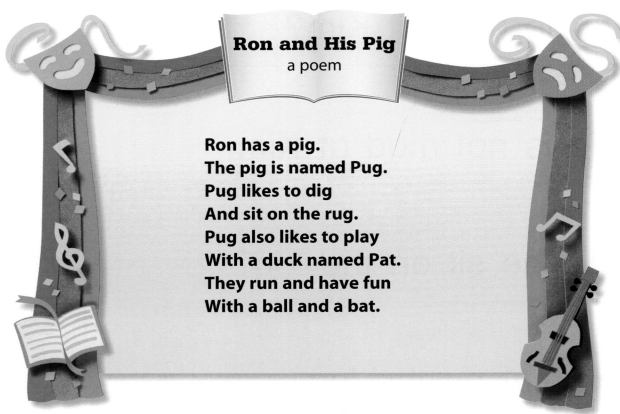

Ron and His Pig
a poem

Ron has a pig.
The pig is named Pug.
Pug likes to dig
And sit on the rug.
Pug also likes to play
With a duck named Pat.
They run and have fun
With a ball and a bat.

Objective: Listen for Words

READ THE POEM Read the poem, "Ron and His Pig." Ask questions such as: *What does Ron have? What does Pug like to do? Where does Pug like to sit?*

> **pig   sit   rug**

LISTEN FOR WORDS Reread the first line of the poem. Then clap as you say each word in the line. Tell children there are four words in the sentence. Then ask children to clap and count as you read the next sentence.

> **The pig is named Pug.**

COUNT WORDS Have children use cubes to count the words in other lines of the poem. Compare the number of words in each sentence. Then have children brainstorm long or short sentences and count the words.

Objective: Listen for Blending Short *a, i, o, u*

LISTEN FOR BLENDING Read the poem. When you read *pig,* emphasize each sound: /p/-/i/-/g/. Then say *pig.* Repeat each time you read *pig.* Tape a picture of a pig to each of the three blocks. Say /p/, and set a block on one end of the table. Say /i/, setting another block in the middle of the table. Say /g/, and place the last block on the opposite end of the table. Point to each block, and say the sounds /p/-/i/-/g/. Push the blocks together as you blend the sounds. Ask children to join in as you repeat the activity.

> **Pug   rug**

SOLVE RIDDLES Remind children that Pug and Pat like to have fun. Invite children to have fun solving riddles. Give two clues, one that includes the sounds in the word.

For example: *You use me for cleaning dishes. What am I?* [/r/-/a/-/g/]

> **rag   map**

Have children blend the sounds to solve the riddle. Repeat the activity by giving clues for other words such as: *map, mop, gum, rig,* and *mug.*

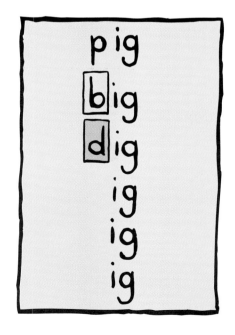

Read Together

From Phonemic Awareness to Phonics

Objective: Relate *a, i, o, u* with Short Vowel Sounds

LISTEN FOR RHYMING WORDS Read the poem. Ask children to name words that rhyme and then write word pairs on the board.

> pig   Pug   Pat
> dig   rug   bat

IDENTIFY THE LETTERS Point to the letters as you say /p/-/i/-/g/. Ask: *How many sounds do you hear?* (three) Identify the letters. Repeat with *dig.* Have children identify the letters *-ig* and the sounds they stand for. Continue with other rhyming words in the poem.

RHYMING WORDS Write the letters of the alphabet on index cards, and give each child a card. Write *pig* on the chalkboard and under it write __ig five times. Point to *pig* and ask: *What rhymes with pig?*

Ask which letter stands for /b/. Have the child with the letter *b* tape it on the board in front of –ig. Point to the word, and say /b/-/ig/. Have children repeat the sounds and then blend the sounds to say *big.* Ask: *Is big a word?* (Yes.) Continue with other letters to find words that rhyme with *pig.*

pig
big
dig
ig
ig
ig

OBJECTIVES

Children will:

- identify /a/*a*, /i/*i*, /o/*o*, /u/*u*
- blend and read short *a*, *i*, *o*, *u* words
- write short *a*, *i*, *o*, *u* words
- review /g/*g*, /p/*p*, /r/*r*, /m/*m*

MATERIALS

- letter cards from the *Word Play Book*

TEACHING TIP

WRITE the following question on the chalkboard, and ask children to read it aloud: *Did the cat go to Meg?* Ask children to draw a circle around the word that begins with the sound /g/. Then ask them to draw a line under the word that ends with the sound /g/.

ALTERNATE TEACHING STRATEGY

BLENDING SHORT
a, i, o, u

For a different approach to teaching this skill, see Unit 1, page T32; Unit 2, page T32; Unit 3, page T30; Unit 4, page T32.

▶ **Visual/Auditory/ Kinesthetic**

Review **Blending with short *a*, *i*, *o*, *u***

TEACH

Identify a, i, o, u as Symbols for /a/, /i/, /o/, /u/

Tell children they will continue to read short *a*, *i*, *o*, *u* words.

- Display the *a, i, o, u* letter cards and say /a/, /i/, /o/, /u/. Have children repeat the sounds /a/, /i/, /o/, /u/ as you point to the cards.

BLENDING Model and Guide Practice

- Place a *g* card before the *o* card. Blend the sounds together and have children repeat after you: *go*.

- Place a *t* letter card after the *g, o* cards. Blend the sounds in the word to read *got*. Have children repeat after you.

Use the Word in Context

- Invite children to use *got* in a sentence, perhaps talking about something they were once given that they really liked.

Repeat the Procedure

- Use the following words to continue modeling and for guided practice with short *a, i , o, u: mug, pig, rag, pat, dig, rug, mop.*

PRACTICE

Complete the Pupil Edition Page

Read aloud the directions on page 264. Identify each picture, and complete the first item together. Work through the page with children, or have them complete the page independently.

ASSESS/CLOSE

Build Short a, i, o, u Words

Observe children as they complete page 264. Then give them letter cards *p, r, m* and have children use them to build one word that begins in *g* and two words that end in *g*, with short *a, i , o,* or *u* in the middle.

Name

1. p i g   pig

2. r u g   rug

3. r a g   rag

4. m u g   mug

Blend the sounds and say the word. • Write the word. • Draw a circle around the
picture that goes with the word.

264   Unit 5   Review Blending with Short *a, i, o, u*

McGraw-Hill School Division

Pupil Edition, page 264

ADDITIONAL PHONICS
RESOURCES

Practice Book, *page 264*
Phonics Workbook

McGraw-Hill School
TECHNOLOGY

Phonics CD-ROM
Activities for Practice with
Blending and Segmenting

PRACTICE BOOK page 264

Meeting Individual Needs for Phonics

EASY	ON-LEVEL	CHALLENGE	LANGUAGE SUPPORT
Write *a, i, o, u* on the chalkboard. Show the following word cards: *pig, rag, mug, got, rug, dig*. Ask children to blend sounds together to read the words aloud; then ask them to point to the letter on the chalkboard that shows the middle sound of each word.	**Show** children pictures of the following: *mug, log, gum, rug, pig, dig, rag*. Have children name the object in each picture, using a word that begins or ends in *g*. Then ask them to write the words and blend sounds to read the words aloud.	**Have** children form a circle and take turns selecting a word card from a hat they pass around. Word cards show words that begin or end in *g*, such as: *dig, log, rug, got, tag, gum*. Ask children to name a word that rhymes with the one on the word card.	**On** the chalkboard write: *dig, dug*. Ask children to repeat after you and blend sounds to read each word. Underline the vowel and ask children to name it. Continue with *rag, rug; pot, pat*. Have children say the words as you point to them.

Guided Instruction

BEFORE READING

PREVIEW AND PREDICT Take a brief picture walk through the book, focusing on the illustrations.

- *Who is Pug? Where is the story taking place?*

- *What do you think Pug will do?*

- *Do you think the story will be realistic, or will it be make-believe? Why?*

SET PURPOSES Discuss with children what they may want to find out about as they read the story. Ask questions, such as: What do they think Pug will do for his mom and dad?

Pug

He got a mug and a cup.

3

McGraw-Hill School Division

Pug got a pot and a pan.

2

McGraw-Hill School Division

Mom and Dad got up.

4

Guided Instruction

☑ **Blending with Short** *a, i, o, u*

☑ **Summarize**

☑ **Concepts of Print**

☑ **High-Frequency Word:** *he*

(1) **CONCEPTS OF PRINT** Have children point to the first letter on the title page. Ask children how it compares in size with the other letters. (It is bigger.) Explain that this is a capital letter and that capital letters are used for titles, to begin sentences, and for people's names.

(2) **BLENDING WITH a, i, o, u** Model: Look on page 2 and find the word that begins with the letter *g*. Let's blend the sounds to read the word: *g-o-t got.*

(3) **HIGH-FREQUENCY WORDS** Ask children to point to the first word on page 3. Read it as you track print. *H e He*

(4) **BLENDING WITH SHORT a** Children point to the third word on page 4. Ask them to blend the letters to say *D a d Dad.*

LANGUAGE SUPPORT

ESL Use props, such as a mug, a cup, a pot, and a pan to help children make word connections. Hold the items as their names appear in the story.

Guided Instruction

BEFORE READING

5 **CONCEPTS OF PRINT** Point out the use of quotation marks on page 5. Ask children to frame the words within the quotation marks and explain that quotation marks are used to show when people are speaking.

6 **USE ILLUSTRATIONS** Look at page 6 and ask children what Pug did for Mom and Dad. (Children's answers will vary.)

7 **MAKE INFERENCES** Point out that on page 7 Pug and his mom and dad look happy. Why? Then, ask children if they have ever surprised their mom and dad. Have them share their experiences.

8 **SUMMARIZE** Ask children to tell what happened, first, next, and last in the story.

ASSESSMENT

SUMMARIZE
HOW TO ASSESS
Have children point out important facts of the story and explain why they are important.

FOLLOW UP Explain to children what Pug is doing in each page of the story and how he will surprise his parents.

"You are in luck,"
said Pug.

5

"I did it for you,"
said Pug.

7

"Is it for Dad and me?" said Mom.

6

Mom and Dad sat to have a sip.

8

Guided Instruction

RETURN TO PREDICTIONS AND PURPOSES
Ask children if their predictions about the story were correct. Ask them how Pug surprised his mom and dad.

RETELL THE STORY Ask children to retell the story using props. Have them show what Pug did first, next, and then what they all did.

LITERARY RESPONSE To help children respond to the story, ask:

Is this story realistic or make-believe? Why?

How did Pug surprise Mom and Dad?

Invite children to draw and write about a breakfast that they would like to make.

CENTER Activity

Cross Curricular: Drama

BREAKFAST IS SERVED Have partners act out cooking something for breakfast. Supply simple classroom props, such as cooking tools, cups, dishes, and silverware. Encourage children to follow a specific sequence. Children may wish to dictate simple breakfast recipes.

▶ Logical/Interpersonal

OBJECTIVES

Children will:

- summarize to understand a story

....

MATERIALS

- *Pug*

TEACHING TIP

INSTRUCTIONAL Talk about ways that children help their parents. Point out that some children may have specific jobs or chores to do. Have children name chores they or their siblings do. Ask: "What special ways can you think of to help your parents?"

Review Summarize

PREPARE

Recall the Story   Ask children to recall the story *Pug*. Ask children who the characters are, where the story takes place, and how the story begins.

TEACH

List Story Events to Summarize   Reread the story together. Then ask children to describe how the story begins, what happens, and how the story ends. Explain that they can summarize a story by recalling the beginning, middle, and ending of a story.

PRACTICE

Complete the Pupil Edition Page   Read the directions on page 267 to the children, and make sure they clearly understand what they are asked to do. Identify each picture, and complete the first item together. Then work through the page with children or have them complete the page independently.

ASSESS/CLOSE

Review the Page   Review children's work, and note children who are experiencing difficulty.

Name_____

✕   ②

[blank box for drawing]

Listen as I read two sentences. • One sentence will tell what the story "Pug" is about. • Circle the number of the sentence that tells what the story is about. • Cross out the number of the sentence that does not tell what the story is about.
1. Pug played with his blocks.
2. Pug made breakfast for his mom and dad.
On the bottom, draw a picture of what "Pug" is about.

Unit 5 Review Summarize   **267**

Pupil Edition, page 267

ALTERNATE TEACHING STRATEGY

SUMMARIZE

For a different approach to teaching the skill, see page T29.

▶ **Visual/Auditory/ Kinesthetic**

PRACTICE BOOK page 267

Meeting Individual Needs for Comprehension

EASY	ON-LEVEL	CHALLENGE	LANGUAGE SUPPORT
Have children use their books to complete the following phrases: *The story begins when ___. Pug wakes up his parents to ____. At the end of the story, ___.* Have children give their responses to you aloud.	**Write** three sentences that describe the beginning, the middle, and the end of a story on sentence strips. Use the sentence strips and have partners put them in order. Then have children use them to retell the beginning, middle, and ending of the story.	**Ask** children to choose a picture book from your classroom library. Read the book to the children. Then have them draw pictures to show the beginning, middle, and end of the story.	**Recite** short, familiar nursery rhymes to the children. Then have them summarize what the rhyme is about. Guide children to describe what happens at the beginning, middle, and end.

267

Develop Phonological Awareness

Listen

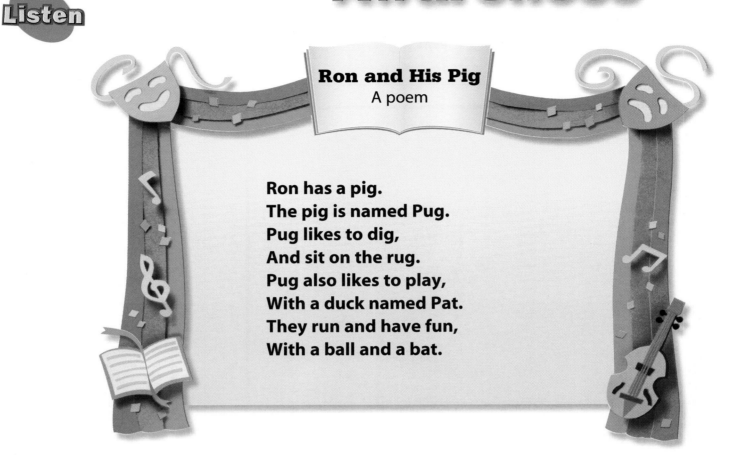

Ron and His Pig
A poem

Ron has a pig.
The pig is named Pug.
Pug likes to dig,
And sit on the rug.
Pug also likes to play,
With a duck named Pat.
They run and have fun,
With a ball and a bat.

Objective: Enhance Listening Skills

READ THE POEM Read the poem "Ron and His Pig."
Ask: *What names did you hear?*

> Ron   Pug   Pat

SIT LIKE PUG Ask children to stand on a classroom
rug if possible. Reread the poem. Invite children to sit
each time they hear *Pug,* then stand again as you continue to read.

LISTEN AND FIND PUG Secretly assign each child a
word from the poem. Assign only one child *Pug.* Identify
a child as *Ron.* Have children scatter throughout the
room and whisper the word they have been assigned.

Explain that *Ron* must find the child who is whispering
Pug. Ron should walk around the room, listening as the
children whisper their assigned words. Once found, *Ron*
introduces *Pug* to the class. Repeat with a new listener
and a new *Pug.*

Objective: Listen for Blending Short *a, i, o, u*

LISTEN FOR BLENDING SHORT o Reread the poem. Say: *Who is this poem about? Here's a clue. /r/-/o/-/n/.* Have the children repeat the sounds, then blend to say *Ron.* Repeat with other names in the poem.

> **Pug   Pat**

DUCK, DUCK, GOOSE Remind children that Pug and Pat like to have fun. Invite children to have fun playing a game similar to "Duck, Duck, Goose." Have children sit in a circle. Ask one child to walk outside the circle, then stop and tap another gently on the shoulder each time you say, "What did they say?"

To play the game, tell children:

Pug and Pat like to play.

Listen to what they have to say.

/t/-/a/-/g/ What did they say?

Encourage all children to figure out the word. Invite the child who was tapped on the shoulder to repeat the sounds, then blend them to say *tag.* Select a new child to walk around the circle. Continue the game by substituting other words.

> **dock   kit   lid   fog   sun   pin   rim**

/t/-/a/-/g/
tag

Read Together

From Phonemic Awareness to Phonics

Objective: Relate *a, i, o, u* to Short Vowel Sounds

LISTEN FOR RHYMING WORDS Read the poem, emphasizing the word *Pug* each time you say it. Ask: *What word in the poem rhymes with Pug?* (rug)

IDENTIFY THE LETTERS Say the sounds /p/-/u/-/g/. As children say each sound, write *Pug* on the board. Identify the letters. Repeat with *rug.* Have children say the sounds /u/-/g/ with you.

FIND RHYME PAIRS Reread the poem. Have children stand when they hear a word that rhymes with Pug. *(rug)* Repeat with other poem pairs.

MORE RHYMING WORDS Write words that rhyme on individual index cards.

> **pig   rig   sit   pit**
> **duck   luck   Pat   cat**
> **lock   dock   fun   sun**

Invite children to find rhyming pairs by matching words with like endings.

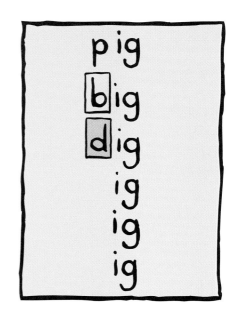

Review

Blending with short *a, i, o, u*

Children will:

- identify /a/*a*, /i/*i*, /o/*o*, /u/*u*
- blend and read short *a, i, o, u* words
- write short *a, i, o, u* words
- review /g/*g*, k/*ck*, /l/*l*, /p/*p*, /r/*r*, /f/*f*, k/*c*, /t/*t*, /m/*m*, /s/*s*, /d/*d*, and /n/*n*.

MATERIALS

- letter cards from the *Word Building Book*

TEACHING TIP

INSTRUCTIONAL Write the word *luck* on the chalkboard. Have children think of other words for that rhyming family. List the words on the chalkboard. Do the same with *rock, tick,* and *sack.*

ALTERNATE TEACHING STRATEGY

BLENDING SHORT
a, i, o, u

For a different approach to teaching this skill, see Unit 1, page T32; Unit 2, page T32; Unit 3, page T30; Unit 4, page T32.

▶ **Visual/Auditory/Kinesthetic**

TEACH

Identify *a, i, o, u* as Symbols for /a/, /i/, /o/, /u/

Tell children they will continue to read words with *a, i, o, u.*

- Display the *a, i, o, u* letter cards and say /a/, /i/, /o/, /u/.
- Have children repeat the sounds as you point to the cards.

BLENDING Model and Guide Practice

- Place an *l* card before the *o* card. Blend the sounds together and have children repeat after you.

- Place a *t* letter card after the *l, o* cards. Blend the sounds to read *lot.* Have children repeat after you.

Use the Word in Context

- Invite children to *use* lot in a sentence, perhaps talking about something they have a lot of or would like to have a lot of.

Repeat the Procedure

- Use these words to continue modeling and for guided practice with short *a, i, o, u: fun, sock, kit, lap, dig, tug, dip.*

PRACTICE

Complete the Pupil Edition Page

Read aloud the directions on page 268. Identify each picture, and complete the first item together. Then work through the page with children, or have them complete the page independently.

ASSESS/CLOSE

Build Short *a, i, o, u* Words

Observe children as they complete page 268. Give them letter cards *k,ck, l, p, r, t, n, d,* and have them build words with short *a, i, o,* or *u.*

Name_____

1. man (mug)

mug

2. sun (sick)

sick

3. (pack) pin

pack

4. run (rock)

rock

Draw a circle around the word that names the picture. • Say the word. • Then write the word.

McGraw-Hill School Division

Pupil Edition, page 268

ADDITIONAL PHONICS RESOURCES

Practice Book, *page 268*
Phonics Workbook

McGraw-Hill School
TECHNOLOGY

Phonics **CD-ROM**
Activities for Practice with Blending and Segmenting

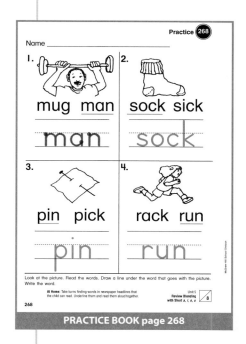

PRACTICE BOOK page 268

Meeting Individual Needs for Phonics

EASY	ON-LEVEL	CHALLENGE	LANGUAGE SUPPORT
Write *a, i, o, u* on the chalkboard. Show the following word cards: *tag, rock, mug, sun, fog, pack, dug*. Ask children to blend sounds together to read the words aloud. Ask children to make the sound of the middle letter of each word.	**Show** children pictures of the following objects: *mug, log, cap, duck, pig, cot, sack, kick*. Have children name the object in each picture. Then ask them to write the words and blend sounds to read their words aloud.	**Have** children form a circle and take turns selecting a word card from a hat that they pass around. Make the following word cards: *fun, lap, not, pit, mad, Nan, did, rod, cut*. Children select a card, read the word, and then name a word that rhymes with it.	**Write** this sentence on the chalkboard: *Tim and the pup ran to the rock.* Ask children to tell which words have the /a/ sound *(and, ran)*. Ask a volunteer to point to the words. Do the same for the /i/ sound (Tim), the /o/ sound (rock), and the /u/ sound (pup).

268

Reread the Decodable Story

Pug

Pug

☑ **Blend with Short *a, i, o, u***
☑ **Summarize**
☑ **High-Frequency Word:** *he*
☑ **Concepts of Print**

Guided Reading

SET PURPOSES Tell children that when they read the story again, they can find out more about what happens. Explain that you also want them to look for words that contain the initial and the medial letter *a*. Remind children that they know the word *he* and they will see it again in this story.

REREAD THE BOOK As you reread the story, keep in mind any problems children experienced during the first reading. Use the following prompts to guide reading:

• **CONCEPTS OF PRINT** Choose a page in the story with two lines and have children practice reading both lines by tracking print left to right and by using a return sweep to begin the second line.

• **MAKE INFERENCES** Ask children to think about what Pug did to surprise his mom and dad. Then ask them how they think Pug feels. (happy and proud)

RETURN TO PURPOSES Ask children if they found out more about what they wanted to know from the story. Have children locate the word *he* in the story. Ask them to whom the word *he* is referring.

LITERARY RESPONSE Have groups of three act out the story, using simple classroom props. Children can use their books as necessary. After children have finished, gather them for a group dicussion.

Ask questions, such as:

• *How did Pug surprise his mom and dad?*

• *What could you do to surprise your mom and dad?*

Read the Patterned Book

Gus and His Dog

Gus and His Dog

by Jose Caparoz
illustrated by Don Madden

☑ **Initial and final /g/g**
☑ **Summarize**
☑ **Concepts of Print**
☑ **High-Frequency Word:** *he*

Guided Reading

PREVIEW AND PREDICT Read the title and the author's and the illustrator's names. Take a **picture walk** through pages 2-4, noting the setting of the story and the characters. Ask if the story seems to be real or a fantasy. Have children make predictions about what will happen in the story.

SET PURPOSES Have children decide what they want to find out from the story and to predict what might happen to the little boy and his dog. Tell them that the story contains words with initial and final *g*.

READ THE BOOK Use the following prompts while the children are reading or after they have read independently. Remind them to run their fingers under each word as they read.

Pages 2-3: Point to the first word on page 3. *Let's read it together: he. Who does he refer to?* (Gus) *High-Frequency Words*

Pages 4-5: Model: I can use what I know about short u to read the word that begins with *t*. Each letter makes its own sound.

Let's blend these sounds together: t u g. Can you think of another word that rhymes with tug? (rug) *Phonics and Decoding*

Pages 6-7: *Read the sentence on page 6. Who can find a word with a capital letter?* (Gus) *A name is a word that begins with a capital letter. What capital letter does your name begin with?* (Answers will vary.) *Concepts of Print*

Page 8: *What is the story about?* (A dog that gets dirty and needs a bath.) *Summarize*

RETURN TO PREDICTIONS AND PURPOSES Ask children if they found out what they needed to know from the story. See if their predictions were correct.

LITERARY RESPONSE The following questions will help focus children's responses:

• What was your favorite part of the story? Why?

• What things do you need to give a dog a bath? Make a picture or a word list in your journal.

Language Arts

A DOG STORY Write the following sentence on sentence strips: He gave the dog a ____. Have children copy the sentence, and complete it. Then have them illustrate their sentences. You may wish to combine the pages to make a class book.

▶ **Linguistic**

OBJECTIVES

Children will:

- identify and read the high-frequency word *he*

MATERIALS

- word cards from the Word Play Book
- *Pug*

TECHNOLOGY TIP

INSTRUCTIONAL Explain that the word *he* is used to refer to a boy or a man. Use sentence pairs to illustrate: *Bob has a red shirt. He has a red shirt.*

Review *he, for, is*

PREPARE

Listen to Words
Explain to the children that they will review the word *he*.

Ask children to say words that rhyme with *he: bee, fee, me, knee, see, she,* and so on.

TEACH

Model Reading the Word in Context
Have children reread the decodable story "Pug." Ask children to listen for the word *he*.

Identify the Word
Ask children to look at their word cards, and then ask them to look for the word in sentences. Have children point to the word *he* on each page as you read the story together. Have volunteers put a self-stick note below the word. (Have children move the self-stick note from page to page.)

Review High-Frequency Words
Give each child one word card of a high-frequency word *(for, is, he, the, a, my, that, I, and, you, said, we, are, have, to, me, go, do)*. Say a word, and have the child who has the word card hold up the card and say it.

PRACTICE

Complete the Pupil Edition Page
Read the directions on page 269 to the children, and make sure they clearly understand what they are asked to do. Complete the first item together. Then work through the page with children or have them complete the page independently.

ASSESS/CLOSE

Review the Page
Review children's work, and note children who are experiencing difficulty or need additional practice.

Name_____

1.

He got a mug for Kim.

2.

He said, "That mug is for Kim."

3.

Kim said, "He got a mug for me."

Read each sentence. **1.** Draw a line under the word *he*. **2.** Draw a line under the word *is*. **3.** Draw a line under the word *for*.

Pupil Edition, page 269

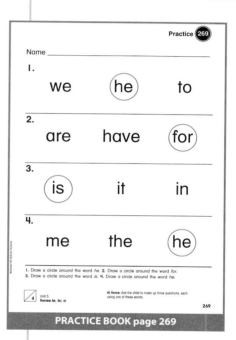

ALTERNATE TEACHING
STRATEGY
....
**HIGH-FREQUENCY
WORDS**
For a different approach
to teaching this skill, see
page T27.

▶ **Visual/Auditory/
Kinesthetic**

Practice **269**

Name_____

1.

| we | (he) | to |

2.

| are | have | (for) |

3.

| (is) | it | in |

4.

| me | the | (he) |

1. Draw a circle around the word *he*. 2. Draw a circle around the word *for*.
3. Draw a circle around the word *is*. 4. Draw a circle around the word *he*.

Unit 5
Review *he, for, is*

At Home: Ask the child to make up three questions, each using one of these words.

269

PRACTICE BOOK page 269

Meeting Individual Needs for Vocabulary

EASY	ON-LEVEL	CHALLENGE	LANGUAGE SUPPORT
Read this nursery rhyme and have children raise their hand when they hear the word *he*: Old King Cole was a merry old soul and a merry old soul was he./He called for his pipe, and he called for his bowl, and he called for his fiddlers three.	**Write** the word *he* and read it together. Then go through the alphabet, substituting each initial letter. Decide if the word is real or nonsense.	**Have** children choose a classroom library book and find the word *he*. As you read the book, stop and ask who *he* is referring to.	**Have** children sit in a circle. Describe a boy using his name: *Evan has brown hair.* Others repeat the sentence, substituting the word *he*: *He has brown hair.*

269

GRAMMAR/SPELLING CONNECTIONS

Model subject-verb agreement, complete sentences, and correct tense so that students may gain increasing control of grammar when speaking and writing.

Interactive Writing

Write a Book of Riddles

Prewrite

LOOK AT THE STORY PATTERN Revisit the book *Any Kind of Dog*. Talk about the pattern in the story: Richard wants a dog. His mother gives him a different animal that looks like a different type of dog. As you go through the book, make a list of the dogs that appear in the book.

Draft

WRITE THE BOOK Explain that children are going to write riddles about the dogs on the list.

- Begin by choosing one of the dogs and writing clues on the chalkboard:

  It is fluffy.

  It is bushy.

  It looks like a lion.

Have children guess the dog, using the book as reference.

- Have children work in small groups to choose one of the dogs, talk about things unique to the dog, and write clues about it. Help as necessary. Children write the clues, and draw the dog on the back of their papers.

Publish

CREATE THE BOOK Compile the pages to make a class book. Invite volunteers to help you make a cover.

Presentation Ideas

MAKE A MASK Have groups work together to make a mask that shows the dog that they wrote about. Children can use classroom art and craft materials.

▶ **Representing/Viewing**

READ THE RIDDLES Have children read their riddles aloud. Children can take turns reading, and one child can wear the costume. Others guess the dog that the riddle describes.

▶ **Speaking/Representing**

COMMUNICATION TIPS

- **Representing** You may find it helpful to assign children specific tasks when they work together. Have children decide beforehand who will read and so on.

TECHNOLOGY TIP

Find Web sites that provide information about various types of dogs.

LANGUAGE SUPPORT

ESL Share a book of simple riddles or jokes with the children. Talk about the funny part of the joke.

Meeting Individual Needs for Writing

EASY	ON-LEVEL	CHALLENGE
Use Pictures Make picture cards of different kinds of dogs. Have children make word lists to describe the dogs.	**Write a Riddle** Invite partners to write riddles about other animals. Have them begin by brainstorming about familiar animals. Remind children to write left to right and top to bottom on the page as they record. Children write their clues and partners guess.	**Find Information** Have children find out more about the dog that they wrote about. Help them to write some interesting facts to share.

A Pet for Ken

Children will read and listen to a variety of stories about working together cooperatively to solve problems.

A Pet for Ken

Listening Library Audiocassette

Decodable Story, pages 277–278 of the Pupil Edition

Meg's Elephant
by Anne Miranda
illustrated by Bob Barner

Patterned Book, page 281B

Winter Days in the Big Woods
by Laura Ingalls Wilder

Teacher Read Aloud, page 275A

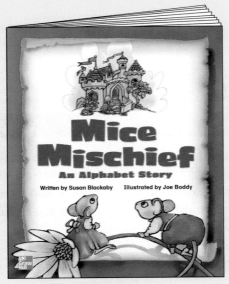

Mice Mischief
An Alphabet Story
Written by Susan Blackaby   Illustrated by Joe Boddy

Listening Library Audiocassette

ABC Big Book, pages 271A–271B

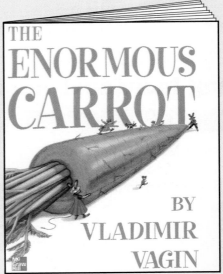

THE ENORMOUS CARROT
BY VLADIMIR VAGIN

Listening Library Audiocassette

Literature Big Book, pages 273A–273B

**Pupil Edition,
pages 270–281**

**Big Book of Real-Life Reading,
page 36**

**Big Book of Phonics Rhymes and
Poems, pages 17, 18**

 Listening
Library
Audiocassette

ADDITIONAL RESOURCES

**Practice Book,
pages 270–281**

- **Phonics Kit**
- **Language Support Book**
- **Alternate Teaching Strategies,** pp T30–T31

McGraw-Hill School
TECHNOLOGY

Phonics CD-ROM Provides
extra phonics support.

interNET CONNECTION Research & Inquiry Ideas.

Visit www.mhschool.com

A Pet for Ken

Suggested Lesson Planner

READING AND LANGUAGE ARTS

- **Phonological Awareness**

- **Phonics** *initial and medial /e/e; blending with short e*

- **Comprehension**

- **Vocabulary**

- **Beginning Reading Concepts**

- **Listening, Speaking, Viewing, Representing**

DAY 1

Focus on Reading Skills

Develop Phonological Awareness, 270G-270H
"Engine, Engine, Number Nine" *Big Book of Phonics Rhymes and Poems*, 17

 **Introduce Initial /e/e**, 270I-270
Practice Book, 270
Phonics/Phonemic Awareness Practice Book

 Phonics CD-ROM

Read the Literature

 Read *Mice Mischief: An Alphabet Story* **Big Book**, 271A-271B
Shared Reading

Build Skills

☑ Action Words, 271C-271
Practice Book, 271

DAY 2

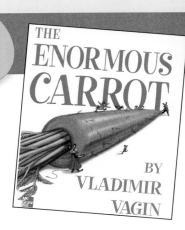

Focus on Reading Skills

Develop Phonological Awareness, 272A-272B
"Ben" *Big Book of Phonics Rhymes and Poems*, 18

 **Introduce Medial /e/e**, 272C-272
Practice Book, 272
Phonics/Phonemic Awareness Practice Book

 Phonics CD-ROM

Read the Literature

 Read *The Enormous Carrot* Big Book, 273A-273B
Shared Reading

Build Skills

☑ Story Structure, 273C-273
Practice Book, 273

- **Cross Curriculum**

 Activity Language Arts, 271B

Activity Math, 273B

- **Writing**

Writing Prompt: Write about what friends do with each other.

Journal Writing, 271B
Letter Formation, 270I

Writing Prompt: Write about how you would help pull the carrot out.

Journal Writing, 273B
Letter Formation, 272C

DAY 3

Winter Days in the Big Woods

Focus on Reading Skills

Develop Phonological Awareness, 274A-274B
"Engine, Engine, Number Nine" and "Ben" *Big Book of Phonics Rhymes and Poems*, 17-18
 **Review /e/e/, 274C-274**
Practice Book, 274
Phonics/Phonemic Awareness
Practice Book

 CD-ROM

Read the Literature

Read "Winter Days in the Big Woods" Teacher Read Aloud, 275A-275B
Shared Reading
Read the Big Book of Real-Life Reading, 36-37
☑ Maps

Build Skills
☑ High-Frequency Words: *she*, 275C-275
Practice Book, 275

 Activity Cultural Perspectives, 275A

 Writing Prompt: What do you like to do when it's cold outside? Write about your ideas.

DAY 4

A Pet for Ken

Focus on Reading Skills

Develop Phonological Awareness, 276A-276B
"Meg and Her Duck"
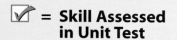 **Review Blending with Short *e*** 276C-276
Practice Book, 276
Phonics/Phonemic Awareness
Practice Book

 **CD-ROM**

Read the Literature

Read "A Pet for Ken" Decodable Story, 277/278A-277/278D

☑ Initial and Medial /e/e: Blending
☑ Story Structure
☑ High-Frequency Words: *she*
☑ Concepts of Print

Build Skills
☑ Story Structure, 279A-279
Practice Book, 279

Activity Drama, 277/278D

 Writing Prompt: If you had a pet, what would you do with it? Write your ideas.

Letter Formation,
Practice Book, 277-278

DAY 5

Meg's Elephant
by Anne Miranda
illustrated by Bob Barner

A Pet for Ken

Focus on Reading Skills

Develop Phonological Awareness, 280A-280B
"Meg and Her Duck"
 **Review Blending with Short *e, u*,** 280C-280
Practice Book, 280
Phonics/Phonemic Awareness
Practice Book

CD-ROM

Read the Literature
Reread "A Pet for Ken" Decodable Story, 281A
Read "Meg's Elephant" Patterned Book, 281B
Guided Reading
☑ Initial and Medial /e/e Blending
☑ Story Structure
☑ High-Frequency Words: *she*
☑ Concepts of Print

Build Skills
☑ High-Frequency Words: *she, he, is, for,* 281C-281
Practice Book, 281

 **Activity** Science, 281B

Writing Prompt: Has your class made anything together? Write about what you made and how you made it.

Interactive Writing, 282A-282B

270F

Develop Phonological Awareness

Listen

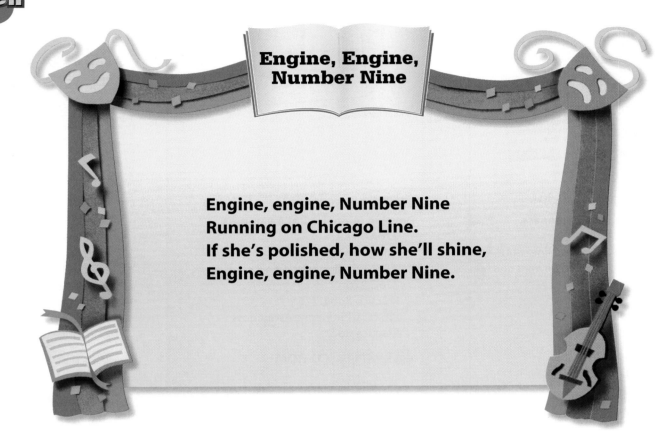

Engine, Engine, Number Nine

Engine, engine, Number Nine
Running on Chicago Line.
If she's polished, how she'll shine,
Engine, engine, Number Nine.

Objective: Listen for Rhyming Words

READ THE POEM Read the poem "Engine, Engine, Number 9." Have children describe what an engine looks like.

Reread each verse. Have children say the words that rhyme.

CREATE NEW WORDS Read the poem again. Change *Number Nine* to *Number Two*. Have children substitute rhyming words for "line." Accept nonsense words, but encourage children to think of real words.

> zoo   blue   flew

THINK OF RHYMING WORDS Say the first line of the poem. Then say the word: *nine*. Ask children to think of a word that rhymes with *nine*.

> pine   line   fine   dine
> mine   vine

Objective: Listen For Initial /e/

LISTEN FOR SOUND

Say the name *Ed*. Emphasize the initial /e/ sound in the name. Have children repeat the sound after you. Then read the title of the poem. Ask which word begins with /o/. Say the following words. Children raise a hand if the word begins with /e/.

> elephant   fox   bed   Ed   enter   cat   exit

DIFFERENTIATE INITIAL SOUNDS
Say the following words: *egg, car, exit*. Ask children to say the two words that begin with /e/. Repeat this activity with the following groups of words:

> **enter, ball, Ed;**
> **Ellen, elephant, fan;**
> **exit, end, bus**

Read Together

From Phonemic Awareness to Phonics

Objective: Identify Initial *e*

IDENTIFY THE LETTER FOR THE SOUND

Explain to children that the letter e stands for the /e/ sound. Ask children to say the sound with you. Display the *Big Book of Phonics and Rhymes and Poems*, page 17. Point to the letters in the corner and identify them. Have children say the sound with you.

REREAD THE POEM

Reread the poem. Have children hold up their letter cards when you say a word that begins with /e/. After reading the poem, point to

each letter *e,* and have children identify it as capital or lowercase.

MATCH LETTERS

Give children letter cards for *E* and *e.* Ask volunteers to match letters with letters in the poem.

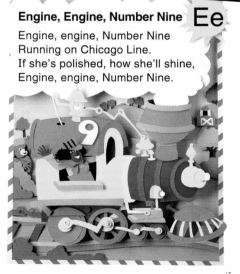

Engine, Engine, Number Nine   Ee

Engine, engine, Number Nine
Running on Chicago Line.
If she's polished, how she'll shine,
Engine, engine, Number Nine.

Big Book of Phonics Rhymes and Poems, 17

270H

OBJECTIVES

Children will:
- identify the letters *E, e*
- identify /e/ *E, e*
- form the letters *E, e*

MATERIALS
- letter cards from the Word Play Book

TEACHING **TIP**

INSTRUCTIONAL Give children a selection of tactile letters *e* and *E*, and ask them to talk about how the letters are similar and different. Point out that both forms open toward the right side, and both have a straight horizontal line. Juxtapose the lowercase form over the capital form to demonstrate these aspects. Then point out how the lowercase letter has a curved line, while the capital letter is made up of straight lines.

ALTERNATE TEACHING STRATEGY

INITIAL /e/e

For a different approach to teaching this skill, see page T30.

▶ **Visual/Auditory/Kinesthetic**

Introduce Initial /e/e

TEACH

Identify /e/ *E, e*   Tell children they will learn to write the sound /e/ with the letters *E,e*. Ask them to say the sound /e/ and to write the letters on the chalkboard. Ask if anyone has a name or knows of a name that begins with /e/; for example: *Ed, Ellen, Emily*. Write the names on the chalkboard, and ask children to repeat them after you.

Form *E, e*   Display the letters *E, e* and, with your back to the children trace them in the air. Ask children to do the same. Talk about how different the two forms are: One is made up of straight lines, the other is mostly a curved line. Have children write both forms of *e* on letter strips and hold up their strips when they recognize a word that begins with /e/. Say: " Ed the elk walked to the end of the road."

PRACTICE

Complete the Pupil Edition Page   Read the directions on page 270 to the children, and make sure they clearly understand what they are being asked to do. Identify each picture, and complete the first item together. Then work through the page with children, or have them complete the page independently.

ASSESS/CLOSE

Identify and Use *E, e*   Display pictures of objects whose names do and do not begin with /e/, such as: *elephant, tiger, egg, hen, hand, elbow*. Help children name the objects, and ask them to identify any words that begin with the sound /e/. Have children write *E, e* for each word.

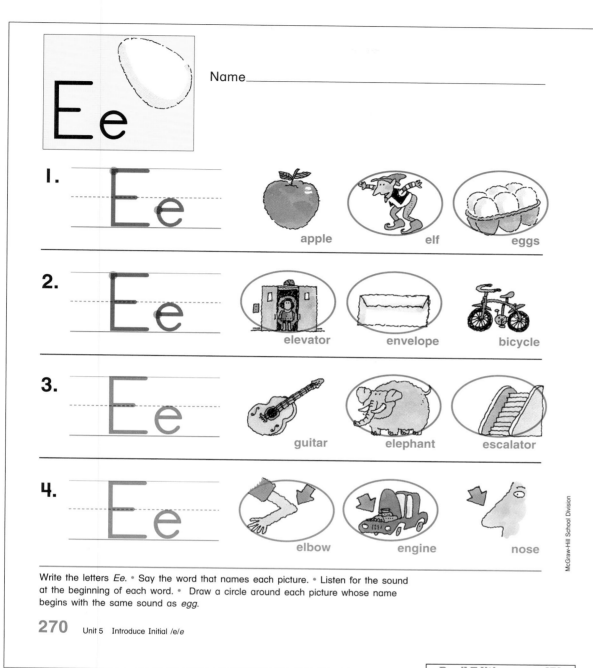

E e

Name _____

I. E e

apple　　elf　　eggs

2. E e

elevator　　envelope　　bicycle

3. E e

guitar　　elephant　　escalator

4. E e

elbow　　engine　　nose

Write the letters *Ee*. • Say the word that names each picture. • Listen for the sound
at the beginning of each word. • Draw a circle around each picture whose name
begins with the same sound as *egg*.

270 Unit 5 Introduce Initial /e/e

McGraw-Hill School Division

Pupil Edition, page 270

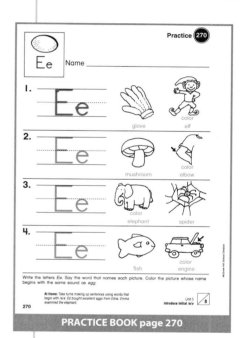

Practice 270

E e Name _____

I. E e

glove　　color elf

2. E e

mushroom　　color elbow

3. E e

color elephant　　spider

4. E e

fish　　color engine

Write the letters *Ee*. Say the word that names each picture. Color the picture whose name
begins with the same sound as *egg*.

At Home: Take turns making up sentences using words that
begin with /e/. Ed bought excellent eggs from Edna. Emma
examined the elephant.

270

Unit 5
Introduce Initial /e/e

8

PRACTICE BOOK page 270

Meeting Individual Needs for Phonics

EASY	ON-LEVEL	CHALLENGE	LANGUAGE SUPPORT
Give each child two paper cutouts in the shape of an egg, and ask them to trace the letters *E* and *e* onto the eggs from their letter cards. Invite them to turn over the cutouts and to write *e* and *E* on the reverse sides to show both forms *E, e* on each egg.	**Ask** children to use words that begin with /e/ to make rhymes with these words: *lend, leg, ledge, Ned, shelf*. Children write an *e* for each rhyming word. You may wish to point out that the initial *e* words are contained within the rhyming words.	**Ask** riddles children can answer using initial e words, such as: *Humpty Dumpty was one.* (egg) *Opposite of beginning.* (end) *Where you go to get out.* (exit) Invite children to think of words that begin with /e/e, and help them make up riddles for their classmates.	**Give** children additional opportunities to listen to words that begin with initial /e/e. Have them clap when they hear a word that begins with /e/. Say: *end, bat, Ed, egg, bit, Emily.*

270

OBJECTIVES

Children will:

- use story details
- recognize words with initial short *e*

LANGUAGE SUPPORT

ESL Help children understand the concepts of *inside* and *outside*. Make a ring using string or yarn, and place small objects outside and inside. Have children identify the position.

Read the Big Book

Before Reading

Develop Oral Language Sing "The Monkey Alphabet Song" with the children. This song is on page 4 in the Big Book of Phonics Rhymes and Poems. Then give children letter cards and sing the song again. Children hold up the appropriate card when they hear that letter.

Remind children that they read a story about two mice. Ask children to describe the mice.

Set Purposes Remind children that they read a story about two mice who have adventures. Explain that they will note which adventures happen inside the palace and which happen outside. They will also say the word that begins with each alphabet letter.

Bink hides behind the **jar**.

"I found an **exit**!" said Dee.

13

Mice Mischief, an Alphabet Story, pages 13-30

During Reading

Read Together

- Before you begin to read, point to the first word in the sentence. Explain that this is where you will begin to read. Continue to track print as you read the story. *Tracking Print*

- As you read the story, omit words that begin with the highlighted letter. Have children say the word, using the picture and the letter. After children supply the key word, confirm the choice by saying, "That's correct. The word *apple* begins with the letter *a*." *Concepts of Print*

- After you read page 2, discuss where the mice are, and determine that the apple tree is outside. Continue with other locations in the story. *Story Details*

- Make the short *e* sound, and have children say it with you. Reread page 9, and ask which word begins with that sound. *(edge) Phonics*

And they **zig-zag** all the way home!

32

Mice Mischief, an Alphabet Story, page 32

After Reading

Literary Response

JOURNAL WRITING Ask children to draw and write about something they like to do outside and something they like to do inside.

ORAL RESPONSE Ask questions such as:

- *Where do you do this activity?*

- *Do you do this alone or with friends?*

ABC Activity Have children sit in a circle. Hold up a letter card for *a* and say, *I like to eat ___.* The first child says a word that begins with the short *a* sound. Continue until children cannot think of new words. Then start over with the letter *b*.

LETTER RECOGNITION
HOW TO ASSESS
Have children turn to a page in the book and identify the letter. Then have them say the letter that comes next. Continue with several pages.

FOLLOW-UP
Help children who experience difficulty by singing the ABC song.

Cross Curricular: Language Arts

INSIDE-OUTSIDE Provide a set of letter cards and pictures of inside and outside locations. Children name the location, such as *kitchen*, and find the letter that stands for the initial sound.

▶ **Linguistic**

OBJECTIVES

Children will:
- describe action words

MATERIALS

- *Mice Mischief: An Alphabet Story*

TECHNOLOGY TIP

MANAGEMENT As children act out action words, help them be aware of their personal space. Demonstrate how to find space to move in place without intruding on other's spaces.

Introduce Action Words

PREPARE

Play a Game
Play a game of "Freeze." Demonstrate how to run in place, and then say "Freeze." Children immediately stop the action. Continue with other action words: *jump*, *walk*, *sway*, and so on.

TEACH

Recognize Action Words
Display the Big Book *Mice Mischief: An Alphabet Story*, and recall the story. Then turn to pages 2–3, and ask what the mice are doing. [climbing] Take a picture walk through the book, and have children note other words that describe actions.

PRACTICE

Find Action Words
Read the directions on page 271 to the children, and make sure they clearly understand what they are asked to do. Complete the first item. Then work through the page with children, or have them complete the page independently.

ASSESS/CLOSE

Review the Page
Check children's work on the Pupil Edition page. Note areas where children need extra help.

Name_____

1.
ten   Sam   (pick)

2.
(kick)   the   Nan

3.
nut   (run)   you

4.
cat   I   (cut)

Circle the word that describes an action.

Unit 5 Introduce Action Words   **271**

Pupil Edition, page 271

ALTERNATE TEACHING STRATEGY
....
For a different approach to teaching this skill, see page T31.

▶ **Visual/Auditory/ Kinesthetic**

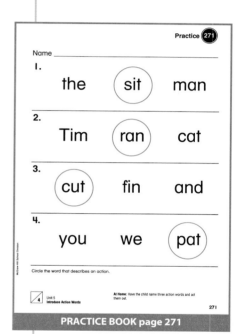

Practice 271

Name _____

1.
the   (sit)   man

2.
Tim   (ran)   cat

3.
(cut)   fin   and

4.
you   we   (pat)

Circle the word that describes an action.

Unit 5
Introduce Action Words

At Home: Have the child name three action words and act them out.

271

PRACTICE BOOK page 271

Meeting Individual Needs for Grammar

EASY	ON-LEVEL	CHALLENGE	LANGUAGE SUPPORT
Invite children to draw a picture of themselves doing an action. Have them use an action word to describe the picture.	**Teach** children the following poem. Then have them act out the action words as they recite the poem. The big, big, puddles that I see, I'll hop over, 1, 2, 3. (jump, skip) No more puddles do I see. I'll just walk home quietly.	**Ask** children to name the steps they take to do a simple task, such as brushing teeth or making a sandwich. Write each step. Then have children identify each action word.	**Have** children talk about how animals move. Note the action words that they use. Then have them pantomime some of the action words.

Develop Phonological Awareness

Listen

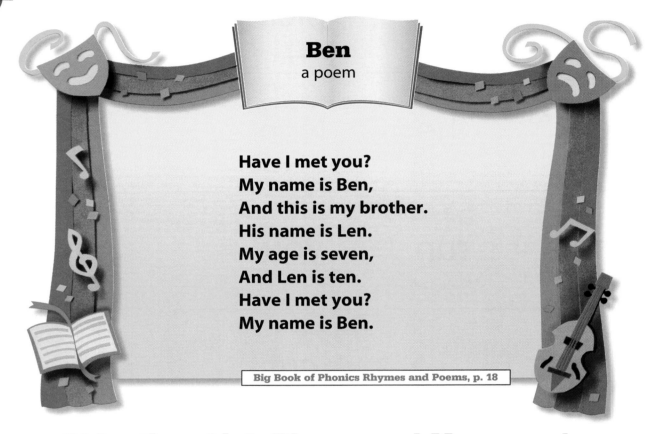

Ben
a poem

Have I met you?
My name is Ben,
And this is my brother.
His name is Len.
My age is seven,
And Len is ten.
Have I met you?
My name is Ben.

Big Book of Phonics Rhymes and Poems, p. 18

Objective: Link Rhyme and Movement

LISTEN TO RHYMES IN THE POEM

- Read the poem "Ben" aloud to the children. Then say the word *Ben*, and have children repeat it with you.
- Repeat the poem slowly. Ask children to raise their hands when they hear a word that rhymes with *Ben*.

> Ben   Len   seven   ten

TAP YOUR FIST FOR SYLLABLES

- Have children sit in a circle with both fists extended in front of them. Ask a volunteer to come to the middle of the circle.

- Children listen to you say the rhyme and join in on words that they remember. The child in the center moves around the circle. He or she gently taps each syllable on each child's fist.
- When a fist is tapped on the last rhyming word of each line, the child puts that fist behind her or his back. Continue until one child has a fist in front. Then that child has a turn tapping out the syllables.

TRY NEW WORDS

- Invite children to substitute other rhyming names for the game.

> Jen   Gwen   Chen

Objective: Listen for Medial /e/

LISTEN FOR MEDIAL *e*

- Say the name *Ben* and emphasize the medial /e/ sound. Have children repeat the sound after you.

- Encourage children to think of other names in which they can hear medial /e/ sound. (*Meg, Helen, Jen, Ken, Mel, Ted,* and so on) Have children repeat each name after you.

REPEAT THE SOUND

- Say the following words from the poem. Ask children to repeat them with you, emphasizing the /e/ sound.

> met   Ben   Len   ten   seven

LISTEN AND COUNT

- Have children count from 10 to 12. Emphasize the medial *e* in each counting word.

> ten   eleven   twelve

10   11   12

Read Together

From Phonemic Awareness to Phonics

Objective: Identify Medial *e*

IDENTIFY THE LETTER FOR THE SOUND

- Explain to children the letter *e* stands for the sound /e/. Say the sound and have children repeat it.

- Then display page 18 in the *Big Book of Phonics Rhymes and Poems.* Point to the letters in the corner of the page and identify them. Have children repeat the sound after you.

REREAD THE POEM

- Read the poem again. When you read a word with medial *e*, stop and have children repeat the word.

- Then read the poem again. Stop before saying the rhyming words, and have children say the words.

LOOK FOR *e*

- Write the letter *e* on small stick-on notes.

- Children look for *e* in the poem, and place the stick-on notes near the letter.

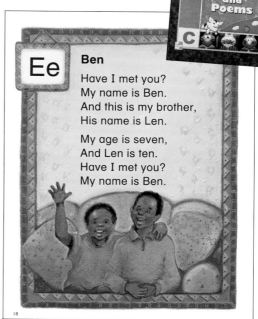

Ee

Ben

Have I met you?
My name is Ben.
And this is my brother,
His name is Len.

My age is seven,
And Len is ten.
Have I met you?
My name is Ben.

18

Big Book of Phonics Rhymes and Poems, 18

OBJECTIVES

Children will:

- identify the letter *e*
- identify /e/ *e*
- form the letters *e*

. . . .

MATERIALS

- letter cards from the Word Play Book

Introduce Medial /e/ e

┌─────────────────────────────┐
TECHNOLOGY TIP

MANAGEMENT Children will continue to write letters with varying degrees of success. Continue to provide dashed letters for children to trace as necessary.
└─────────────────────────────┘

ALTERNATE TEACHING STRATEGY
. . . .

MEDIAL /e/e

For a different approach to teaching this skill, see page T30.

▶ **Visual/Auditory/ Kinesthetic**

TEACH

Identify /e/ e Tell children they will learn to write the sound /e/ in the middle of a word with the letter *e*. Ask them to say the sound /e/ and to write *pet* on the chalkboard. Read the word aloud. Then write *Have you fed your pet yet?* Read the sentence as you point to each word, and invite volunteers to underline the words that have /e/e in the middle.

Form *e* Display the letter e and, with your back to the children, trace it in the air. Ask children to do the same. Then help them fold a sheet of paper in sixths and write the letter *e* in each of the spaces. Say the following sentence: Ken let the net get wet. Tell children that each time they hear a word with /e/ in the middle, they should draw a circle around an *e* on their paper.

PRACTICE

Complete the Pupil Edition Page Read the directions on page 272 to the children, and make sure they clearly understand what they are being asked to do. Identify each picture, and complete the first item together. Then work through the page with children, or have them complete the page independently.

ASSESS/CLOSE

Identify and Use *e* Show the following pictures, and have children write *e* on self-stick labels for every picture that shows an object whose name has the sound /e/ in the middle: *pen, fan, leg, ten, run, net*.

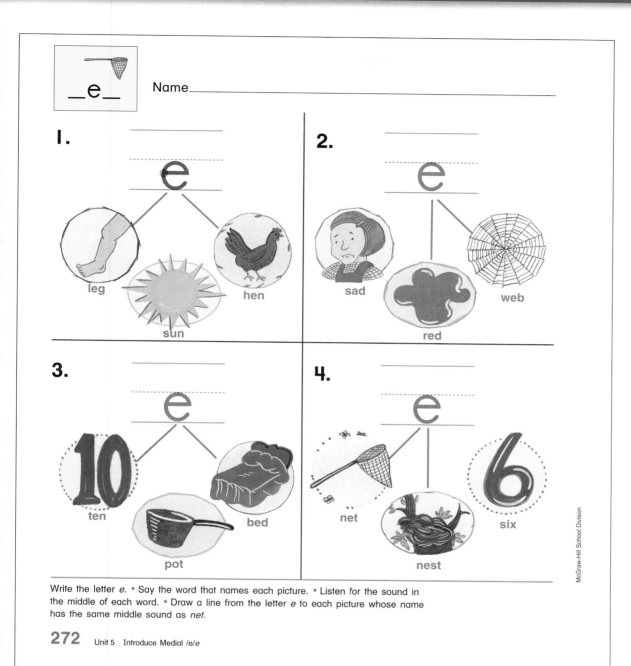

_e_   Name_____

1.
_____
e

leg   sun   hen

2.
_____
e

sad   red   web

3.
_____
e

ten   pot   bed

4.
_____
e

net   nest   six

Write the letter *e*. • Say the word that names each picture. • Listen for the sound in the middle of each word. • Draw a line from the letter *e* to each picture whose name has the same middle sound as *net*.

272   Unit 5   Introduce Medial /e/e

McGraw-Hill School Division

Pupil Edition, page 272

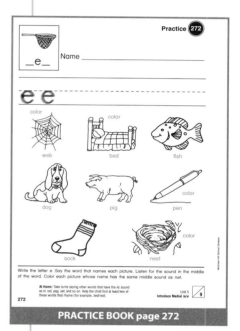

ADDITIONAL PHONICS RESOURCES

Practice Book *page 272*
Phonics Workbook

McGraw-Hill School
TECHNOLOGY

Phonics CD-ROM
Activities for practice with Medial Letters

PRACTICE BOOK page 272

Meeting Individual Needs for Phonics

EASY	ON-LEVEL	CHALLENGE	LANGUAGE SUPPORT
Give each child a sheet of paper with large letter e printed on it. Have children dip their fingers in white glue, trace the letter, and then sprinkle it with colored sand or glitter. After the glue is dry, invite children to draw a border of *e*s around the large letter.	**Have** children fill in the missing words with ones that have /e/e in the middle: *In the morning I ___ up. I make my ___. Then I ___ the table. I wear my ___ jacket to school.* Each time children say a medial *e* word, have them write the letter *e*.	**Say** an initial consonant, and have children complete the word using medial /e/e and a final consonant. Give clues as necessary, such as: *Bears sometimes live in a d___. (den) I like the color r___. (red) You can p___ the dog. (pet)*	**Reinforce** ESL children's recognition of medial /e/. Have them raise their hands and say the /e/ sound when they hear it in the following story: *Ted has a pet cat. It lives in the den. It has a red collar.*

272

OBJECTIVES

- recognize words with medial *e*
- understand story structure

VLADIMIR VAGIN worked in a Moscow publishing house before he moved to the United States. He remembers a version of this story called "The Turnip" when he was a child. Mr. Vagin has written several other books for young readers, including "The Nutcracker Ballet" and "The Twelve Days of Christmas." He lives in Vermont with his family.

LANGUAGE SUPPORT

ESL Ask children what the word *enormous* means. If necessary, help by explaining that *enormous* means very, very big. Invite children to draw a picture of something that is enormous. Ask questions about the pictures.

Before Reading

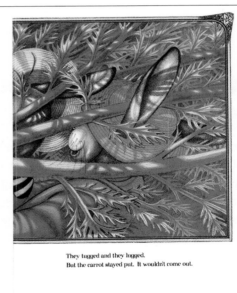

Build Background

EVALUATE PRIOR KNOWLEDGE Show children some fresh, raw carrots, preferably with the greens attached. Have children describe the carrots in terms of shape, color, texture, and taste. Explain that carrots are root vegetables that grow in the ground.

HOW DOES YOUR GARDEN GROW? Draw a simple garden plot on chart paper. Invite children to draw pictures of vegetables that might grow in the garden. You may wish to show some seed packets or pictures of vegetables.

Preview and Predict

DISCUSS AUTHOR AND ILLUSTRATOR Display the Big Book cover and read the title. Then read the author's name, and share some background information about him with the children.

TAKE A PICTURE WALK Ask what is unusual about the carrot pictured on the cover of the book. Then take a **picture walk** through about a third of the book, and talk about what children see.

MAKE PREDICTIONS Look at the pictures on pages 16-17 and ask children what they think might happen if all these characters work together.

Set Purposes

Ask children what they want to find out about the enormous carrot. Tell children you will read the story to find out if the animals will pull the carrot out of the ground.

Then Daisy and Floyd tried together
to pull the carrot out of the ground.

They tugged and they tugged.
But the carrot stayed put. It wouldn't come out.

12

The Enormous Carrot, pages 12-13

During Reading

Read Together

- Before you begin to read, point to the first word in the first sentence. Explain that this is where you will begin to read. Continue to track print as you read the story. *Tracking Print*

- Reread pages 23-25, pointing to the words. Ask: *Why do you think the words are getting bigger and bigger? How should these words be read? Concepts of Print*

- After you read the story, point out that the story is cumulative—characters are added who repeat the same action in the story. Revisit the illustrations, Ask children: *Can you identify the characters who join the story? Who joins the story first? Who is the last character to help pull out the carrot? Understand Story Structure*

- Review the short *e* sound. Then reread the first sentence on page 13, and ask children to say the words with that sound. *(then, friend, Henry)* Repeat with the second sentence. *(help) Phonics and Decoding*

The Enormous Carrot, p. 5

After Reading

Return to Predictions and Purposes

Return to the predictions that children made and the vote that children did before reading the story. Discuss the results.

Literary Response

Ask children to draw a picture of some of the animals trying to get the carrot out of the ground. Then ask them to write about what the animals are doing.

Ask questions such as:

- *Which animals are helping?*

- *What are the animals doing?*

CENTER Activity

Cross Curricular: Math

COMPARING CARROTS Provide cut-outs of carrots of several different lengths. Have children arrange them from shortest to longest. Then ask children to compare the carrot lengths with lengths of other objects in the classroom. Ask children to compare their measurements and discuss their findings.

▶ **Logical/Mathematical**

OBJECTIVES

Children will:

- understand story structure

....

MATERIALS

- *The Enormous Carrot*

TEACHING TIP

INSTRUCTIONAL Guide pairs of children to share familiar books and talk about their favorite parts of the stories. In a class discussion, have partners summarize their books by stating what happened in the beginning, the middle and the end of the story.

Review Story Structure

PREPARE

Warm-Up: Recall a Story
Ask children to recall the story *The Enormous Carrot*. Take a picture walk through several spreads, and ask children how the story begins. Tell children that all stories have beginnings, middles and ends.

TEACH

Recall Middle and End
Continue through the story, and ask children to explain the problem. Determine that in the middle of the story, the animals are trying different ways to solve the problem.

When you finish the story, ask children to recount how the problem is solved. Guide them to recall specific pictures and events from each part of the story. Remind children that they can remember a story by briefly explaining what happens at the beginning, the middle, and the end of the story.

PRACTICE

Show What Happens Next
Read the directions on page 273 to the children, and make sure they clearly understand what they are asked to do. Identify each picture, and complete the first item together. Then work through the page with children, or have them complete the page independently.

ASSESS/CLOSE

Review the Page
Review children's work, and guide children who are experiencing difficulty.

Name_____

1.

2   3   Answers may vary.   1

2.

1   3   2

3.

3   1   2

Look at the pictures. • Tell a story about each row of pictures. • Write *1* on the line under the picture that shows the beginning of the story. • Write *2* on the line under the picture that shows the middle of the story. • Write *3* on the line under the picture that shows the end of the story.

Unit 5 Review Story Structure   **273**

Pupil Edition, page 273

Practice **273**

Name_____

1.

3   2   1

2.

3   2

3.

2   3

Look at the pictures. Write *1* on the line under the picture that shows the beginning of the story. Write *2* on the line that shows the middle of the story. Write *3* on the line that shows the end of the story.

9 | Unit 5 Review Story Structure

At Home: Ask about the child's day at school. Fold a piece of paper into three sections. Have the child draw what happened in the beginning, the middle, and the end of the day.   273

PRACTICE BOOK page 273

Meeting Individual Needs for Comprehension

EASY	ON-LEVEL	CHALLENGE	LANGUAGE SUPPORT
Ask children to choose an activity in your classroom, and draw three pictures showing the beginning, the middle, and the end of the activity. Have them summarize the activity aloud while showing their drawings.	**Reread** a familiar story to the children, and have them summarize by asking: "How does the story begin? What is the problem? How does the story end?" Give children opportunities to respond by elaborating on story details.	**Have** children pretend to be news reporters. Guide pairs of students to summarize what happened to Daisy, Floyd, and their friends. Have them present their summaries in a newscaster format. Encourage them to experiment with voice and gestures.	**Revisit** the story by adapting the words to "The Farmer in the Dell": The carrot won't come up, The carrot won't come up, Heigh ho the derrio, The carrot won't come up. Then Mabel came to call.... Repeat verses, adding the names of Daisy and Floyd's friends.

Develop Phonological Awareness

Listen

Engine, Engine #9
a poem

Ben
a poem

Engine, Engine, Number Nine
Engine, Engine, Number Nine
Running on Chicago Line

If she's polished, how she'll shine,
Engine, Engine, Number Nine.

Have I met you?
My name is Ben.
And this is my brother,
His name is Len.

My age is seven.
And Len is ten.
Have I met you?
My name is Ben.

Big Book of Phonics Rhymes and Poems, p.17 p.18

Objective: Listen for Rhythmic Pattern

READ THE POEM Read the poem "Engine, Engine #9" aloud. Ask: *What word repeats?*

Engine

MOVE LIKE A TRAIN Model how to move your arms like a train's wheels as you chant: *Chug-a-chug-a-chug-a.* Invite children to move like a train as they join in the chant.

Have children form a line and move in rhythmic unison. Suggest children chant *Chug-a-chug-a* to match their movements. Then reread the poem and have children move like a train to the poem's rhythm.

VARY THE SPEED Talk about how a train's speed might change going uphill. Reread the poem slowly and then quickly. Encourage children to listen and match their train movements to the speed of your voice.

chug-a chug-a

Objective: Listen for /e/

LISTEN FOR INITIAL /e/ Read the title "Engine, Engine, #9." Emphasize the /e/ sound in *engine*. Have children repeat the sound with you.

CRACK AN EGG FOR /e/ Say the word *egg*. Ask: *Does the word* egg *have the same beginning sound as* engine? Invite children to listen as you say some words. If a word begins with /e/, the children pretend to crack an egg.

> elm   line   elf   hat

LISTEN FOR MEDIAL /e/ Read the poem "Ben," emphasizing the words with medial /e/. Have children repeat the words with you.

SHOW TEN FOR /e/ Randomly say words from "Ben." Have children show ten fingers each time they hear the /e/ sound.

> name   Ben   met   my   you   ten

SHOW ANOTHER TEN Repeat the previous activity, using words children might encounter in their everyday language experiences.

> bed   peg   pit   tell   Tom
> hem   pen   hot   get

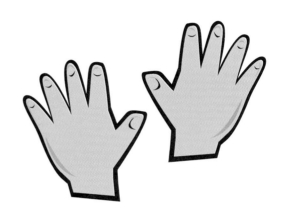

Read Together

From Phonemic Awareness to Phonics

Objective: Identify /e/ *E, e*

IDENTIFY THE LETTER Explain that the letters *E* and *e* stand for the /e/ sound. Have children say the sound.

Display pages 17 and 18 in the *Big Book of Phonics Rhymes and Poems*. Point to the letters and identify them. Say the sound.

REREAD THE POEMS Read the poems. Point to each word, emphasizing those with /e/.

FIND WORDS WITH E, e Have children place stick-on dots under the words in the poems with *E* or *e*.

Engine, Engine, Number Nine Ee

Engine, engine, Number Nine
Running on Chicago Line.
If she's polished, how she'll shine,
Engine, engine, Number Nine.

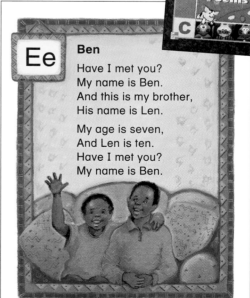

Ee **Ben**

Have I met you?
My name is Ben.
And this is my brother,
His name is Len.

My age is seven,
And Len is ten.
Have I met you?
My name is Ben.

Big Book of Phonics Rhymes and Poems, page 17, page 18

274B

OBJECTIVES

Children will:

- identify and discriminate between initial and medial /e/ *E,e*

- write and use the letters *E,e*

MATERIALS

- letter cards and picture cards from the *Word Building Book*

TEACHING TIP

INSTRUCTIONAL

Remind children of the rules of capitalization, then say a sentence that includes words with *e* at the beginning or in the middle. Ask children to hold up the *E* or *e* letter card to show which form a word uses, for example: *Ed fed his pet.*

ALTERNATE TEACHING STRATEGY

LETTER /E/E

For a different approach to teaching this skill, see page T30.

▶ **Visual/Auditory/ Kinesthetic**

Review /e/e

TEACH

Identify and Discriminate Between initial and Medial /e/ E,e

Tell children they will review the sound /e/ at the beginning and in the middle of words and write the letters *E,e*. Write *e___* on one side of the chalkboard, and *__e__* on the other side, and have children make the /e/ sound with you. Ask children to point to the *e* that shows the position of that letter in the name of each object they see, and show pictures of: *egg, leg, net, exit, red, elbow.*

Write and Use E,e

Write the following sentence on the chalkboard: *Ed has ten pets.* Read it aloud as you point to each word. Ask children to clap when they hear a word with the sound *e* in the beginning or the middle. Have children identify the position of the *e*'s in each word and write the letter on a letter strip.

PRACTICE

Complete the Pupil Edition Page

Read the directions on page 274 to the children, and make sure they clearly understand what they are being asked to do. Identify each picture, and complete the first item together. Then work through the page with children, or have them complete the page independently.

ASSESS/CLOSE

Identify and Use E,e

Place word cards on the chalkboard ledge that have the letter *e* in the beginning or the middle of the word, such as: *let, led, pen, set, egg, Ed.* Have children write a black *e* or *E* for each word that begins with /e/ and a red *e* for each word that has /e/ in the middle.

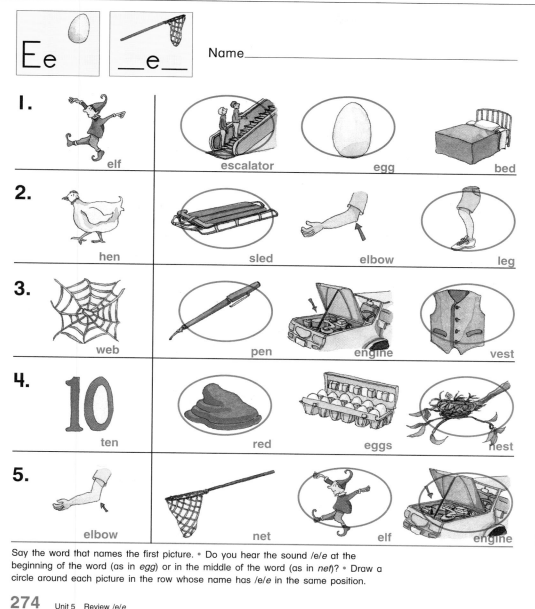

Ee | **_e_** | Name_____

1. elf | escalator | egg | bed

2. hen | sled | elbow | leg

3. web | pen | engine | vest

4. ten | red | eggs | nest

5. elbow | net | elf | engine

Say the word that names the first picture. • Do you hear the sound /e/e at the beginning of the word (as in *egg*) or in the middle of the word (as in *net*)? • Draw a circle around each picture in the row whose name has /e/e in the same position.

McGraw-Hill School Division

274 Unit 5 Review /e/e

Pupil Edition, page 274

ADDITIONAL PHONICS RESOURCES

Practice Book, *page 274*
Phonics Workbook

McGraw-Hill School
TECHNOLOGY

Phonics CD-ROM
Activities for practice with Initial and Medial Letters

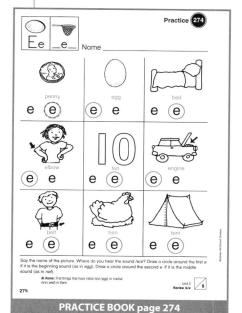

Practice **274**

Ee _e_ Name_____

penny | egg | bed
e (e) | (e) e | e (e)

elbow | ten | engine
(e) e | e (e) | (e) e

belt | hen | tent
e (e) | e (e) | e (e)

Say the name of the picture. Where do you hear the sound /e/e? Draw a circle around the first *e* if it is the beginning sound (as in *egg*). Draw a circle around the second *e* if it is the middle sound (as in *net*).

At Home: Find things that have initial /e/e (*egg*) or medial /e/e (*nest*) in them.

274

Unit 5 Review /e/e

McGraw-Hill School Division

PRACTICE BOOK page 274

Meeting Individual Needs for Phonics

EASY	ON-LEVEL	CHALLENGE	LANGUAGE SUPPORT
Give children pictures of objects whose names have *e* in the beginning or the middle, and have them sort for the position of *e*. For example: *egg, elbow, pen, net, red*. Read the words, and have children trace the letter *e* in each with their fingers.	**Ask** children to write *e___* and *___e___* three times each on six squares of paper. Then have them arrange the paper squares to copy word cards you place on the chalkboard ledge, such as: *Ned, egg, set, exit, Ed, den*. Rearrange the words and repeat the activity.	**Tell** riddles that children can answer using words that have *e* at the beginning or in the middle, such as: *Something to write with.* (pen) *Mother of a chicken.* (hen) *What the hen lays.* (egg) *More than one man.* (men)	**Say** the following sentence: *At the end of the story the red hen lays an egg.* Ask children to hold up *e* letter cards each time they hear a word that begins with /e/ or has /e/ in the middle. Have them tell whether the *e* is at the beginning or in the middle of the word.

274

Teacher Read Aloud

 **Listen**

Winter Days in the Big Woods
by Laura Ingalls Wilder

Once upon a time, a little girl named Laura lived in the Big Woods of Wisconsin in a little house made of logs.

Laura lived in the little house with her Pa, her Ma, her big sister Mary, her baby sister Carrie, and their good old bulldog Jack.

Winter was coming to the Big Woods. Soon the little house would be covered with snow. Pa went hunting every day so that they would have meat during the long, cold winter.

Ma, Laura, and Mary gathered potatoes and carrots, beets and turnips, cabbages and onions, and peppers and pumpkins from the garden next to the little house.

By the time winter came, the little house was full of good things to eat. Laura and Mary thought the attic was a lovely place to play. They played house by using the round orange pumpkins as tables and chairs, and everything was snug and cozy.

Soon the first snow came, and it was very cold. In the mornings the windows were covered with beautiful frost pictures of trees and flowers and fairies.

Continued on page T4

Oral Comprehension

LISTENING AND SPEAKING Ask children to think about what life might have been like before there were cars and electricity. Explain to children that they will hear a true story about a family who lived long ago. Point out that Laura Ingalls Wilder is a famous author who wrote many books based on her life when she was young.

After you read, focus on the story structure and ask: *What did the family do in the morning? What did they do in the afternoon? What did the family do at night when Pa came home?*

Activity Help children fold a sheet of paper into thirds. Have them draw a picture of something they do in the morning; in the afternoon; in the evening. Talk about how their activities are similar to and how they are different from Laura's activities.

▶ **Spatial/Linguistic**

Real-Life Reading

Can you find all the words in this picture?

EXIT

COUNTRY FAIR on Friday

FLOUR

DANGER DO NOT TOUCH

BIG BOOK OF REAL LIFE READING

Door
Funnel
Engine
Cars
Wheels

Big Book of Real-Life Reading, pages 36–37

Objective: Read Environmental Print

READ THE PAGE Write the words *Danger*, *Do not touch*, and *Exit* on the chalkboard. Read the words and discuss their meanings. Discuss where children might see these words. Ask children if they remember the story about Laura and her family. Explain that children will see a picture of the family kitchen in which they will see these signs. Read the question, and talk about the picture. Ask the children to point out all the places where words appear.

ANSWER THE QUESTION Ask volunteers to point to the safety signs. Ask: *What do the signs mean? Why might this sign be near the stove?* Invite children to mention other signs they have seen on other places. Discuss why it is important to pay attention to safety signs.

CULTURAL PERSPECTIVES

PAPER DOLLS Paper dolls have been favorite toys of children in America and Europe for over a hundred years. Paper dolls were first made in France.

Activity Make a paper doll out of yourself! Provide large rolls of paper. Pair each child with a partner. While one child lies on the paper, the partner draws the outline of that child. When both outlines are completed, the children can draw in their features and clothes and cut out the outlines.

▶ **Interpersonal/Kinesthetic**

MATERIALS

- word cards from the Word Play Book

TEACHING TIP

INSTRUCTIONAL Make sure children understand that the word *she* refers to another girl or woman. Say the sentences: *Mia likes to swim. She swims every day.* Ask who *she* refers to. Repeat with the other sentences.

Introduce High-Frequency Words: *she*

PREPARE

Listen to Words

Explain to the children that they will be learning a new word: *she.* Say the following sentence: *She was small.* Say the sentence again, and ask children to raise a hand when they hear the word *she.* Repeat with the sentence: *She made a castle.*

TEACH

Model Reading the Word in Context

Give a word card to each child, and read the word. Reread the sentences, and have children raise their word cards when they hear the word.

Identify the Word

Write the sentences above on the chalkboard. Track print and read each sentence. Children hold up their word card when they hear the word *she.* Then ask volunteers to point to and underline the word *she* in the sentences.

PRACTICE

Complete the Pupil Edition Page

Read the directions on page 275 to the children, and make sure they clearly understand what they are asked to do. Complete the first item together. Then work through the page with children or have them complete the page independently.

ASSESS/CLOSE

Review the Page

Review children's work, and note children who are experiencing difficulty or need additional practice.

Name_____

1.

Did she get a pet?

_____

2.

She got a pet.

_____

3.

Did she get a cat?

_____

4.

She got a tan pup.

_____

Read the sentence. • Then draw a line under the word *she* in the sentence.

Unit 5   Introduce High-Frequency Words: *she*   **275**

ALTERNATE TEACHING STRATEGY

HIGH-FREQUENCY WORDS: *she*

For a different approach to teaching this skill, see page T27.

▶ **Visual/Auditory/Kinesthetic**

Practice **275**

Name_____

1.

Can she run?

_____

2.

She can run!

_____

3.

She is a lot of fun!

_____

4.

She is my cat, Dot.

_____

Read each sentence. Then draw a line under the word she in each sentence.

4 | Unit 5
Introduce High-Frequency Words: she

At Home: Look through a magazine together. Have the child find a picture of a girl or woman and say what she is doing.

275

PRACTICE BOOK page 275

Meeting Individual Needs for Vocabulary

EASY	ON-LEVEL	CHALLENGE	LANGUAGE SUPPORT
Give each child a word card for *she*. Then sit in a circle, point to the first girl and say: *She is wearing (jeans)*. The children go around the circle, saying something else about the girl and holding up their word card when they say the word.	**Have** children draw a picture of a female relative. Then ask them to say three things about that person using the word *she*.	**Have** children pick a story from the classroom library that has a girl in it. Have children put stick-on notes under the word *she* each time they find one. Have children read and count how many times the word appeared.	**Write** the word *she* on chart paper and read it together. Then say statements, and ask children to restate them, using the word *she*: Gwen is 5 years old. *She is 5 years old.* Jane is wearing a hat. *She is wearing a hat.*

275

Develop Phonological Awareness

Listen

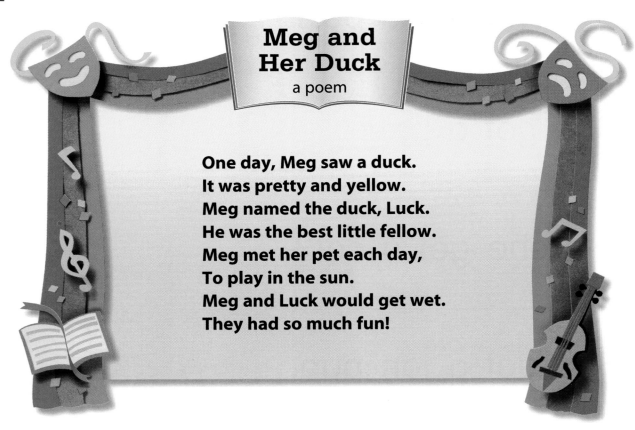

Meg and Her Duck
a poem

One day, Meg saw a duck.
It was pretty and yellow.
Meg named the duck, Luck.
He was the best little fellow.
Meg met her pet each day,
To play in the sun.
Meg and Luck would get wet.
They had so much fun!

Objective: Develop Ability to Listen

READ THE POEM Read the poem "Meg and Her Duck." Ask children to name a color word used in the poem.

> yellow

COLOR MY WORLD Show children a yellow crayon. Ask them to listen as you name familiar objects. Tell children to quack like a duck if the object could be yellow.

> sun   grape   tomato
> banana   chalk   milk   butter

LISTEN TO A LIST Ask children to close their eyes and listen to a series of color names. Repeat the sequence, but omit one color name. Have children name the color that was omitted. Start with three color names in the series and build to more.

Objective: Blending with Short *e*

LISTEN FOR BLENDING Read the title of the poem. Then say /m/-/e/-/g/. Model how to set out a connecting cube for each sound. Touch each cube as you say each sound. Move the cubes closer together as you blend the sounds. Finally, connect the cubes as you say *Meg*. Ask children to set out a cube for each sound they hear as you say /m/-/e/-/g/. Have children touch each cube as they repeat /M/-/e/-/g/. Tell children to push the cubes together as they blend the sounds to say *Meg*.

MORE NAMES WITH SHORT *e* Tell children that Meg was not the only one to see the duck. Explain that they must listen to the sounds and then guess who saw the duck.

> **Who saw the duck?**
> **/K/-/e/-/n/ saw the duck.**

MORE BLENDING Have children set out cubes for each sound they hear, moving cubes together as they blend the sounds. Invite children to raise their hands when they know who saw the duck. Repeat with other short *e* names.

> **Ben   Ted   Ned   Peg**

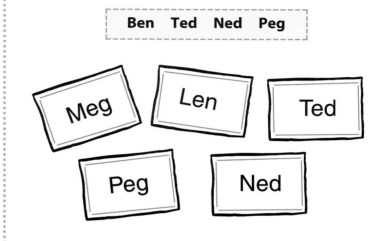

Read Together

From Phonemic Awareness to Phonics

Objective: Identify Words with Short *e*

LISTEN FOR SHORT *e* Read the poem. Emphasize *Meg* each time you say it.

IDENTIFY THE LETTERS Say the sounds /M/-/e/-/g/. Ask: *How many sounds do you hear?* (three) Write *Meg* on the board. Identify the letters and ask children to say the sounds these letters stand for. Repeat the activity with other words from the poem that contain short *e*.

> **met   pet   get   wet**

MAKE THE RHYMING WORDS Write *pet* and *wet* in list form on chart paper. Point to each letter, and say the sound it represents. Have children say the words with you. Invite children to name words that rhyme with *pet* and *wet*.

> **let   met   set   net**

Write children's ideas under *pet* and *wet*. Invite volunteers to circle the letters that are the same in each word. Repeat by having children name words that rhyme with *red*.

OBJECTIVES

Children will:

- identify /e/*e*
- blend and read short *e* words
- write short *e* words
- review /g/*g*, /k/*k*, *ck*, /l/*l*, /p/*p*, /r/*r*, /f/*f*, /k/*c*, /t/*t*, /m/*m*, /s/*s*, /d/*d*, and /n/*n*

MATERIALS

- letter cards from the *Word Building Book*

TEACHING **TIP**

INSTRUCTIONAL Display the following word cards on the chalkboard ledge: *let, met, men.* Ask children to tell how *let* and *met* are different, and how *met* and *men* are different. Continue with *men* and *pen, pen* and *pet, pet* and *let.*

ALTERNATE TEACHING STRATEGY

BLENDING SHORT *e*

For a different approach to teaching this skill, see page T30.

▶ **Visual/Auditory/ Kinesthetic**

Introduce Blending with short *e*

TEACH

Identify *e* as the Symbol for /e/

Tell children that they will be reading and writing words with *e*.

- Display the *e* letter card and say /e/. Have children repeat /e/ as you point to the card.

BLENDING Model and Guide Practice

- Place the *t* letter card after the *e* card. Blend the sounds together and have children repeat after you.

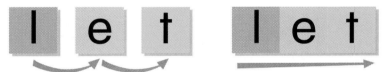

- Place an *l* letter card before the *e* card. Blend the sounds in the word to read *let*. Have children repeat after you.

Use the Word in Context

- Ask children to use *let* in a sentence, perhaps talking about how they share things with siblings or friends.

Repeat the Procedure

- Use the following words to continue modeling and for guided practice with short *e*: *get, Ken, red, pet, pen, leg, set.*

PRACTICE

Complete the Pupil Edition Page

Read aloud the directions on page 276. Identify each picture, and complete the first item together. Then work through the page with children, or have them complete the page independently.

ASSESS/CLOSE

Build Short *e* Words

Observe children as they complete page 276. Then give them letter cards *g, l, p, r, t, m, d, n.* Ask them to build four short *e* words, using a different first and last letter for each.

Name_____

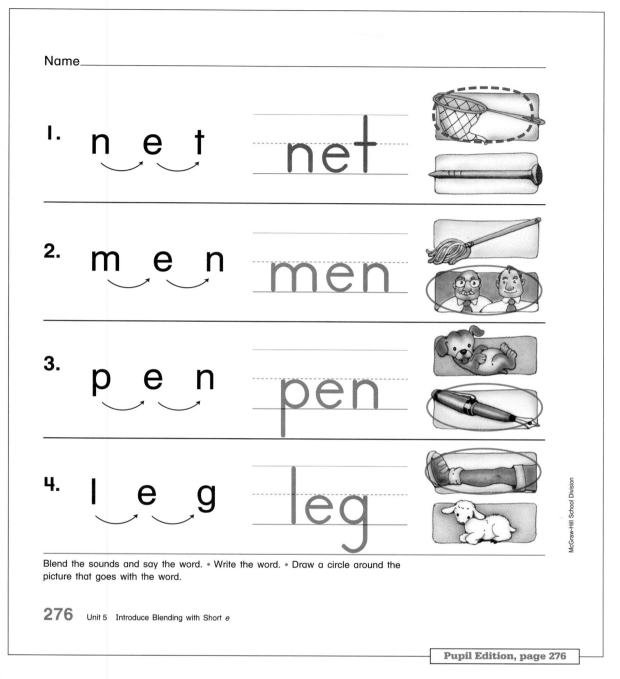

1. n e t   net

2. m e n   men

3. p e n   pen

4. l e g   leg

Blend the sounds and say the word. • Write the word. • Draw a circle around the
picture that goes with the word.

McGraw-Hill School Division

276   Unit 5   Introduce Blending with Short *e*

Pupil Edition, page 276

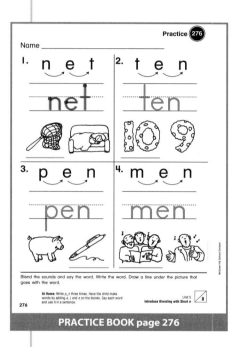

PRACTICE BOOK page 276

Meeting Individual Needs for Phonics

EASY	ON-LEVEL	CHALLENGE	LANGUAGE SUPPORT
Ask children to clap when they hear short *e* words and say: *red, rod, pan, pen, set, sit*. Write *red* and *rid* on the chalkboard and ask children which one is pronounced *red*. Continue with *pan, pen,* and *set, sit,* asking children to identify the short *e* word.	**Read** this story through once, and then ask children to fill in the blanks with short *e* words: *My (pet) is not a dog or cat. She must be (fed) dried corn. I go to (get) eggs from her each day. She is my little (red) hen.* Ask children to write the missing words.	**Help** children list as many short *e* words as they can that begin or end in *g, k, ck, l, p, r, f, c, t, m, s, d, n.* Then ask them to work in small groups and make up stories using as many of the words as they can. Record the stories and invite groups to act them out.	**Write** the following sentence on the chalkboard and ask children to read it aloud with you: *Ken and Ned met in the den.* Ask volunteers to underline and say each word that has the sound /e/. Be sure to review the meanings of the word *met* and *den*.

276

Guided Instruction

BEFORE READING

PREVIEW AND PREDICT Take a brief **picture walk** through the book, focusing on the illustrations.

- *Who is the story about?*

- *What things do you think Ken and his pup will do together?*

- *Do you think the story will be realistic, or will it be make-believe? Why?*

SET PURPOSES Discuss with children what part of the story looks most interesting to them. Then ask them why. Ask children questions such as: *What do you think the boy and his dog like to do?*

TEACHING TIP

To put book together:

1. Tear out the story page.

2. Cut along the dotted line.

3. Fold each section on fold line.

4. Assemble book.

INSTRUCTIONAL Ask children to share any experiences that they have about pets. Talk about pet needs, such as food, water, exercise, and medical care.

A Pet for Ken

"My pup can sit up," said Ken.

3

"I have a pup, and
she is red," said Ken.

2

"I let my pup lick me,"
said Ken.

4

Guided Instruction

DURING READING

☑ **Blending with Short *e***

☑ **Story Structure**

☑ **High-Frequency Word:** *she*

☑ **Concepts of Print**

1 **CONCEPTS OF PRINT** Ask children to identify the second and the fourth words on the title page. (Pet, Ken) Then ask children to match each word with the picture.

2 **BLENDING WITH SHORT *e*** Model: Find the word that begins with *r* on page 2. Let's blend the sounds to read the word: *r e d red.* What other word has the /e/ sound? (Ken)

3 **USE ILLUSTRATIONS** Look at the picture on page 3. What is the boy holding? Why? (He is holding a treat as a reward for the dog.)

4 **STORY STRUCTURE** After reading page 4, explain to children that they have now read the beginning and the middle of the story. Ask children to describe Ken's pet and what he can do so far in the story.

LANGUAGE SUPPORT

ESL Have children pantomime the actions of the story while you read it. (sitting, licking, fetching, swimming, running) Then ask them to connect the words with the actions as they read the story.

Guided Instruction

BEFORE READING

⑤ HIGH-FREQUENCY WORDS Ask children to point to the first word on page 5. (she) Have children read it as they track print *s-h-e she*.

⑥ BLENDING WITH SHORT *e* Have children locate the last word on page 6. (Ken) Have them blend the sounds to read the word *K-e-n Ken*. Then ask children to isolate the letter *e* and to practice making the short *e* sound.

⑦ CONCEPTS OF PRINT Have children point to the last word on the second line of page 7. (Ken) Ask them to count the letters in the word. *(3)* Ask them how many words on that page have 3 letters. *(7)*

⑧ STORY STRUCTURE After children read page 8, ask them to think about what happens on each page of the story. (Ken does something different with his dog.)

ASSESSMENT

STORY STRUCTURE

HOW TO ASSESS Have children draw a picture of something that happened in the beginning, in the middle, and at the end of the story.

FOLLOW UP Have children point out a beginning page, a middle page, and an ending page.

"She can get a sock for me," said Ken.

5

"My pup and I can run and run," said Ken.

7

"She and I can go for a dip," said Ken.

6

"My pup and I have fun," said Ken.

8

Guided Instruction

RETURN TO PREDICTIONS AND PURPOSES
Ask children if their prediction about what they thought the boy and the dog would do were correct. Discuss some of the things Ken did with his dog.

RETELL THE STORY Have children work with partners to role-play retelling the story. Ask one child to be Ken and the other to be the pup. Allow children to switch roles as time permits.

LITERARY RESPONSE To help children respond to the story, ask:

Would you like to have a dog like Ken's pup? Why or why not?

Invite children to draw and write about a dog they would like to have. Encourage them to name the dog.

Activity

Cross Curricular: Drama

DOG CARE 101 Provide a stuffed animal dog, and dog equipment: brush, dog dish, leash, and so on. Children role-play taking care of a dog. Have them discuss what they need to do each day to take care of a pet.

▶ Intrapersonal/Linguistic

OBJECTIVES

Children will:

- use story structure to understand a story

MATERIALS

- *A Pet for Ken*

TEACHING **TIP**

INSTRUCTIONAL Make sure children understand the concepts of beginning, middle and end. You may wish to demonstrate with simple actions. For instance:
First, I write a letter.
Then, I address and stamp it.
Last, I mail a letter.

PREPARE

Recall the Story
Have children recall the story *A Pet for Ken*. Ask who the story is about. Then ask them to remember something that Ken and his pet do together.

TEACH

Review Events in the Story
Reread the story together. As you read, talk about the series of events. Ask: *What are Ken and his pup doing at the end of the story?* Explain that most stories have a beginning, a middle part, and an end.

PRACTICE

Complete the Pupil Edition Page
Read the directions on page 279 to the children, and make sure they clearly understand what they are asked to do. Identify each picture, and complete the first item together. Then work through the page with children or have them complete the page independently.

ASSESS/CLOSE

Review the Page
Review children's work, and note children who are experiencing difficulty.

Name_____

I.

2.

3.

Look at the first picture. • Then look at the second picture. • Think about what is happening in the story. • In the last box, draw what you think will happen at the end of the story.

Pupil Edition, page 279

ALTERNATE TEACHING
STRATEGY
....
STORY STRUCTURE
For a different approach to teaching this skill, see page T26.

▶ **Visual/Auditory/ Kinesthetic**

PRACTICE BOOK page 279

Meeting Individual Needs for Comprehension

EASY	ON-LEVEL	CHALLENGE	LANGUAGE SUPPORT
Have children show parts of the story by making a class comic strip. Give pairs of children large squares of paper, and assign each pair one part of the story. Then put the squares together to make a big comic strip.	**Have** children make a word web to describe Ken and his pup. As children dictate their ideas to you, have them focus on what Ken and the pup do together.	**Invite** children to contribute to a story map for the book. Have them dictate their ideas for the title, characters, and events in the story.	**Use** a stuffed animal and have children act out the story as you read it. Show the illustration and say: *What does Ken do next with his pup?*

279

Develop Phonological Awareness

Listen

Meg and Her Duck
a poem

One day, Meg saw a duck.
It was pretty and yellow.
Meg named the duck, Luck.
He was the best little fellow.
Meg met her pet each day,
To play in the sun.
Meg and Luck would get wet.
They had so much fun!

Objective: Identify and Make Rhymes

READ THE POEM Read the poem "Meg and Her Duck," emphasizing rhyming words at the end of lines. Ask: *Which word in the poem rhymes with duck? (Luck)* Repeat this with other word pairs from the poem.

> yellow   fellow   fun   sun

MORE WORD PAIRS Help children brainstorm other animals Meg might see. Encourage them to think of a name that rhymes with the animal's name. For example, *fish/wish*. Have children use their ideas to complete this sentence frame. Meg saw a _____ named _____.

> cat   Pat   dog   Fog
> bird   Third   snake   Jake

REVISE THE POEM Reread the first four lines of the poem but substitute an animal word children have suggested for the word *duck* in the first line. Tell children to complete the third line of the poem by saying the name. Repeat with other word pairs children suggested.

Objective: Blending Short *e* and *u*

LISTEN FOR BLENDING Read the title of the poem, emphasizing duck as you say it. Say the sounds /d/-/u/-/k/, then duck. Have children repeat. Then read the poem, segmenting words with short *u*. Invite children to say the sounds, then blend the sounds into words.

> **duck Luck sun fun**

Repeat, segmenting words from the poem that contain short *e*.

> **Meg met pet get wet**

WHAT'S IN MY NET? Write words that contain short *u* or *e* on index cards cut in the shape of fish. Provide a small fishing net. Place the fish cards in the net. Extend the fishing net toward the children.

Say: *Look, look in my net.*
Listen, listen, what did I get?

Pause while one child pulls a fish card from the net. Then read the word on the card by segmenting the sounds, for example, /m/-/u/-/d/. Have children blend the sounds to say the word on the card: *mud*. Repeat the refrain, and invite another child to pull a card.

> **rug   duck   pet   Len**
> **cup   fun   men   Ken**

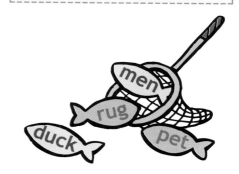

Read Together

From Phonemic Awareness to Phonics

Objective: Relate *e, u* to Short Vowel Sounds

LISTEN FOR RHYMING WORDS
Read the poem. Ask: *What word in the poem rhymes with duck? sun? pet?*

> **Luck   fun   wet**

IDENTIFY THE LETTERS Say the sounds /d/-/u/-/k/. Write the word *duck* on the board as children say each sound. Identify the letters. Repeat with *Luck*. Invite a volunteer to underline the letters in the words that are the same. Ask children to say the sounds these letters stand for. Continue the activity with other rhyming words from the poem.

MATCH RHYMING WORDS
Write these words on index cards: *red, fed, dug, rug*. Give each pair of children one set of cards and tell them to make rhyming pairs.

Write each word pair in list form on the board as a volunteer reads it. Challenge children to name words that rhyme with the word pairs. Add children's words to the appropriate lists.

> **bed   led   Ned   Ted**
> **bug   hug   jug   mug   tug**

OBJECTIVES

Children will:

- identify /e/*e,* /u/*u*
- blend and read short *e* and *u* words
- write short *e* and *u* words
- review /g/*g,* /k/*k, ck,* /l/*l,* /p/*p,* /r/*r,* /f/*f,* /k/*c,* /t/*t,* /m/*m,* /s/*s,* /d/*d,* and /n/*n*

MATERIALS

- letter cards from the *Word Building Book*

TEACHING TIP

INSTRUCTIONAL Have children look in a mirror and repeat the short vowel sounds /e/ and /u/ several times. Talk about how the shape of the mouth changes. Ask them to repeat: *Don't get mud on the red rug.* Ask children to identify a short *e* word and a short *u* word in the sentence.

ALTERNATE TEACHING STRATEGY

BLENDING SHORT *e, u*

For a different approach to teaching this skill, see page T30 and Unit 4, page T32.

▶ **Visual/Auditory/ Kinesthetic**

Review Blending with short *e, u*

TEACH

Identify *e* as the Symbol for /e/

Tell children they will continue to read words with *e* and *u*.

- Display the *e* letter card and say /e/. Have children repeat the sound /e/ after you as you point to the card.

BLENDING Model and Guide Practice

- Place a *d* letter card after the *e* card. Blend the sounds together and have children repeat after you.

- Place an *f* letter card before the *e* card. Blend the sounds in the word to read *fed*. Have children repeat after you.

Use the Word in Context

- Ask children to use *fed* in a sentence, perhaps talking about a real or an imaginary pet.

Repeat the Procedure

- Use the following words to continue modeling and guided practice with short *e* and *u: ten, tug, den, met, mud, net, nut.*

PRACTICE

Complete the Pupil Edition Page

Read aloud the directions on page 280. Identify each picture, and complete the first item together. Then work through the page with children, or have them complete the page independently.

ASSESS/CLOSE

Build Short *e* and Short *u* Words

Observe children as they complete page 280. Then give them letter cards *g, l, p, r, t, m, d, n.* Ask them to build two short *e* words and two short *u* words. Help them write all the words on a chart.

Name _____

1. (duck) den

    duck

2. pan (pen)

    pen

3. set (sun)

    sun

4. (red) rat

    red

Draw a circle around the word that names the picture. • Say the word. • Then write the word.

McGraw-Hill School Division

280   Unit 5   Review Blending with Short *e, u*

Pupil Edition, page 280

ADDITIONAL PHONICS RESOURCES

Practice Book, *page 280*
Phonics Workbook

McGraw-Hill School
TECHNOLOGY

Phonics CD-ROM
Activities for practice with Blending and Segmenting

Practice **280**

Name _____

1. leg let   2. rug red
    leg   rug

3. pet pen   4. fin fed
    pet   fed

Look at the picture. Read the words. Draw a line under the word that goes with the picture. Write the word.

At Home: Take turns rhyming words with these short *e* and short *u* words: *red, leg, set, mug, fun, up.*

280   Unit 5   Review Blending with Short *e, u*   8

PRACTICE BOOK page 280

Meeting Individual Needs for Phonics

EASY	ON-LEVEL	CHALLENGE	LANGUAGE SUPPORT
Have children draw a picture of an object that has either the sound /e/ or /u/ in the middle. Suggest to children that they frame their pictures with capital and lowercase *e*'s or *u*'s.	**Ask** children to answer riddles using words with short *e* and *u* in the middle, such as: *below your head is your (neck); it disappears at night (sun); in the poem "Humpty Dumpty," all the king's (men).* Invite children to make up more riddles for one another.	**Have** children form a circle. Say a short *e* or *u* word to one child, who then must say a word that begins with the last letter of your word, such as: *set, tug, gum, mud, den, net.* Words can be repeated. See how many different words children can say.	**Have** children act out the phrases with short *e* and *u* words, such as: *I pet the dog. I am having fun. The sun is hot.* See if they can recognize the *e* and *u* words. Invite children to make up their own phrase to act out.

280

Reread the Decodable Story

A Pet for Ken

☑ **Blend with Short *e***
☑ **Story Structure**
☑ **High-Frequency Word:** *she*
☑ **Concepts of Print**

A Pet for Ken

INFORMAL ASSESSMENT

BLEND WITH SHORT *e*
HOW TO ASSESS Write the word *pen*, and ask children to blend the sounds to read the word. Continue with *ten, den,* and *men*.

FOLLOW UP With children, blend the words *pen, ten, den,* and *men*. Have children point out which letters are the same in each word.

Guided Reading

SET PURPOSES Tell children that when they read the story again, they can find out more about what happened. Explain that you also want them to look for words containing the short *e* sound. Remind children that they know the word *she* and will see it again in this story.

REREAD THE BOOK As you reread the story, keep in mind any problems children experienced during the first reading. Use the following prompts to guide reading.

• **STORY STRUCTURE** Ask children to tell you in their own words how the story begins. Then ask them to tell you how the story ends.

• **CONCEPTS OF PRINT** Ask children to point out which word in the story contains only one letter. (A) Ask children to identify the word.

RETURN TO PURPOSES Ask children if they found out more about what they wanted to know from the story. Then ask children to look at the title and locate the letter *e*'s. Ask children if they are found at the beginning, in the middle, or at the end of the word.

LITERARY RESPONSE Make a class book by having each child complete the sentence: *My pup can ___.* Children write or dictate their ideas, and illustrate their page for the book.

Read the Patterned Book

Meg's Elephant

Meg's Elephant

by Anne Miranda
illustrated by Bob Barner

☑ **Short** *e*
☑ **Story Structure**
☑ **High-Frequency Word:** *she*

Guided Reading

PREVIEW AND PREDICT Read the title and the author's and the illustrator's names. Ask children what the author does and what the illustrator does. Take a **picture walk** through pages 2-4, noting the setting of the story and the characters. Have children make predictions about the story.

SET PURPOSES Have children decide what they want to find out from the story and predict what might happen to the little girl and her elephant. Tell them that the story contains words with short *e*.

READ THE BOOK Use the following prompts while the children are reading or after they have read independently. Remind them to run their fingers under each word as they read.

Pages 2-3: Point to the last word on page 3. *Let's use what we know about short e to read the word that begins with pe. Let's blend the sounds together: p e t. Phonics and Decoding*

Point to the first word on page 3. *Let's read it together: she. Who does she refer to?* (Meg) *High-Frequency Words*

Pages 4-5: *Let's think about the story so far. What does Meg do on each page?* (She gets something for her elephant.) *Story Structure*

Pages 6-7: *Listen as I read the sentence on page 7. Which words have the /e/ sound?* (Meg, pet, elephant, teddy) *Phonological Awareness*

RETURN TO PREDICTIONS AND PURPOSES Ask children if they found out what they needed to know from the story. See if their predictions were correct.

LITERARY RESPONSE These questions will help focus children's responses:

• How do you know that this story is a fantasy?

• What would you do if you had an elephant as a pet? Write and draw in your journal.

CENTER Activity

Science

ANIMALS OF AFRICA Explain to children that some elephants live in Africa. Have animal picture books available, and have children find other animals that live in Africa. Children make a picture or a word list to show their findings.

▶ **Spatial**

Review *she, he, for, is*

OBJECTIVES

Children will:

• identify and read the high-frequency word *she*

MATERIALS

• word cards from the Word Play Book

• *A Pet for Ken*

TECHNOLOGY TIP

INSTRUCTIONAL Explain that the word *she* is used to refer to a girl or woman. Use sentence pairs to illustrate: Susan has a new coat. *She* has a new coat.

PREPARE

Listen to Words Explain to the children that they will review the word *she*.

Read the following sentence, and have children raise a hand when they hear the word *she: She is coming to dinner. Is she your aunt?*

TEACH

Model Reading the Word in Context Have children reread the decodable book. Ask children to listen for the word *she*.

Identify the Word Ask children to look at their word cards, and then ask them to look for the word in sentences. Have children to point to the word *she* on each page as you read the story together. Have volunteers put a self-stick note below the word. (Have children move the self-stick note from page to page.)

Review High-Frequency Words Give each child one word card of a high-frequency word (*he, for, is, she, the, a, my, that, I, and, you, said, we, are, have, to, me, go, do*). Say a word, and have the child who has the word hold up the card and say it.

PRACTICE

Complete the Pupil Edition Page Read the directions on page 281 to the children, and make sure they clearly understand what they are asked to do. Complete the first item together. Then work through the page with children or have them complete the page independently.

ASSESS/CLOSE

Review the Page Review children's work, and note children who are experiencing difficulty or need additional practice.

Name_____

1.

Did <u>she</u> get a cap (for) Ron?

_____

2.

She and <u>he</u> got a cap and a mug.

_____

3.

She got a cap that <u>is</u> red.

_____

Read each sentence. **1.** Draw a line under the word *she*. Draw a circle around the word *for*. **2.** Draw a line under the word *he*. **3.** Draw a line under the word *is*.

Unit 5   Review *she, he, for, is*   **281**

Pupil Edition, page 281

ALTERNATE TEACHING STRATEGY

HIGH-FREQUENCY WORDS

For a different approach to teaching this skill, see page T27.

▶ **Visual/Auditory/ Kinesthetic**

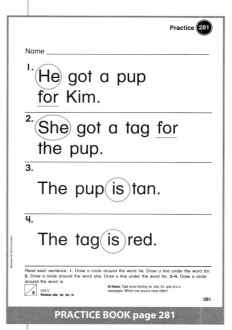

Practice **281**

Name_____

1. (He) got a pup for Kim.

2. (She) got a tag <u>for</u> the pup.

3. The pup (is) tan.

4. The tag (is) red.

Read each sentence. **1.** Draw a circle around the word *he*. Draw a line under the word *for*. **2.** Draw a circle around the word *she*. Draw a line under the word *for*. **3–4.** Draw a circle around the word *is*.

Unit 5
Review *she, he, for, is*

At Home: Take turns finding *he, she, for,* and *is* in a newspaper. Which one occurs most often?

281

PRACTICE BOOK page 281

Meeting Individual Needs for Vocabulary

EASY	ON-LEVEL	CHALLENGE	LANGUAGE SUPPORT
Give the children word cards for the word *she*. Then sing "I Know an Old Lady Who Swallowed a Fly." Have children hold up their cards when they hear the word *she*.	**Write** the word *she* on chart paper. Then describe a girl in the class: *She has blonde hair. She likes to draw. She is wearing a blue skirt.* Children guess who you are describing, and point to the word *she*.	**Ask** children to draw a picture of a girl or woman that they know. Have them write a sentence about the person, using the word *she*.	**Have** children sit in a circle. Describe a girl, using her name: *Lauren has blue eyes.* Others repeat the sentence, substituting the word *she*: *She has blue eyes.*

281

GRAMMAR/SPELLING
CONNECTIONS
Model subject-verb agreement, complete sentences, and correct tense so that students may gain increasing control of grammar when speaking and writing.

Interactive Writing

Write a New Episode

Prewrite

LOOK AT THE STORY PATTERN
Reread *The Enormous Carrot* together. Talk about the pattern in the story: another character joins the group and tries to pull out the carrot. Then brainstorm another vegetable that might grow to be enormous. Write a list on the chalkboard.

Draft

WRITE A NEW STORY EPISODE Have children choose one of the vegetables from the list. Explain that children will write a new episode for the story.

- Begin by having children decide if the characters will remain the same, or if children want to include new or additional characters.

- Have children tell the story as you write it on chart paper. Encourage children to focus on the beginning, middle, and end.

- Have pairs of children decide on a part of the story to write and illustrate.

Publish

CREATE THE BOOK Compile the text and illustrations into a book. Reread it together.

They tried to pull the celery off the stalk.
But the celery stayed put.
It wouldn't come out.

Presentation Ideas

MAKE PROPS Have children make props for the new story episode. Children can show the new vegetable by using clay, paper, papier mâché, and so on.

▶ **Representing/Viewing**

ACT OUT THE STORY Have groups of children use their props and act out the new story. Children may also wish to make simple costumes.

▶ **Speaking/Representing**

COMMUNICATION TIPS

- **Representing** When children role play, encourage them to speak loudly and clearly.

- **Viewing** As children watch others perform, remind them to listen and refrain from talking.

TECHNOLOGY TIP

Help children to input parts of their story on the computer.

LANGUAGE SUPPORT

ESL Show pictures of vegetables, and have children identify and describe them.

Meeting Individual Needs for Writing

EASY	ON-LEVEL	CHALLENGE
Describe a Carrot Display a carrot, and work with children to write a word web that describes the carrot. Then slice the carrot for children to sample.	**Write Dialogue** Have children choose a character from the story. Help them generate some thoughts that the character might be thinking and record them.	**New Ending** Invite children to write a new ending to the story. Remind children to sound out words as they write. Have them illustrate and share their endings.

A Big Bug

The variety of literature in this lesson will offer children opportunities to read and listen to stories about friends solving problems.

A Big Bug

Decodable Story, pages 289–290 of the Pupil Edition

Listening Library Audiocassette

Patterned Book, page 293B

Winnie the Pooh Gets Stuck

Teacher Read Aloud, page 287A

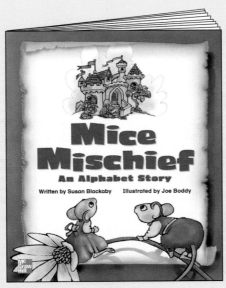

Listening Library Audiocassette

ABC Big Book, pages 283A–283B

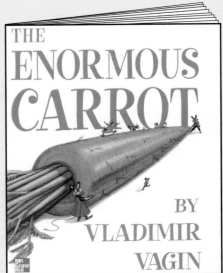

Listening Library Audiocassette

Literature Big Book, pages 285A–285B

**Pupil Edition,
pages 282–293**

**Big Book of Real-Life Reading,
page 38**

**Big Book of Phonics Rhymes and
Poems, pages 10, 11**

 Listening
Library
Audiocassette

ADDITIONAL RESOURCES

**Practice Book,
pages 282–293**

- **Phonics Kit**
- **Language Support Book**
- **Alternate Teaching Strategies,** pp. T32–T33

McGraw-Hill School
TECHNOLOGY

Phonics **CD-ROM** Provides
extra phonics support.

*inter***NET**
CONNECTION Research & Inquiry Ideas.

Visit www.mhschool.com

A Big Bug

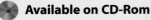
READING AND LANGUAGE ARTS

- **Phonological Awareness**

- **Phonics** *initial and final /b/b; blending with short a, e, i, o, u*

- **Comprehension**

- **Vocabulary**

- **Beginning Reading Concepts**

- **Listening, Speaking, Viewing, Representing**

DAY 1

Focus on Reading Skills

Develop Phonological Awareness, 282G-282H
"Bounce the Ball" *Big Book of Phonics Rhymes and Poems*, 10

**Introduce Initial /b/b,** 282I-282
Practice Book, 282
Phonics/Phonemic Awareness
Practice Book

 **CD-ROM**

Read the Literature

Read *Mice Mischief: An Alphabet Story*
Big Book, 283A-283B
Shared Reading

Build Skills

☑ Action Words, 283C-283
Practice Book, 283

DAY 2

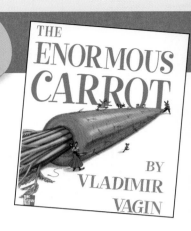

Focus on Reading Skills

Develop Phonological Awareness, 284A-284B
"Tub Time" *Big Book of Phonics Rhymes and Poems*, 11

Introduce Final /b/b, 284C-284
Practice Book, 284
Phonics/Phonemic Awareness
Practice Book

CD-ROM

Read the Literature

Read *The Enormous Carrot* **Big Book,**
285A-285B
Shared Reading

Build Skills

☑ Summarize, 285C-285
Practice Book, 285

- **Cross Curriculum**

 Language Arts, 283B

a  Social Studies, 285B

- **Writing**

 Writing Prompt: Write about something special you and a friend do together.

 Journal Writing, 283B
Letter Formation, 282I

 Writing Prompt: Which animal did you li* in the story? Draw a picture of it and tell v

 Journal Writing, 285B
Letter Formation, 284C

☑ = **Skill Assessed in Unit Test**

DAY 3

Winnie the Pooh Gets Stuck

Focus on Reading Skills

Develop Phonological Awareness, 286A-286B
"Bounce the Ball" and "Tub Time"
Big Book of Phonics Rhymes and Poems, 10-11

 **Review /b/b,** 286C-286
Practice Book, 286
Phonics/Phonemic Awareness
Practice Book

 **CD-ROM**

Read the Literature

Read "Winnie the Pooh Gets Stuck"
Teacher Read Aloud, 287A-287B
Shared Reading
Read the Big Book of Real-Life Reading, 38-39
☑ Maps

Build Skills

☑ High-Frequency Words: *has,* 287C-287
Practice Book, 287

 **Art,** 287B

 Writing Prompt: How would you help Winnie if you were one of his friends? Write about what you would do.

DAY 4

A Big Bug

Focus on Reading Skills

Develop Phonological Awareness, 288A-288B
"Rob the Hog"
 **Review Blending with Short *a, e, i, o, u,*** 288C-288
Practice Book, 288
Phonics/Phonemic Awareness
Practice Book

 CD-ROM

Read the Literature

Read "A Big Bug" Decodable Story, 289/290A-289/290D

☑ Initial and Final /b/b:
Blending
☑ Summarize
☑ High-Frequency Words: *has*
☑ Concepts of Print

Build Skills

☑ Summarize, 291A-291
Practice Book, 291

 Science, 289/290D

 Writing Prompt: Write a story about how you would catch a bug without harming it.

Letter Formation,
Practice Book, 289-290

DAY 5

A Big Bug

Bob's Bath
by Sally Joyce
illustrated by Brian Cody

Focus on Reading Skills

Develop Phonological Awareness, 292A-292B
"Rob the Hog"
 **Review Blending with Short *a, e, i, o, u,*** 292C-292
Practice Book, 292
Phonics/Phonemic Awareness
Practice Book

CD-ROM

Read the Literature

Reread "A Big Bug" Decodable Story, 293A
Read "Bob's Bath" Patterned Book, 293B
Guided Reading
☑ Initial and Final /b/b;
Blending
☑ Summarize
☑ High-Frequency Words: *has*
☑ Concepts of Print

Build Skills

☑ High-Frequency Words: *has, he, she, me, for,* 293C-293
Practice Book, 293

 Language Arts, 293B

 Writing Prompt: Is there something you would like to make with friends? Write about it.

Interactive Writing, 294A-294B

Develop Phonological Awareness

Listen

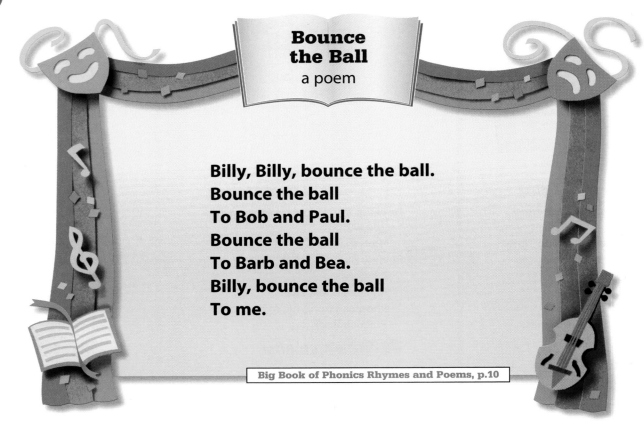

Bounce the Ball
a poem

Billy, Billy, bounce the ball.
Bounce the ball
To Bob and Paul.
Bounce the ball
To Barb and Bea.
Billy, bounce the ball
To me.

Big Book of Phonics Rhymes and Poems, p.10

Objective: Identify Words That Rhyme

LISTEN TO THE RHYMES IN THE POEM

- Have children stand in a circle. Read the poem "Bounce the Ball" aloud. Have children point out the words that rhyme in the poem. *(ball/Paul; Bea/me)*

PLAY RHYMING GAME

- Bounce a ball to a child, and ask the child to bounce it back. Repeat several times.
- Give the ball to a volunteer and say the name *Billy*. The child says a word that rhymes with *Billy* and bounces the ball to another child, who does the same. Children continue saying rhyming words. Accept nonsense words, but encourage children to think of real words.

silly   Willy   chilly   filly   hilly   lily

CONTINUE RHYMING OTHER WORDS

- Continue the game by rhyming other words from the poem: *ball, Bob, me.*

ball, call, fall, hall, wall

Objective: Listen for Initial /b/

SEGMENTING

- Say the word *ball*. Emphasize the /b/ sound, and have children repeat it after you. Have them segment the sound.

> **b-all**

- Then say the word *Bob* and ask if the word has the same beginning sound as *ball*. Have children segment the initial sound (B-ob).

BOB FOR *b*

- Say words from the poem. Ask children to repeat each word and to determine if the word begins with /b/. If it does, the children should bob their heads.

> **ball   and   to   Barb   Paul   me**

ADD THE /b/ SOUND

- Then say the *b* words from the poem without the /b/ sound. Have children add the sound to say the word.
- Repeat with other *b* words.

> **ob/Bob   illy/Billy   all/ball**

From Phonemic Awareness to Phonics

Objective: Identify Initial /b/B,b

IDENTIFY THE LETTER FOR THE SOUND

- Explain to children that the letters *B,b* stand for the sound /b/. Say the sound and have children say it with you.
- Display the *Big Book of Phonics Rhymes and Poems*, page 10. Point to the letters in the corner. Identify them, and have children say the /b/ sound.

REREAD THE POEM

- Reread the poem. Have children pretend to bounce a ball when they hear a word that begins with /b/.

FIND *B* AND *b*

- Use a sheet of paper to highlight each line in the poem. Have children count all the *B*'s and *b*'s.
- Keep a tally. Then determine whether there are more capital or lowercase *b*'s in the poem.

FIND MATCHING WORDS

- Have children find matching words and say each letter name aloud. Then have children put stick-on notes under both words.

> **Billy/Billy   To/To   ball/ball**

Bb

Bounce the Ball

Billy, Billy, bounce the ball.
Bounce the ball
To Bob and Paul.
Bounce the ball
To Barb and Bea.
Billy, bounce the ball
To me.

Big Book of Phonics Rhymes and Poems, 10

282H

OBJECTIVES

Children will:

- identify the letters *B,b*
- identify /b/ *B,b*
- form the letters *B,b*

....

MATERIALS

- letter cards from the *Word Building Cards*

TEACHING TIP

INSTRUCTIONAL As children form the letters *B,b,* first by tracing in the air and then by writing them, observe and give individual help with letter formation, as necessary. You may also want to have them trace *B,b* on the palms of their hands.

ALTERNATE TEACHING STRATEGY

....

INITIAL /b/*b*

For a different approach to teaching this skill, see page T32.

▶ **Visual/Auditory/ Kinesthetic**

Introduce Initial /b/ b

TEACH

Identify /b/ B,b   Tell children they will learn to write the sound /b/ with the letters *B,b*. Ask them to repeat the /b/ sound. Write the word *bed* on the chalkboard, and say it aloud, emphasizing the initial sound /b/. Write *boy* and say it aloud. Say some boys' names, and ask children to *bounce* in their seats when they hear a name that *begins* with /b/, for example: *Bill, Matt, Bob, Bud, Victor, Burt, Ben, Arturo.* Invite children to suggest *B* names for girls. Write all of the *B* names on the chalkboard.

Form B,b   Display the letters *B,b* and, with your back to the children, trace them in the air. Ask children to do the same, then have them trace their *B,b* letter cards. Give them each a picture of a ball. Have them write the letters *B,b* several times under the picture of the ball.

PRACTICE

Complete the Pupil Edition Page   Read the directions on page 282 to the children, and make sure they clearly understand what they are being asked to do. Identify each picture, and complete the first item together. Then work through the page with children, or have them complete the page independently.

ASSESS/CLOSE

Identify and Use B,b   Say the sentence, "Ben has a ball and bat." Have children hold up their letter cards when they hear a word that begins with /b/*b*. Write the sentence on the chalkboard, and invite volunteers to draw a line under the words that begin with *B,b*.

Name _____

1.   balloon  pencil  bird

2.   ring bicycle butterfly

3.   bee  ball mop

4. sun bus button

Write the letters *Bb*. • Say the word that names each picture. • Listen for the sound at the beginning of each word. • Circle each picture whose name begins with the same sound as *balloon*.

McGraw-Hill School Division

282 Unit 5 Introduce Initial /b/b

Pupil Edition, page 282

ADDITIONAL PHONICS RESOURCES

Practice Book *page 282*
Phonics Workbook

McGraw-Hill School
TECHNOLOGY

Phonics **CD-ROM**
Activities for practice with Initial Letters

PRACTICE BOOK, page 282

Meeting Individual Needs for Phonics

EASY	ON-LEVEL	CHALLENGE	LANGUAGE SUPPORT
Say several words, some of which will begin with /b/b and some of which won't. Ask children to say, "Bingo!" every time you say a word that begins with b. (Suggested words: *bet, fun, bath, boy, cot, Mom, big, have, baby, bank*.)	**Have** children look through magazines and cut out pictures of objects whose names begin with the sound /b/. Then have children paste their pictures onto construction paper and label them with the letters *B,b* or with a word label.	**Begin** the following story, and invite children to add on to it. They can make up sentences or suggest words that begin with b: *The big, blue bird flew into a berry bush. It bit into some berries. The branch began to bend.*	Some ESL children may have trouble distinguishing between initial /b/ and /v/. Have them repeat words after you. Then write the word on the chalkboard, underlining the initial letters, for example: *bug, bit, bad, vet, very.*

282

○BJECTIVES

Children will:

- summarize a story
- recognize words with initial *b*
- understand alphabetical order

MATERIALS

- picture cards and letters from the Word Building Cards

TEACHING TIP

Provide picture and reference books about different types of animals. Include them in your library corner, and encourage children to think about how the animals are different and the same.

Read the Big Book

Before Reading

Develop Oral Language Reread "The Alphabet Name Game" with children on page 5 in the Big Book of Phonics Rhymes and Poems. Have children use their last names and do the actions to the song.

Have children retell what happened to the mice in Mice Mischief. Discuss the title and have children explain how Dee and Bink get into mischief.

Set Purposes Tell children that, as they reread the story, they should pay close attention to the problems the mice face in the castle. Do the mice solve their problems? Have children think about whether or not Dee and Bink work together to solve their problems. Have children predict what letter the word in dark print will begin with before you read each page.

"Let's try the **window**!" said Dee.

28

29

Mice Mischief, an Alphabet Story, pages 28-29

During Reading

Read Together

- Before you begin to read, point to the first word in the sentence. Explain that this is where you will begin to read. Continue to track print as you read the story. *Tracking Print*

- After you read pages 2-3, ask which two letters will come next. Then turn the page and confirm. Continue as you read the story. *Phonics*

- Make the /b/ sound, and ask children to say it with you. Then read page 4, and ask which word begins with that sound. (bed) *Phonics*

- After you read page 6, ask children to tell what has happened in the story so far. *Summarize*

Then Bink tears his **vest**!

27

Mice Mischief, an Alphabet Story, page 27

After Reading

Literary Response

JOURNAL WRITING Ask children to draw a picture of and write about what one of the animals did in the story.

ORAL RESPONSE Ask questions such as:

- What did one of the mice do to get away from the cat?

- Do you think this was a good idea?

ABC Activity

Say the first three letters of the alphabet and stop. Then ask a volunteer to say the next three letters. Continue, choosing beginning letters at random.

CENTER Activity

Cross Curricular: Language Arts

ANIMAL MATCH Have children gather 10 of the animal picture cards from the Word Building Manipulative Cards (the camel, dinosaur, elephant, mouse, ostrich, pig, raccoon, seal, turtle, and fox).

Also use the letter cards that correspond to the initial letter of each animal (such as the l letter card to go with the picture card of the lion.)

Have one child hold up an animal card and say the animal's name. The partner finds the card with the letter that stands for the beginning sound.

▶ Linguistic

OBJECTIVES

Children will:

- identify and describe action words

....

MATERIALS

- *The Enormous Carrot*

TECHNOLOGY TIP

INSTRUCTIONAL Give children some examples of words that name people, places, and things. Then invite children to make a phrase with a name word and an action word, for example, *Mom reads*.

Review Action Words

PREPARE

Play a Game
Ask children to guess an action word you are thinking of. Give clues about people and animals such as: *Cats do this to get up a tree.* (climb) *A mouse does this when it sees a cat.* (runs) Encourage children to think of various action words that fit the clue.

TEACH

Describe Actions
Display the Big Book *The Enormous Carrot*, and have volunteers retell the story. Look at pages 6–7, and have children name the actions that the rabbits are doing. Continue through the story, having children note action words. You may wish to have volunteers pantomime some of the words.

PRACTICE

Find Action Words
Read the directions on page 283 to the children, and make sure they clearly understand what they are asked to do. Read the words. Complete the first item. Then work through the page with children, or have them complete the page independently.

ASSESS/CLOSE

Review the Page
Check children's work on the Pupil Edition page. Note areas where children need extra help.

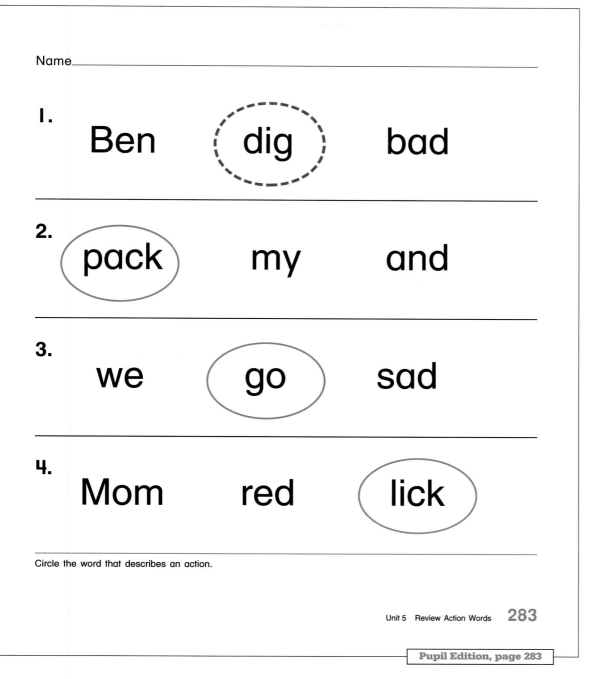

Name_____

1. Ben (dig) bad

2. (pack) my and

3. we (go) sad

4. Mom red (lick)

Circle the word that describes an action.

Pupil Edition, page 283

ALTERNATE TEACHING
STRATEGY

IDENTIFY ACTION
WORDS

For a different approach
to teaching this skill, see
page T31.

▶ Visual/Auditory/
Kinesthetic

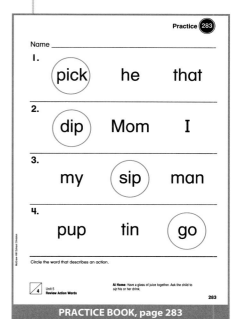

Practice 283

Name_____

1. (pick) he that

2. (dip) Mom I

3. my (sip) man

4. pup tin (go)

Circle the word that describes an action.

Unit 5
Review Action Words

At Home: Have a glass of juice together. Ask the child to
sip his or her drink.

283

PRACTICE BOOK, page 283

Meeting Individual Needs for Grammar

EASY	ON-LEVEL	CHALLENGE	LANGUAGE SUPPORT
Teach children the following action rhyme: *Two little feet go tap, tap, tap.* *Two little hands to clap, clap, clap.* *A quick little jump from the chair,* *Two little arms reach high in the air.* Children identify the action words and act out the poem.	**Help** children fold drawing paper into fourths. Have children illustrate a different action word from *The Enormous Carrot* in each section. Help them to label their pictures.	**Invite** children to think about actions they do during the school day. Have partners work together to make a picture/word list of these words. Then have children compare lists.	**Talk** about the action words *push* and *pull*. Have children pantomime each word and give examples of when they *push* and *pull*.

283

Develop Phonological Awareness

Listen

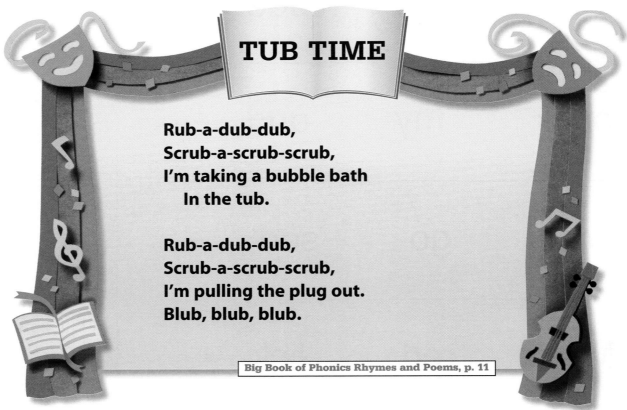

TUB TIME

Rub-a-dub-dub,
Scrub-a-scrub-scrub,
I'm taking a bubble bath
  In the tub.

Rub-a-dub-dub,
Scrub-a-scrub-scrub,
I'm pulling the plug out.
Blub, blub, blub.

Big Book of Phonics Rhymes and Poems, p. 11

Objective: Listen for Rhymes

LISTEN TO THE POEM
- Read the poem "Tub Time" aloud. Then read it again, and invite children to pantomime taking a bath as they listen.

NAME THE RHYMES
- When you read the poem, emphasize the final word in each line except the sixth. Say the word *dub* and read the next line. Ask which word rhymes with *dub*. Then continue through the poem. Have children pantomime taking a bath when the other rhyming word is named.

> dub   scrub   blub

LISTEN AND MOVE
- Ask children to pretend that they are washing their arms when you say, "rub-a-dub-dub." Have them pretend to wash their legs when you say, "scrub-a-scrub-scrub."

- When you say, "blub, blub, blub," have children pantomime pulling out the plug.

VARY THE PACE
- Read the poem at different speeds. Point out to children that their actions will become faster or slower.

Objective: Listen for Final /b/

LISTEN FOR SOUNDS

- Read the poem "Tub Time" aloud. Ask children to notice how the words in the poem sound a bit like blowing bubbles under water.
- Make the /b/ sound and stretch it to say *b-b-b-b-b*. Have children repeat the sound after you.

REPEAT THE SOUNDS

- Invite children to pretend that they are underwater creatures who have a bubbly way of talking. Say the word *rub*. Then say *rub-b-b-b-b,* and have children repeat after you.

TRY OTHER WORDS

- Say *tub,* and ask children to stretch the /b/ sound to say *tub-b-b-b*.
- Continue with the words *scrub* and *blub*. Have children think of other words to try.

Read Together

From Phonemic Awareness to Phonics

Objective: Identify Final /b/*b*

RELATE THE LETTER AND THE SOUND

- Explain to children that the letter *b* stands for /b/. Say the sound and have children repeat it after you. Tell children that sometimes the /b/ sound comes at the end of a word.

IDENTIFY THE LETTERS

- Display page 11 in the Big Book of Phonics Rhymes and Poems. Point to the *b* in the corner, identify it, and repeat the sound. Have children say the sound after you.

REREAD THE POEM

- Reread the poem "Tub Time," tracking words as you read. Emphasize the words that end with /b/.

FIND WORDS WITH FINAL /b/

- Ask volunteers to find the words in each line that end with *b*.
- Say each word and have children repeat.

Tub Time

Rub-a-dub-dub,
Scrub-a-scrub-scrub,
I'm taking a bubble bath
In the tub.

Rub-a-dub-dub,
Scrub-a-scrub-scrub,
I'm pulling the plug out.
Blub, blub, blub.

Big Book of Phonics Rhymes and Poems, 11

Introduce Final /b/ *b*

Children will:

- identify the letter *b*
- identify /b/*b*
- form the letter *b*

MATERIALS

- letter cards from the *Word Building Cards*

TEACHING TIP

INSTRUCTIONAL

Remind children that when b falls at the end of a word, the letter will always be in its lower-case form. Explain that a word might begin with a capital B if it is the name of a person, place, or thing, or if it is at the beginning of a sentence

ALTERNATE TEACHING STRATEGY

FINAL /b/*b*

For a different approach to teaching this skill, see page T32.

▶ **Visual/Auditory/ Kinesthetic**

TEACH

Identify /b/*b*   Tell children they will learn to write the ending sound /b/ with the letter *b*. First have children repeat the sound /b/; then say, "rub-b-b-b-a-dub-b-b-b". Ask children to repeat this. Write *rub* and *dub* on the chalkboard, and read the words aloud as you point to them. Write and say the names *Ron, Rod, Rob,* and ask children which name ends in /b/. Repeat this for *Deb, Dan, Dad.*

Form *b*   Display the letter *b*, and trace it with your finger in the air, with your back to the children. Ask them to trace *b* on their tables. Give each child four index cards, and ask them to write the letter *b* on each card.

PRACTICE

Complete the Pupil Edition Page   Read the directions on page 284 to the children, and make sure they clearly understand what they are being asked to do. Identify each picture, and complete the first item together. Then work through the page with children, or have them complete the page independently.

ASSESS/CLOSE

Identify and Use *b*   Make the following word cards and place them on the chalkboard ledge. Ask children to hold up a *b* card when you point to a word that ends in *b: cub, cut, tub, fib, dog, rib.* Invite volunteers to place a letter card on the final letter of every word that ends with the letter *b*.

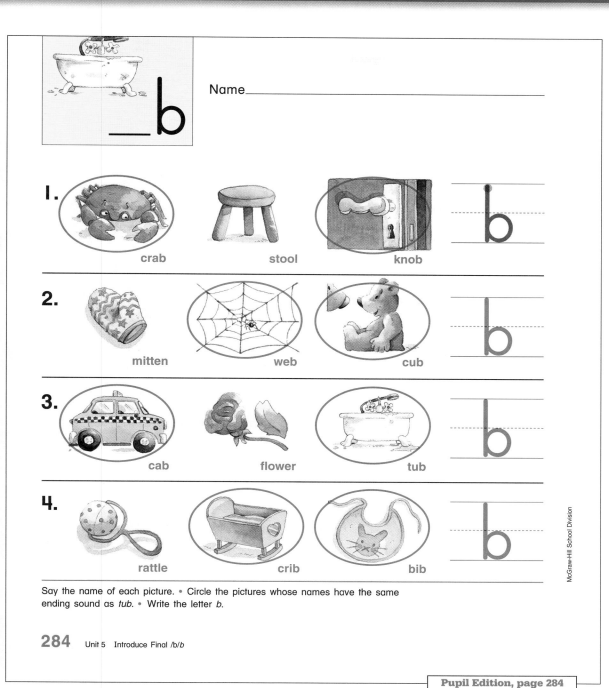

Name_____

1. crab   stool   knob   b

2. mitten   web   cub   b

3. cab   flower   tub   b

4. rattle   crib   bib   b

Say the name of each picture. • Circle the pictures whose names have the same ending sound as *tub*. • Write the letter *b*.

McGraw-Hill School Division

284   Unit 5   Introduce Final /b/b

Pupil Edition, page 284

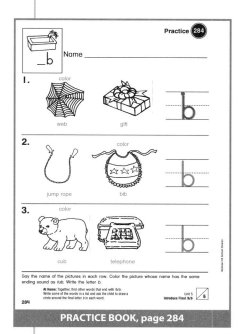

PRACTICE BOOK, page 284

Meeting Individual Needs for Phonics

EASY	ON-LEVEL	CHALLENGE	LANGUAGE SUPPORT
Say the following to children: *Did you stub your toe? Then soak it in the tub.* Have them raise a *b* letter card each time they hear a word that ends in /b/. Ask them to raise their cards to show how many words ended in *b*.	**Show** pictures of the following: *cub, cat, tub, crib, bus, crab*. Have children name each object shown, and ask them to write a *b* for each word that ends in /b/.	**Tell** riddles, and have children guess the answers using words that end in *b*, for example: *What is a baby bear called?* (cub) *What does a baby wear?* (bib) Invite them to create their own final *b* riddles.	Second-language learners may have difficulty distinguishing between final /b/ and /v/ sounds. Ask them to hold a mirror and say *b-b-b*, then *v-v-v*. Have them repeat the sounds and practice saying the following: *have, cab, save, tub, rib, drive.*

284

OBJECTIVES

Children will:

- summarize a story
- identify /b/ *b*

TEACHING TIP

Sing familiar cumulative songs with the children, such as "I Know An Old Lady Who Swallowed a Fly" and "I'm Being Swallowed by a Boa Constrictor." Talk about how the cumulative style of the songs are similar to "The Enormous Carrot."

Read the Big Book

Before Reading

Develop Oral Language

Teach children the following song to the tune of "Row, Row, Row Your Boat."

Plant, plant, plant the seeds,
Plant them in a row.
If you weed and water them,
The sun will make them grow.

Invite children to act out the song and to talk about what is necessary to make a garden grow. Remind children about how the rabbits cared for the garden in "The Enormous Carrot."

Set Purposes

Model: We know that this story is about an enormous carrot that wouldn't come out of the ground. Let's read the story and think about how the animals worked together to solve the problem.

THE
ENORMOUS
CARROT
BY
VLADIMIR
VAGIN

Then Daisy, Floyd, Mabel, Henry, Gloria, Buster, Claire, Lester, and all

their friends ate every bit of that enormous carrot until it was all gone.

30

31

The Enormous Carrot, pages 30-31

During Reading

Read Together

• Before you begin to read, point to the first word in the first sentence. Explain that this is where you will begin to read. Continue to track print as you read the story. *Tracking Print*

• *After you read page 17, ask children to find a word on the page that begins with the letter* b (by). *Phonics*

• After you read the story, ask children how the story began, how the animals worked together, and how the story ended. *Summarize the Story*

Just then, their friend Henry came by.
"Will you help us pull this carrot out?" asked Mabel.
"Glad to," said Henry.

The Enormous Carrot, p. 17

After Reading

Retell the Story

Ask children to summarize the story by explaining how the story began, what the animals did, and how the story ended. Cut out a large carrot from construction paper, and have children make simple masks for each character from paper plates. Small groups can act out the story.

Literary Response

JOURNAL WRITING Invite children to think of a different enormous vegetable that might grow in the garden. Have children write about or draw a picture of their vegetable and what might happen in the story.

ORAL RESPONSE Engage children in a discussion about their drawings and/or writings by asking the following questions:

• *Which vegetable did you draw?*

• *Did it stay in the ground, or did the animals pull it out?*

CENTER Activity

Cross Curricular: Social Studies

BRAINSTORMING PROJECTS

With children brainstorm a "to do" list of classroom or community projects. Have children work together to devise a plan for cooperatively completing the projects.

▶ Interpersonal

School Projects
1. Clean up school yard.
2. Have a Bake Sale.
3. Plan a Science Fair.
4. Have a Holiday Assembly Show.

Children will:
- summarize to understand a story

MATERIALS
- *The Enormous Carrot*

TEACHING TIP

MANAGEMENT Guide pairs of children to share familiar books and talk about their favorite parts of the stories. In a class discussion, have partners summarize their books and share their favorite parts in a class discussion.

Review Summarize

PREPARE

Recall the Story
Ask children to recall the story *The Enormous Carrot*. Take a picture walk through several spreads, and ask children how the story begins.

TEACH

Summarize Story Events
Continue through the story, and ask children to explain the problem. When you finish the story, ask children to recount how the problem is solved. Guide them to recall specific pictures and events from each part of the story. Remind children that they can remember a story by summarizing. Tell children that summarizing is briefly explaining what *the important parts of the story are.*

Extend the activity by having groups of five children come to the front of the room. Assign each child an important event in the story The Enormous Carrot. (For example, Daisy and Floyd plant the seeds, discover the huge carrot, ask many friends to help pull out the carrot, finally pull it out, and have a party). Then have the children line up in correct story order and state a brief explanation of their part of the story.

PRACTICE

Complete the Pupil Edition Page
Read the directions on page 285 to the children, and make sure they clearly understand what they are asked to do. Identify each picture, and complete the first item together. Then work through the page with children, or have them complete the page independently.

ASSESS/CLOSE

Review the Page
Review children's work, and guide children who are experiencing difficulty.

Name____

~~1~~ ~~2~~ (3)

Listen as I read three sentences. • One sentence will tell what the story "The Enormous Carrot" is about. • Circle the number of the sentence that tells what the story is about. • Cross out the number of each sentence that does not tell what the story is about.

1. A girl teaches her brother how to play hopscotch.
2. Two rabbits have fun playing together.
3. A group of friends works together to pull out an enormous carrot.

On the bottom, draw a picture of what "The Enormous Carrot" is about.

Unit 5 Review Summarize 285

Pupil Edition, page 285

ALTERNATE TEACHING STRATEGY

SUMMARIZE

For a different approach to teaching this skill, see page T29.

▶ **Visual/Auditory/Kinesthetic**

Practice 285

Name ________________________

1.

2.

3.

4.

Look at the pictures in each row. Draw a circle around the picture that shows something that happened in "The Enormous Carrot." Then use the pictures you circled to retell the story.

At Home: Take turns telling each other what a favorite movie was about.

Unit 5 Review Summarize

285

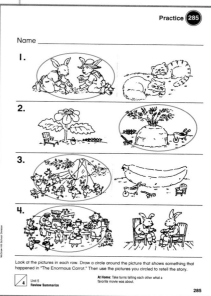

PRACTICE BOOK, page 285

Meeting Individual Needs for Comprehension

EASY	ON-LEVEL	CHALLENGE	LANGUAGE SUPPORT
Ask children to choose an activity in your classroom. Have them draw three or four pictures showing important parts of the activity.. Have them summarize the activity aloud while showing their drawings.	**Reread** a familiar story to the children, and have them summarize by asking: *What are the important parts of the story?* Give children opportunities to respond by elaborating on story details.	**Have** children pretend to be news reporters. Guide pairs of students to summarize what happened to Daisy, Floyd, and their friends. Have them present their summaries in a newscaster format. Encourage them to experiment with voice and gestures.	**Revisit** the story by adapting the words to "The Farmer in the Dell": The carrot won't come up, The carrot won't come up, Heigh ho the derrio, The carrot won't come up Then Mabel came to call, …. Repeat verses, adding the names of Daisy and Floyd's friends.

Develop Phonological Awareness

Listen

Bounce the Ball
a poem

Tub Time
a poem

Billy, Billy, bounce the ball.
Bounce the ball
To Bob and Paul.
Bounce the ball
To Barb and Bea.
Billy, bounce the ball
   To me.

Rub-a-dub-dub,
Scrub-a-scrub-scrub,
I'm taking a bubble bath
   In the tub.
Rub-a-dub-dub,
Scrub-a-scrub-scrub,
I'm pulling the plug out.
Blub, blub, blub.

Big Book of Phonics Rhymes and Poems, pp. 10–11

Objective: Listen for Names

READ THE POEM Read the poem "Bounce the Ball" aloud. Then read the poem a second time and have children clap each time they hear a person's name.

Billy   Bob   Paul   Barb   Bea

CLAP OUT SYLLABLES Ask volunteers to clap for each syllable in the five names in the poem. Then have children take turns saying their names aloud while they clap out the number of syllables.

LISTEN AND BOUNCE Have children stand in a circle. Model how to gently bounce a ball. Then give the ball to one of the children. Reread the poem slowly, substituting the names in the poem with the names of children in your class or with names they suggest.
Encourage children to listen carefully. Have the child with the ball gently bounce it to the next child when a name is said.

Objective: Listen for /b/

LISTEN FOR INITIAL /b/ Read the title "Bounce the Ball," emphasizing the initial /b/ sound. Ask which words in the title begin with /b/.

> **Bounce   Ball**

LISTEN FOR FINAL /b/ Read the title "Tub Time," emphasizing the final /b/ sound. Ask which word in the title ends with /b/.

> **Tub**

IDENTIFY WORDS WITH /b/ Reread the poem "Tub Time" line by line. Have children pretend to bounce a ball each time they hear a word that begins with /b/. Repeat the poem, but this time have children pretend to scrub their desks each time they hear a word that ends with /b/.

BLOW BUBBLES FOR /b/ Have children listen to the following sentences and pretend to blow bubbles when they hear a word that begins or ends with /b/.

> Bernie likes his bubble bath.
> Deb bakes tasty brownies.
> Rob the clown makes balloon pets.

Read Together

From Phonemic Awareness to Phonics

Objective: Identify /b/ B, b

IDENTIFY THE LETTER Explain to children that the letters *B* and *b* stand for the sound /b/. Have children repeat the sound after you.

Display pages 10 and 11 in the *Big Book of Phonics Rhymes and Poems*. Point to the letters and identify them. Say the /b/ sound and have children say the sound with you.

REREAD THE POEMS Emphasize words with initial or final /b/. Have children repeat the words.

FIND B, b Have children point to words that begin or end with B or b.

Bb

Bounce the Ball

Billy, Billy, bounce the ball.
Bounce the ball
To Bob and Paul.
Bounce the ball
To Barb and Bea.
Billy, bounce the ball
To me.

10

Bb

Tub Time

Rub-a-dub-dub,
Scrub-a-scrub-scrub,
I'm taking a bubble bath
In the tub.

Rub-a-dub-dub,
Scrub-a-scrub-scrub,
I'm pulling the plug out.
Blub, blub, blub.

11

Big Book of Phonics Rhymes and Poems, pp. 10–11

286B

Review /b/ b

OBJECTIVES

Children will:

- identify and discriminate between initial and final /b/ *B,b*

- write and use the letters *B,b*

TECHNOLOGY TIP

INSTRUCTIONAL Write the letters *B,b* on the chalkboard. Invite children to come forward and paint the letters on the chalkboard using a paintbrush dipped in water.

ALTERNATE TEACHING STRATEGY

IDENTIFY /b/ *B,b*

For a different approach to teaching this skill, see page 32.

▶ **Visual/Auditory/ Kinesthetic**

TEACH

Identify and Discriminate Between Initial and Final /b/ *B,b*
Tell children they will review the sound /b/ at the beginning and the end of words and write the letters *B,b*. Ask them to raise their hands if a word begins or ends in /b/, and say: *The big bear cub was named Ben.*

Write and Use *B,b*
Write *B,b* on one part of the chalkboard and __*b* on another part. Show pictures of objects whose names begin or end in *b*, and ask children to point to the side of the chalkboard that shows the position of the letter *b*. For example: *tub, boy, bike, crib, web.*

PRACTICE

Complete the Pupil Edition Page
Read the directions on page 286 to the children, and make sure they clearly understand what they are being asked to do. Identify each picture, and complete the first item together. Work through the page with children, or have them complete the page independently.

ASSESS/CLOSE

Identify and Use *B,b*
Have children write *b*__ and __*b* three times each on six squares of paper. Make the following word cards and arrange them on the chalkboard: *bin, bag, cub, bed, rib, tab.* Have children arrange their paper squares to match the pattern of initial and final *b* in the six words.

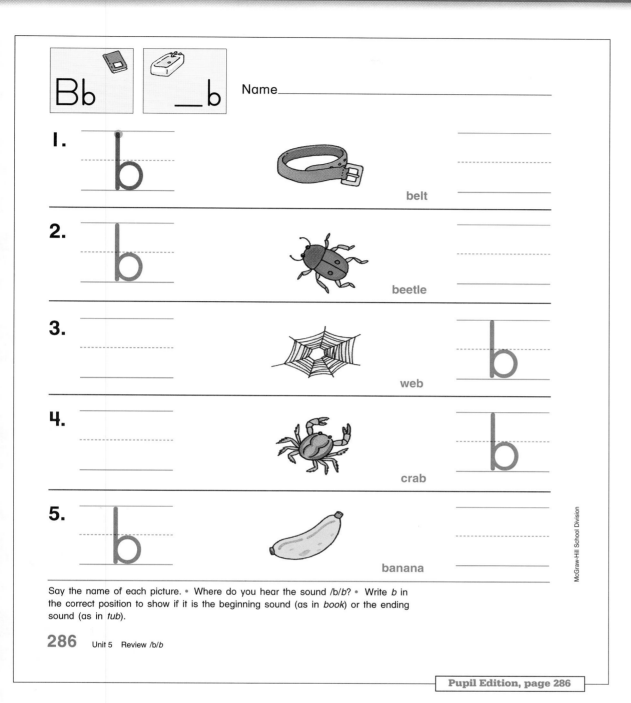

Bb **_b** Name_____

1. b — belt

2. b — beetle

3. web — b

4. crab — b

5. b — banana

Say the name of each picture. • Where do you hear the sound /b/b? • Write b in the correct position to show if it is the beginning sound (as in *book*) or the ending sound (as in *tub*).

286 Unit 5 Review /b/b

McGraw-Hill School Division

Pupil Edition, page 286

ADDITIONAL PHONICS RESOURCES

Practice Book, *page 286*
Phonics/Phonemic Awareness Practice Book

McGraw-Hill School
TECHNOLOGY

Phonics **CD-ROM**
Activities for practice with Initial and Final Letters

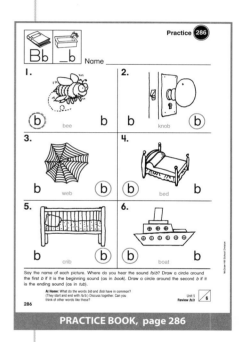

PRACTICE BOOK, page 286

Meeting Individual Needs for Phonics

EASY	ON-LEVEL	CHALLENGE	LANGUAGE SUPPORT
Say the following words, and ask children to identify whether each begins or ends with *b*: *bed, bud, cub, big, bag, rub, tub, bat*. Then ask children to select one of the words and draw a picture of it. Have children label their pictures with the letter *b* or with the word.	**Give** children pictures of objects whose names begin or end in *b*, such as: *ball, knob, bat, cab, tub, bud*. Ask them to name each object and then to sort the pictures into two groups: objects whose name begins with *b* and the objects whose name ends in *b*.	**Give** children pictures of animals and objects whose names begin or end in *b*. Have children name the pictures, write *b* on stick-on notes, and place them in the right- or left-hand corner of each picture depending on where /b/ occurs.	**Play** "What Did You Buy?" Have children form a circle. One turns to the next and says, *What did you buy?* The next child replies using a word that begins or ends in /b/, such as: *tub, cab, bacon, bubble bath, book*.

286

Teacher Read Aloud

Listen

Winnie the Pooh Gets Stuck

Pooh always liked a little something at eleven o'clock in the morning, and he was very glad to see Rabbit getting out the plates and mugs; and when Rabbit said, "Honey or condensed milk with your bread?" he was so excited that he said, "Both," and then, so as not to seem greedy, he added, "But don't bother about the bread, please." And for a long time after that he said nothing . . . until at last, humming to himself in a rather sticky voice, he got up, shook Rabbit lovingly by the paw, and said that he must be going on.

"Must you," said Rabbit politely.

"Well," said Pooh, "I could stay a little longer if it—if you—" and he tried very hard to look in the direction of the larder.

"As a matter of fact," said Rabbit, "I was going out myself directly."

"Oh, well, then, I'll be going on. Good-bye."

"Well, good-bye, if you're sure you won't have any more."

"Is there any more?" asked Pooh quickly.

Continued on page T5

Oral Comprehension

LISTENING AND SPEAKING Ask children how friends sometimes help each other out of "tight spots." Tell children that they will hear a story about a familiar character, Winnie the Pooh. Explain that the story is make-believe, but that the animal characters talk and act like humans. Discuss the plot of the story by asking, "What is Winnie the Pooh's problem? How do his friends try to help?"

After you finish reading, have children summarize the story. Ask: What are the important parts?

Activity Have children use clay to show Winnie the Pooh stuck in a hole. Ask children to create their own solutions to Pooh's problem.

▶ **Kinesthetic**

Real-Life Reading

The bear is stuck. Read the signs. How are his friends helping him?

PULL

PUSH

Big Book of Real-Life Reading, pages 38–39

Objective: Read Signs

READ THE PAGE Ask children if they know what it means to push or to pull. Explain that to push means to move something away from you. Share that to pull something means to pull something toward you. Remind children of the story "Winnie the Pooh Gets Stuck," and ask children to retell the story. Explain that they will see a picture of Winnie the Pooh and his friends. Discuss the picture and the signs.

ANSWER THE QUESTION Point to each sign, and read the word. Ask if the friends should push or pull and why. Ask: *Why is it important to read signs?* Elicit that *Push* and *Pull* signs help to stay safe. Ask: *Have you ever seen a sign saying* Push *or* Pull? Share that these signs are often seen on doors of stores and other buildings.

Cross Curricular: Art

SIGN FUN Provide index cards and art materials. First have children create their own *Exit, Push, Pull,* and *Danger* signs on the index cards. Provide a model so that they can write the letters.

Next, have children choose one of their signs and draw a picture of where they might see that a sign (i.e., an *Exit* sign on a store door). Children should then glue their sign on their picture as a label.

Have children share their pictures and signs with the class.

▶ **Linguistic/Spatial**

OBJECTIVES

Children will:

- identify and read the high-frequency word *has*

MATERIALS

- word cards from the *Word Building Cards*

TEACHING **TIP**

INSTRUCTIONAL Have children sit in a circle. Ask children to think about a pet that another classmate might have. Invite them to complete the sentence: (*Name of classmate*) *has a* _____. Then have the child next to that child repeat what the child before has said and then add their own sentence using *has*.

has

Introduce High-Frequency Words: *has*

PREPARE

Listen to Words
Explain to the children that they will be learning a new word: *has*. Say the following sentence: *Pooh has to get thin.* Say the sentence again, and ask children to raise a hand when they hear the word *has*. Repeat with the sentence: *He has to eat.*

TEACH

Model Reading the Word in Context
Give a word card with *has* to each child, and read the word. Reread the sentences, and have children raise their hands when they hear the word.

Identify the Word
Write the sentences above on the chalkboard. Track print and read each sentence. Children hold up their word card when they hear the word *has*. Then ask volunteers to point to and underline the word *has* in the sentences.

PRACTICE

Complete the Pupil Edition Page
Read the directions on page 287 to the children, and make sure they clearly understand what they are asked to do. Complete the first item together. Then work through the page with children or have them complete the page independently.

ASSESS/CLOSE

Review the Page
Review children's work, and note children who are experiencing difficulty or need additional practice.

Name_____ | has

I. Ben <u>has</u> a big cat.

2. The cat <u>has</u> a red tag.

3. Pam <u>has</u> a big pup.

4. The pup <u>has</u> a tan tag.

Read the sentence. • Then draw a line under the word *has* in the sentence.

Unit 5 Introduce High-Frequency Words: *has* **287**

Pupil Edition, page 287

Practice 287

Name _____

I. Kim <u>has</u> a bug in a bag.

2. Ben <u>has</u> a duck in a pen.

3. Min <u>has</u> a cat on the bed.

4. Ron <u>has</u> a bug, a duck, and a cat!

Read the sentence. Then draw a line under the word *has.*

4 Unit 5
Introduce High-Frequency Words: *has*

At Home: Use *has* in a sentence such as: "A monkey has a tail." If the sentence is true, have the child spell the word *has* in the air. Repeat with other sentences.

287

PRACTICE BOOK, page 287

Meeting Individual Needs for Vocabulary

EASY	ON-LEVEL	CHALLENGE	LANGUAGE SUPPORT
Have children sit in a circle to play a color game. Start by showing the word card *has.* Say: *Kim has yellow on. I have red.* Then pass the word card to the child next to you. Then the child repeats *Mrs. _____ has red on. I have green.* Continue until all children have had a chance.	**Distribute** word cards for *has* to each child. Then give clues about animals, such as: *It has a mane. It has a tail. People ride this animal.* When you say the word *has,* children hold up their cards. Call on children to give their answers. Continue with similar riddles.	**Draw** an outline of a house on chart paper. Then invite a volunteer to draw something for the house, such as a door. The child completes the phrase: *The house has a (door).*	**Have** children use the word *has* to describe each other: *Rob has brown hair. Gina has blue eyes.* Have them point to the word *has* when they say it.

287

Develop Phonological Awareness

Listen

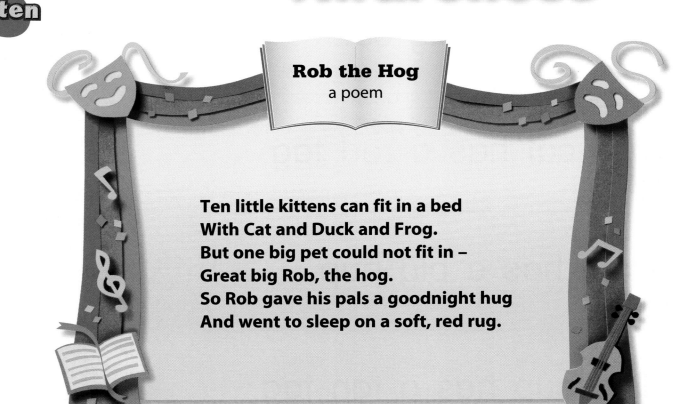

Rob the Hog
a poem

Ten little kittens can fit in a bed
With Cat and Duck and Frog.
But one big pet could not fit in –
Great big Rob, the hog.
So Rob gave his pals a goodnight hug
And went to sleep on a soft, red rug.

Objective: Develop Listening Skills

READ THE POEM Read the poem "Rob the Hog." To help children focus attention on details, ask: *Who was in bed? Who couldn't fit in the bed? Why? What did Rob do?*

> Frog   Rob   hug

LISTENING FOR RHYMING WORDS Reread the first four lines of the poem, emphasizing the last word in lines two and four. Invite children to identify the rhyming words. Read the last two lines of the poem and have children identify the rhymes.

SUBSTITUTE WORDS IN THE POEM Invite children to substitute the last word in line one, such as *Ten little kittens can fit on the couch.*

THINK OF ACTION WORDS Read the last line of the poem. Help children brainstorm other actions Rob might do on a soft, red rug.

> nap   read   rest
> color   doze   sing   jump

Objective: Blending with Short *a, e, i, o, u,* and *b*

LISTEN FOR BLENDING Read the poem aloud. When you get to the word *big,* say: /b/-/i/-/g/. After reading, say: *Listen again. /b/-/i/-/g/.* Have children repeat the sounds, and then blend them to say *big.* Repeat with other words in the poem that contain short vowels and /b/ sounds.

> **Rob   bed   but**

WHO CAN FIT IN THE BED? Explain that even though Rob can't fit in the bed, there is still room for others. Tell children, "Only animals with /b/ in their names can fit in the bed."

Say: *Guess who wants to go to bed? /b/-/e/-/n/. Can Ben go to bed?*

Pause while children blend the sounds to say *Ben* and respond to the question.

Repeat with other names. If the name has /b/, emphasize it when you pose the question.

> | Pam | Abe | Bev | Red |
> |-----|-----|-----|-----|
> | Tim | Deb | Bob | Tom |
> | | Bud | Gus | |

From Phonemic Awareness to Phonics

Objective: Relate *a, e, i, o, u* to Short Vowel Sounds

LISTEN FOR /b/ Read the poem, emphasizing /b/ in *Rob* and *bed* as you read.

IDENTIFY THE LETTERS Say /r/-/o/-/b/. Write *Rob* on the board as children say each sound. Identify the letters. Repeat with *bed.* Continue the activity with other words from the poem that contain /b/.

> **but   big**

FIND RHYMING WORDS Write words on index cards: *but, cut, cab, dab, Bob, cob, bat, beg, bin, bag.* Set out two words that rhyme and two that do not. Ask children to find words with the same ending letters. Segment, then blend the sounds. For example: /k/-/ab/, *cab.* Challenge children to name other words that rhyme with *cab* and *dab.* Then have them think of words that end the same as the words on the other two cards.

> | cab |
> |-----|
> | dab |
> | gab |
> | lab |
> | nab |
> | tab |

> cab
> dab

> **lab   nab**

 **Review Blending with short _a, e, i, o, u_**

OBJECTIVES

Children will:

- identify /a/*a*, /e/*e*, /i/*i*, /o/*o*, /u/*u*
- blend and read short *a, e, i, o, u* words
- write short *a, e, i, o, u* words
- review /b/*b*

MATERIALS

- letter cards from the *Word Building Cards*

TECHNOLOGY TIP

INSTRUCTIONAL Have children look at one another and repeat the sound /b/ several times. Ask them to describe the shape of their mouth when they say *b-b-b-b-b*.

ALTERNATE TEACHING STRATEGY

BLENDING SHORT
a, e, i, o, u

For a different approach to teaching this skill, see Unit 1, page T32; Unit 2, page T32; Unit 3, page T30; Unit 4, page T32; Unit 5, page T30.

▶ **Visual/Auditory/ Kinesthetic**

TEACH

Identify *a, e, i, o, u* as symbols for /a/, /e/, /i/, /o/, /u/

Tell children they will read words with *a, e, i, o, u.*

- Display the *a, e, i, o, u* letter cards and say /a/, /e/, /i/, /o/, /u/. Have children repeat the sounds as you point to the cards.

BLENDING Model and Guide Practice

- Place a *b* card before the *i* card. Blend the sounds together and have children repeat after you.

b i   **b i**

- Place a *g* letter card after the *b, i* cards. Blend the sounds in the word to read *big*. Have children repeat after you.

b i g   **b i g**

Use the Word in Context

- Invite children to use the word *big* in a sentence. Ask them to name some things that are big.

Repeat the Procedure

- Use the following words to continue modeling and for guided practice with short *a, e, i, o, u*: *bug, tan, pin, get, Kim, lock.*

PRACTICE

Complete the Pupil Edition Page

Read aloud the directions on page 288. Identify each picture, and complete the first item together. Work through the page with children, or have them complete the page independently.

ASSESS/CLOSE

Write Short *a, e, i, o, u* Words

Observe children as they complete page 288. Then ask them to write five words that begin or end with *b* and have short *a, e, i, o, u* in the middle.

Name

1. b a g   bag

2. b e d   bed

3. b a t   bat

4. c u b   cub

Blend the sounds and say the word. • Write the word. • Draw a circle around the
picture that goes with the word.

McGraw-Hill School Division

Pupil Edition, page 288

ADDITIONAL PHONICS
RESOURCES

Practice Book, *page 288*
**Phonics/Phonemic Awareness
Practice Book**

McGraw-Hill School
TECHNOLOGY

Phonics CD-ROM
**Activities for practice with
Initial and Final Letters**

Practice 288

Name

1. b u g   2. b e d
   bug   bed

3. t u b   4. d i g
   tub   dig

Blend the sounds and say the word. Write the word. Draw a line under the picture that
goes with the word.

At Home: Put a, e, i, o, and u on pieces of paper. Take
turns choosing a letter and making a word by writing a
letter on each side of it. Use the word in a sentence.

288   Review Blending with Short a, e, i, o, u   Unit 5   8

McGraw-Hill School Division

PRACTICE BOOK, page 288

Meeting Individual Needs for Phonics

EASY	ON-LEVEL	CHALLENGE	LANGUAGE SUPPORT
Create the following word cards: *bit, bed, bag, rub, bog, bad, bet, cub*. Write *a, e, i, o, u* on the chalkboard. Ask children to point to the letter that stands for the middle sound of each word. Blend sounds and have children repeat.	**Write** the word *bin* on the chalkboard. Have a volunteer pronounce the word. Ask children what letter in *bin* needs to change to make the word *big*. After children respond that n needs to change to *g*, write *big* below *bin*. Continue this procedure with these words: *bug, bud, bad, bet*, asking children what letter needs to change to make each new word.	**Write** *a, e, i, o, u* on one side of the chalkboard and *g, k, ck, l, p, r, f, c, t, m, s, d, n* on the other side. Brainstorm *b* words with children and have them make a list. They can work alone or in groups to make up stories using words that begin or end with *b*.	**Have** children repeat after you as you blend common initial and final *b* words: *but, bet, big, bag, tab, back*. Some children may have trouble distinguishing between the /b/ and /v/ sounds.

288

Guided Instruction

BEFORE READING

PREVIEW AND PREDICT Take a brief **picture walk** through the book, focusing on the illustrations.

- *What kind of bug is on the cover?* (grasshopper) *Have you ever seen this kind of bug?*

- *What do you think will happen to the bug?*

SET PURPOSES Encourage children's discussion of what might happen in the story. Have volunteers pose questions, such as why the bug might be in the house or what might happen to the bug.

A Big Bug

It is a big bug!

3

McGraw-Hill School Division

A bug is on the rug.

2

McGraw-Hill School Division

Mom can not get the bug.

4

Guided Instruction

DURING READING

☑ **Initial and Final *b***

☑ **Summarize**

☑ **Concepts of Print**

☑ **High-Frequency Word: *has***

① CONCEPTS OF PRINT Model how to run your finger from left to right under each word as you read. Have children repeat the words after you as they track print.

② INITIAL AND FINAL *b* Ask children to find the word on page 2 that starts with the letter *b*. (bug) Have them say the individual sounds in the word, as you write it on the chalkboard. Then, have children blend the sounds and read the word.

③ USE ILLUSTRATIONS Ask children to describe the bug, noting as many details as possible from page 3 of the story.

④ SUMMARIZE Isolate pages 1–4 and have volunteers read them aloud. Invite children to summarize what they know about the story up to this point.

LANGUAGE SUPPORT

ESL Make sure children realize the meaning of *not* on page 4. Have them compare Mom on page 4 with Meg on page 5, focusing on the word *not* as a negative meaning.

Guided Instruction

BEFORE READING

5 **USE ILLUSTRATIONS** Ask children to look at page 5 and tell what Meg is holding. (magnifying glass, net) Have children predict what Meg will do with each of these items.

6 **HIGH-FREQUENCY WORDS** Ask children to point to the word *has* on page 6. Track print as you read it together. Invite volunteers to use the word *has* in an original sentence.

7 **PHONICS** Have children identify the word *let* on page 7. Ask children to look for words in the story that rhyme with *let*. (net, get on page 6)

8 **SUMMARIZE** Ask children to summarize the story by describing the important events in the story. (A bug was in the house. Meg caught the bug. She put the bug outside.)

INFORMAL ASSESSMENT

SUMMARIZE

HOW TO ASSESS Have children summarize the action of the story. If some children have difficulty remembering the story, have them work with a partner. You may wish to ask children to use the pictures in their book to aid their recall.

FOLLOW-UP Have pairs of children act out the story. Ask other children to tell if the main parts of the story were correctly summarized by the "actors."

But Meg can get the bug.

5

Meg can let the bug go.

7

Meg has a bug net
to get the bug.

6

The big bug has fun
on a rock.

8

Guided Instruction

AFTER READING

RETURN TO PREDICTIONS AND PURPOSES
Ask children if their predictions about the story were correct. Check to see if they have any unanswered questions about the story.

RETELL THE STORY Have partners retell the story. Have children use picture clues from the story if they have difficulty recalling the sequence of events.

LITERARY RESPONSE To help children respond to the story, ask:

- *What did Meg use to catch the bug?*

- *Why would the bug prefer to be outside?*

Invite children to draw and write about a bug they have seen. You may wish to provide books or other reference materials that have photographs or illustrations of insects.

CENTER Activity

Cross Curricular: Science

BUILD A BUG Create a simple diagram of an insect, showing its head, thorax, abdomen, and legs. Then provide art materials, such as cotton balls, egg cartons, pipe cleaners, and so on. Invite children to design an insect. Encourage them to write or tell about where their insect lives, what it eats, and its name.

▶ **Spatial/Linguistic**

OBJECTIVES

Children will:
- summarize a story

MATERIALS
- *A Big Bug*

TEACHING TIP

INSTRUCTIONAL Model summarizing informally by giving children frequent examples of a summary as you talk about stories, films, and TV programs.

Review Summarize

PREPARE

Recall the Story   Ask children to recall the story *A Big Bug*. Ask what the story is about. Encourage volunteers to give their interpretations.

TEACH

List Events in the Story to Summarize   Reread the story together. After you read, ask what the important parts of the story are. Explain that a summary tells what the story is about in a very few words. Remind children that they can tell what happens using their own choice of words when they want to summarize a story.

PRACTICE

Complete the Pupil Edition Page   Read the directions on page 291 to the children, and make sure they clearly understand what they are asked to do. Identify each picture, and complete the first item together. Then work through the page with children or have them complete the page independently.

ASSESS/CLOSE

Review the Page   Review children's work, and note children who are experiencing difficulty.

Name _____

⨉ 1 ② ⨉ 3

[blank box for drawing]

Listen as I read three sentences. • One sentence will tell what the story "A Big Bug" is about. • Circle the number of each sentence that tells what the story is about. • Cross out the numbers of the sentences that do not tell what the story is about.

1. Meg helped her Dad cook breakfast.
2. Meg caught a bug and set it free.
3. Meg and her brother played outside.

On the bottom, draw a picture of what "A Big Bug" is about.

Pupil Edition, page 291

ALTERNATE TEACHING STRATEGY

SUMMARIZE

For a different approach to teaching the skill, see page T29.

▶ Visual/Auditory/ Kinesthetic

PRACTICE BOOK, page 291

Meeting Individual Needs for Comprehension

EASY	ON-LEVEL	CHALLENGE	LANGUAGE SUPPORT
Have children use the illustrations on pages 2, 5, and 7 of *A Big Bug* to tell what the story is mainly about. Help them to focus on these main actions.	**Have** children work in groups of three or four. Each child draws a picture to show an important part of the story. Help children use their pictures to summarize the story.	**Invite** children to choose a familiar classroom picture book. Have children summarize the main events of the story.	**Divide** a story into three or four important parts and have children act out each one. Help the rest of the group tell about each of the parts in order to summarize the story.

Develop Phonological Awareness

Listen

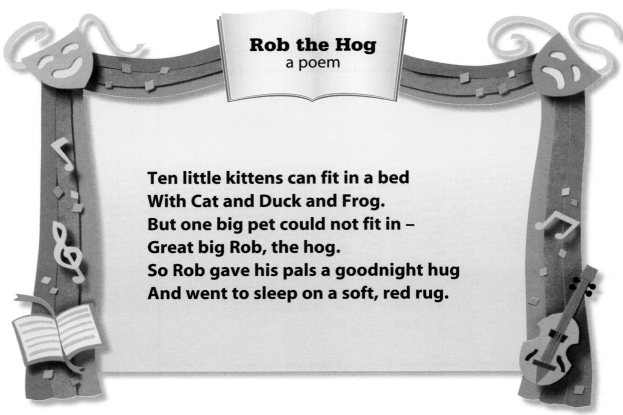

Rob the Hog
a poem

Ten little kittens can fit in a bed
With Cat and Duck and Frog.
But one big pet could not fit in –
Great big Rob, the hog.
So Rob gave his pals a goodnight hug
And went to sleep on a soft, red rug.

Objective: Enhance Awareness of Sounds

READ THE POEM Read the poem "Rob the Hog." Have children close their eyes and listen for sounds. Ask: *What sounds do you hear in the classroom now?*

> **people talking   someone walking**
> **a clock   a chair moving**

Explain that the animals in the poem are getting ready to sleep. Ask: *What sounds do you hear at night?*

> **clock ticking   water running**
> **someone brushing teeth   people snoring**
> **pets walking**

IDENTIFY SOUNDS Ask children to close their eyes and listen as you make some common classroom sounds

such as: writing on a chalkboard, sharpening a pencil, shaking a tambourine. Have children guess each sound.

Repeat the activity with other isolated sounds—or extend the activity by producing two sounds in a sequence. Invite volunteers to be the sound-makers.

Objective: Blending with Short *a, e, i, o, u*

BLEND THE SOUNDS Assign each sound to a child as you say: /p/-/a/-/l/. Tell the three children to stand apart from each other at the front of the room. Have the children move closer together as the class says /p/-/a/-/l/. Continue until the three children are standing next to each other as the class says *pal*. Repeat the activity with other words from the poem.

> cat   pet   fit   Ron   duck

WHAT TO GIVE? Read the last two lines of the poem. Ask: "What did Rob give his pals?" (a hug) Mention that Rob wants to give his pals other things, too. Tell children you will give them clues so they can guess what else Rob will give. Ask children to raise their hands when they think they know the answer.

Say: "Rob would like to give his pals and you,
A great big hug and a /c/-/o/-/t/, too."

Pause while children blend the sounds aloud to determine the word *cot*.

Repeat the activity, substituting other words for *cot*. You might add additional descriptors before a word you are going to segment such as a *recycling /b/-/i/-/n/.*

> kit   duck   map   fig
> pen   sack   lab   rock

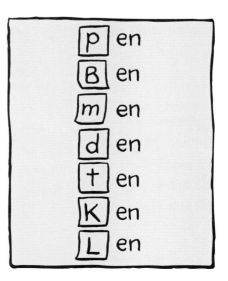

Read Together

From Phonemic Awareness to Phonics

Objective: Relate *a, e, i, o, u* to Short Vowel Sounds

LISTEN FOR SHORT VOWEL SOUNDS Read the poem, emphasizing each sound in *bed* as you say it.

IDENTIFY THE LETTERS Say: /b/-/e/-/d/. Ask: *How many sounds do you hear?* (3) Write *bed* on the chalkboard as children say each sound. Identify the letters. Ask children to say the sounds these letters stand for. Repeat the activity with the following words:

> ten   can   duck   fit   Rob

MAKE RHYMING WORDS Write these letters on self-stick notes: *b, g, k, ck, l, p, r, f, c, t, m, s, d, n.* Write _____*en* in list form on paper.

Have children place letters one at a time on the chart paper to the left of –*en*. Tell children to say the sounds, such as /p/-/en/, then blend the sounds to say *pen*. After a word is made, leave the self-stick note on the chart paper. Guide children to see that all words in the list end with –*en*.

p	en
B	en
m	en
d	en
t	en
K	en
L	en

Review Blending with short *a, e, i, o, u*

TESTED
✓ **OBJECTIVES**

Children will:

- identify /a/*a*, /e/*e*, /i/*i*, /o/*o*, /u/*u*
- blend and read short *a, e, i, o, u* words
- write short *a, e, i, o, u* words
- review /b/*b*, /g/*g*, /k/*k,ck,* /l/*l*, /p/*p*, /r/*r*, /f/*f*, /k/*c*, /t/*t*, /m/*m*, /s/*s*, /d/*d*, and /n/*n*

MATERIALS

- letter cards from the *Word Building Cards*

TEACHING TIP

INSTRUCTIONAL Say a word that children can read and write such as: *cat, Ben, sick, dot, get, fin*. Ask them to write a word that rhymes. Remind them that rhyming words have the same ending, such as *bug, rug, tug, mug, dug*. Display letter cards for all the words children are reviewing.

ALTERNATE TEACHING STRATEGY

BLENDING SHORT *a, e, i, o, u*

For a different approach to teaching this skill, see Unit 1, page T32; Unit 2, page T32; Unit 3, page T30; Unit 4, page T32; Unit 5, page T30.

▶ **Visual/Auditory/ Kinesthetic**

TEACH

Identify *a, e, i, o, u* as symbols for /a/, /e/, /i/, /o/, /u/

Tell children they will continue to read words with *a, e, i, o, u.*

- Display the *a, e, i, o, u* letter cards and say /a/, /e/, /i/, /o/, /u/. Have children repeat the sounds as you point to the cards.

BLENDING Model and Guide Practice

- Place an *o* card before the *ck* card. Blend the sounds together and have children repeat after you.

- Place an *r* letter card before the *o, ck* cards. Blend and read *rock.*

Use the Word in Context

- Invite children to use *rock* in a sentence. Ask them to tell some things they know about rocks.

Repeat the Procedure

- Use the following words to continue modeling and for guided practice with short *a, e, i, o, u: back, rug, bat, get, Meg, net, fun.*

PRACTICE

Complete the Pupil Edition Page

Read aloud the directions on page 292. Identify each picture, and complete the first item together. Then work through the page with the children, or have children complete the page independently.

ASSESS/CLOSE

Write Short *a, e, i, o, u* Words

Observe children as they complete page 292. Then ask them to write five words that have short *a, e, i, o,* or *u* in the middle and begin or end in any combination of *b, g, k, ck, l, p, r, f, c, t, m, s, d, n.*

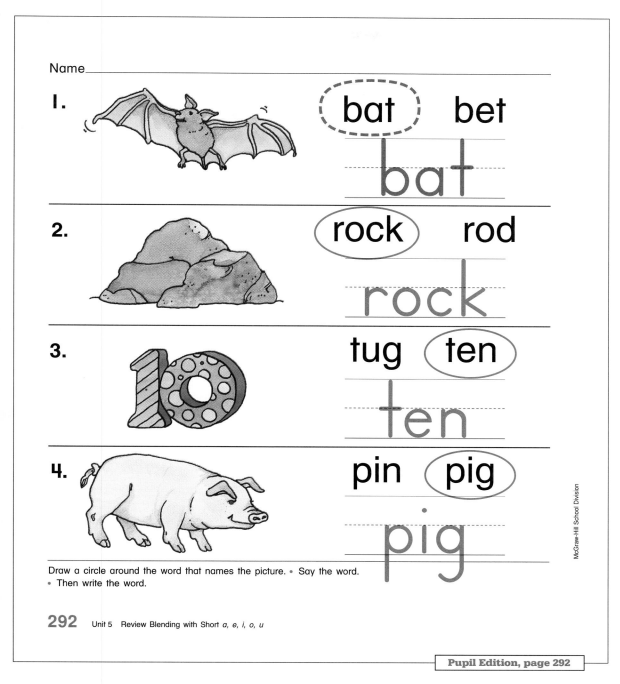

Name _____

1. bat bet

bat

2. rock rod

rock

3. tug ten

ten

4. pin pig

pig

Draw a circle around the word that names the picture. • Say the word.
• Then write the word.

292 Unit 5 Review Blending with Short *a, e, i, o, u*

McGraw-Hill School Division

Pupil Edition, page 292

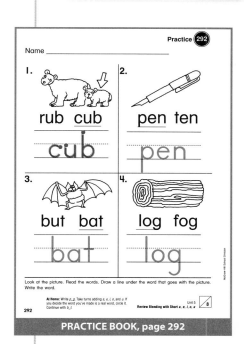

ADDITIONAL PHONICS RESOURCES

Practice Book, *page 292*
Phonics/Phonemic Awareness Practice Book

McGraw-Hill School
TECHNOLOGY

Phonics CD-ROM
Activities for Practice with Blending and Segmenting

Practice 292
Name _____

1. rub cub
   cub
2. pen ten
   pen
3. but bat
   bat
4. log fog
   log

Look at the picture. Read the words. Draw a line under the word that goes with the picture. Write the word.

At Home: Write *p_p*. Take turns adding *a, e, i, o,* and *u.* If you decide the word you've made is a real word, circle it. Continue with *b_t.*

292 Review Blending with Short *a, e, i, o, u* Unit 5 8

PRACTICE BOOK, page 292

Meeting Individual Needs for Phonics

EASY	ON-LEVEL	CHALLENGE	LANGUAGE SUPPORT
Show letter cards *a, e, i, o, u* on the chalkboard ledge and ask children to say each sound as you point to a letter and name it. Write some decodable words (see Word List, pp. T72-T75) and ask children to read them and identify the medial letter and sound.	**Select** a decodable word (see Word List, pp. T72-T75) that answers a riddle, such as: *the opposite of little (big); use this to hit a ball (bat); baby lion or tiger (cub); baby goat (kid); baby dog (pup)*. Invite children to guess the answers and then make up their own riddles.	**Show** letter cards *a, e, i, o, u* and then write incomplete words on the chalkboard such as: *b_n, c_b, g_t, t_ck, s_p, l_d*. Ask children to select a middle letter from the cards and write a word they can either define or use in a sentence.	**Have** children repeat after you as you blend the sounds in the following words: *rug, bat, Meg, net, fun*. Show pictures and use gestures where possible, to help children understand the meaning of each word.

Reread the Decodable Story

☑ **Initial and Final** *b*
☑ **Summarize Story Events**
☑ **High-Frequency Word:** *has*
☑ **Concepts of Print**

A Big Bug

Guided Reading

SET PURPOSES Have children discuss what their purpose is for rereading the story. Children may have questions about the story.

REREAD THE BOOK As you reread the story, keep in mind any problems children experienced during the first reading.

- **PHONICS** Ask children to look at the last two words on page 3. Have children blend the sounds and read: *b i g big/b u g bug*. Then focus children's attention on medial *i* and ask them to blend and read the three words on the page with the short /i/ sound: *it, is, big*.

- **SUMMARIZE** Review the main events of the story with the children and ask them how they think Meg feels and how her mother feels.

RETURN TO PURPOSES Ask children if they found out what they needed to know from the story. See if they have any unanswered questions.

LITERARY RESPONSE Ask children to draw a picture of their favorite kind of bug. Then ask the following questions to prompt discussions about their drawings:

- *Where does your bug live and what does it eat?*

- *What name have you given to your bug? Why?*

TEACHING TIP

INSTRUCTIONAL You may wish to have several children read the story aloud for the rest of the class. Other children can follow along with the group reading.

INFORMAL ASSESSMENT

SUMMARIZE STORY EVENTS

HOW TO ASSESS Have children draw on index cards simple pictures that illustrate the story. Then have children put the cards in order and summarize the story.

FOLLOW-UP For those children who are experiencing difficulties, guide them through the story. Summarize the events on pages 4, 6, and 8.

Read the Patterned Book

Bob's Bath

☑ **Initial and final /b/ *b***
☑ **Summarize**
☑ **High-Frequency Word:** *has*
☑ **Concepts of Print**

Guided Reading

PREVIEW AND PREDICT Read the title and the author's and the illustrator's names. Ask who wrote the story and who drew the pictures. Take a **picture walk** through pages 2-4, noting the setting of the story and the characters. Have children make predictions about the story

SET PURPOSES Have children decide what they want to find out from the story and predict what might happen as the dog takes a bath. Tell them that the story contains words with initial and final *b*.

READ THE BOOK Use the following prompts while the children are reading or after they have read independently. Remind them to run their fingers under each word as they read.

Pages 2-3: Point to the second word on page 2. *Let's read it together:* has. *High-Frequency Words*

Pages 4-5: *Model: I can use what I know about sounds to read the word that begins with* b. *Let's blend these sounds together:* b-a-c-k. *Back. Phonics and Decoding*

Pages 6-7: *Listen as I read the sentence on page 6. Which words have the /b/ sound?* (Bob, scrub) *Phonics and Decoding*

Page 8: *What is the story about?* (A dog who takes a bath) *Summarize*

RETURN TO PREDICTIONS AND PURPOSES Ask children if they found out what they needed to know from the story. See if their predictions were correct.

LITERARY RESPONSE The following questions will help focus children's responses:

• Would you like to have a dog as a pet? Why or why not?

• What kind of dog would you like to have? What would you name the dog? Write about the dog and draw a picture.

Activity

Language Arts

STEP-BY-STEP BATH Make a set of picture/word cards that show the steps needed to give a dog a bath. Have children arrange the cards in the correct sequence. Children may wish to make their own set of cards.

▶ **Logical/ Mathematical**

Children will:

- identify and read the high-frequency word *has*

MATERIALS

- word cards from the *Word Building Cards*
- *A Big Bug*

TEACHING TIP

INSTRUCTIONAL Remind children that the word *has* refers to ownership. Have them form sentences to describe another child in the classroom, using the word: *Ben has black hair. Tara has glasses.*

Review has, he, she, me, for

PREPARE

Listen to Words Tell children that they will review the word *has*. Read the following sentence, and have children raise their hands when they hear the word *has: The bug has long legs.*

TEACH

Model Reading the Word in Context Reread the decodable book. Ask children to listen for the word *has* (pages 6 and 8).

Identify the Word Have children display their *has* word card. Tell them to first look at their word cards, and then to look for the word in the story. Read the story, tracking print, and ask children to point to the word *has* in their book. Have them put a stick-on note below the word.

Review High-Frequency Words Hold up word cards for the following words: *the, a, my, that, I, and, you, said, we, are, is, have, to, me, go, do, for, he,* and *she.* Have children take turns reading the words.

PRACTICE

Complete the Pupil Edition Page Read the directions on page 293 to children, and make sure they clearly understand what they are being asked to do. Complete the first item together. Then work through the page with children or have them complete the page independently.

ASSESS/CLOSE

Review the Page Review children's work, and guide children who are experiencing difficulty or need additional practice.

Name_____

I.

Ken <u>has</u> a mug for me.

_____

2.

<u>He</u> has a big bag <u>for</u> Nan.

_____

3.

<u>She</u> has a red fan for <u>me</u>.

_____

Read each sentence.   **I.** Draw a line under the word *has*.   **2.** Draw a line under the words *he* and *for*.   **3.** Draw a line under the words *she* and *me*.

Unit 5   Review *has, he, she, me, for*   **293**

Pupil Edition, page 293

ALTERNATE TEACHING
STRATEGY
....

**HIGH-FREQUENCY
WORDS:** *has*

**For a different approach to
teaching the skill,
see page T27.**

▶ **Visual/Auditory/
Kinesthetic**

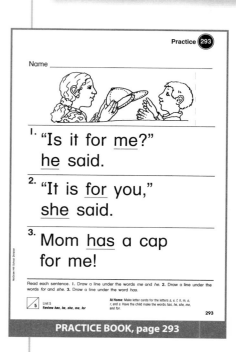

Practice 293

Name _____

I. "Is it for <u>me</u>?"
<u>he</u> said.

2. "It is <u>for</u> you,"
<u>she</u> said.

3. Mom <u>has</u> a cap
for me!

Read each sentence. **I.** Draw a line under the words *me* and *he*. **2.** Draw a line under the words *for* and *she*. **3.** Draw a line under the word *has*.

Unit 5
Review *has, he, she, me, for*

At Home: Make letter cards for the letters *a, e, f, h, m, o, r,* and *s.* Have the child make the words *has, he, she, me,* and *for.*

293

PRACTICE BOOK, page 293

Meeting Individual Needs for Vocabulary

EASY	ON-LEVEL	CHALLENGE	LANGUAGE SUPPORT
Write the following words on chart paper: *has, her, hat, has, he, had, he, has, ham, has.* Tell children to find the word *has.* Read the other words aloud together.	**Play** a memory game called "In My Suitcase." Prompt one child to complete a sentence using *has: He has a ___ in his suitcase.* Have children continue adding other items, taking turns repeating the items in a list order.	**Make** a pet graph on chart paper. Include pets, such as cats, dogs, fish, birds, and hamsters. Tell children to fill in a square indicating the pet they have or would like to have. Ask them to write their names next to the square. Then ask: *Who has or would like to have a cat?*	**Have** children sit in a circle. Write the word *has* and read it together. **Describe** a child, using her or his name: *Sam has a green shirt.* Have children follow the word pattern using *has* to describe a classmate's clothing, hair, or eye color.

Interactive Writing

Write a New Ending

GRAMMAR/SPELLING CONNECTIONS

Model subject-verb agreement, complete sentences, and correct tense so that students may gain increasing control of grammar when speaking and writing.

Prewrite

LOOK AT THE STORY PATTERN Revisit *The Enormous Carrot*, having children identify the cumulative pattern of the story. Talk about how each new character joined the group and how the animals finally pulled the carrot out. Then talk about how the story ended.

Draft

WRITE A NEW ENDING Explain that the children are going to think of a new ending to the story. Brainstorm different endings to the story, and write them on the chalkboard.

- Have the children choose one of the endings. You may wish to have children vote.

- Children dictate text for the new story ending as you write the sentences on chart paper. Then reread the sentences, making revisions as necessary.

- Have pairs of children write parts of the new text on drawing paper to make pages. Remind children to move left-to-right across the page as they rewrite the sentences. Children illustrate the text.

Publish

CREATE THE BOOK Compile the pages to make a book. Reread the book aloud.

So together they dug a hole around the carrot.

Presentation Ideas

MAKE A PAPER PLATE MASK Have children choose a character from the story and draw the character's face on a paper plate. Attach yarn or string to make a mask. Children take turns wearing the mask and telling parts of the new story.

▶ **Representing/Viewing**

ACT OUT THE ENDING Have children work in small groups to act out the new ending. Children may wish to act out the ending as you read, or say their own dialogue.

▶ **Speaking/Representing**

COMMUNICATION TIPS

• **Speaking** Invite children to make their voice sound like the character in the book. Have them experiment with different types of voices.

• **Listening** Suggest that children listen attentively and quietly while the new ending is being performed. Have them say what they liked best about the show.

TECHNOLOGY TIP

Look up *The Enormous Carrot* on a website for an online bookstore. Read the reviews and descriptions to the children.

LANGUAGE SUPPORT

ESL Ask children to name and describe their favorite vegetables. Make a list, and then have children vote to find the class favorite.

Meeting Individual Needs for Writing

EASY	ON-LEVEL	CHALLENGE
Draw Pictures Have children draw pictures of their favorite vegetables. Help them to label their pictures.	**Answer Riddles** First show children pictures of some garden vegetables. Then give them clues, and have them say the vegetable you are thinking of. Help children write the name of the vegetable they guess.	**Journal Entry** Invite children to write a journal entry for one of the characters in the original or new story. Help children to generate ideas before writing by asking how the character might be feeling and why.

A Pup and a Cat

Children will read and listen to a variety of stories about sharing ideas for solving problems.

**Decodable Story,
pages 301–302 of the
Pupil Edition**

Listening
Library
Audiocassette

**Patterned Books,
page 305B**

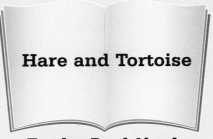

Hare and Tortoise

**Teacher Read Aloud,
page 299A**

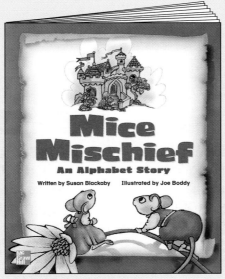

**ABC Big Book,
pages 295A–295B**

Listening
Library
Audiocassette

**Literature Big Book,
pages 297A–297B**

Listening
Library
Audiocassette

Pupil Edition,
pages 294–305

Big Book of Real-Life Reading,
page 32

Big Book of Phonics Rhymes and
Poems, pages 10, 11, 22, 29, 30

Listening
Library
Audiocassette

ADDITIONAL RESOURCES

Practice Book,
pages 294–305

- **Phonics Kit**
- **Language Support Book**
- **Alternate Teaching Strategies,** pp T24–T33

McGraw-Hill School
TECHNOLOGY

Phonics **CD-ROM** Provides
extra phonics support.

*inter***NET**
CONNECTION   Research & Inquiry Ideas.

Visit www.mhschool.com

A Pup and a Cat

Suggested Lesson Planner

 Available on CD-Rom

READING AND LANGUAGE ARTS

- **Phonological Awareness**
- **Phonics** *review*
- **Comprehension**
- **Vocabulary**
- **Beginning Reading Concepts**
- **Listening, Speaking, Viewing, Representing**

DAY 1

Focus on Reading Skills

Develop Phonological Awareness, 294G-294H
"Katie's Kangaroo" and "Bounce the Ball" *Big Book of Phonics Rhymes and Poems*, 10, 29

Review Initial /k/k, /g/g, /b/b, 294I-294
Practice Book, 294
Phonics/Phonemic Awareness Practice Book

 **CD-ROM**

 Read the Literature

Read *Mice Mischief: An Alphabet Story* **Big Book,** 295A-295B
Shared Reading

Build Skills

- ☑ Naming Words and Action Words, 295C-295
  Practice Book, 295

DAY 2

Focus on Reading Skills

Develop Phonological Awareness, 296A-296B
"Miss Mary Mack," "Little Pig," "Tub Time" *Big Book of Phonics Rhymes and Poems*, 11, 22, 30

Introduce Final /k/k, /g/g, /b/b, 296C-296
Practice Book, 296
Phonics/Phonemic Awareness Practice Book

 **CD-ROM**

 Read the Literature

Read *Any Kind of Dog* **Big Book,** 297A-297B
Shared Reading

Build Skills

- ☑ Story Structure, 297C-297
  Practice Book, 297

- **Cross Curriculum**

   Language Arts, 295B

   Social Studies, 297B

- **Writing**

   Writing Prompt: Write your own adventure about visiting a castle.

  Journal Writing, 295B
  Letter Formation, 294I

   Writing Prompt: Write about a time you worked together with a friend.

  Journal Writing, 297B
  Letter Formation, 296C

☑ = **Skill Assessed in Unit Test**

DAY 3

Hare and Tortoise

Focus on Reading Skills

Develop Phonological Awareness, 298A-298B

"Katie's Kangaroo" and "Gobble, Gobble" *Big Book of Phonics Rhymes and Poems,* 21, 29

 **Review /k/k, /k/ck, /g/g, /b/b,** 298C-298
Practice Book, 298
Phonics/Phonemic Awareness
Practice Book

 **CD-ROM**

Read the Literature

 Read "Hare and Tortoise" Teacher Read Aloud, 299A-299B
Shared Reading
Read the Big Book of Real-Life Reading, 32-33
☑ Maps

Build Skills

☑ High-Frequency Words: *for, he, she, has,* 299C-299
Practice Book, 299

 Activity Science, 299A

 Writing Prompt: Which do you like better—a hare or a tortoise? Draw a picture of your favorite and explain why you like it.

DAY 4

A Pup and a Cat

Focus on Reading Skills

Develop Phonological Awareness, 300A-300B

"Pets in a Tub"
 **Review Blending with Short *a, e, i, o, u,*** 300C-300
Practice Book, 300
Phonics/Phonemic Awareness
Practice Book

Phonics CD-ROM

Read the Literature

Read "A Pup and a Cat" Decodable Story, 301/302A-301/302D

☑ Initial and Final *k, ck, g, e, b;* Blending
☑ Summarize
☑ High-Frequency Words: *for, he, she, has*
☑ Concepts of Print

Build Skills

☑ Summarize, 303A-303
Practice Book, 303

 Activity Cultural Perspectives, 301/302D

 **Writing Prompt:** Write about the last time you made a new friend.

Letter Formation,
Practice Book, 301-302

DAY 5

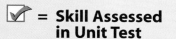
A Pup and a Cat

Just For the Duck
by Anne Miranda
illustrated by Kristen Goeters

Focus on Reading Skills

Develop Phonological Awareness, 304A-304B

"Pets in a Tub"
 **Review Blending with Short *a, e, i, o, u,*** 304C-304
Practice Book, 304
Phonics/Phonemic Awareness
Practice Book

Phonics CD-ROM

Read the Literature

Reread "A Pup and a Cat" Decodable Story, 305A
Read "Just for the Duck" Patterned Book, 305B
Guided Reading
☑ Review *k, ck, g, e, b;* Blending
☑ Summarize
☑ High-Frequency Words: *for, he, she, has,*
☑ Concepts of Print

Build Skills

☑ High-Frequency Words: *for, he, she, has,* 305C-305
Practice Book, 305

 Activity Social Studies, 305B

Writing Prompt: Write about a problem that you solved with a friend.

Interactive Writing, 306A-306B

Develop Phonological Awareness

Listen

Katie's Kangaroo

Katie has a kangaroo.
She keeps it on her bed.
Katie has a kangaroo.
It sleeps by Katie's head.

Katie has a kangaroo.
And five koalas, too.
She has so many animals,
Her room looks like a zoo!

Big Book of Phonics Rhymes and Poems, 29

Objective: Review Initial /k/ *K,k*

IDENTIFY THE SOUND Read "Katie's Kangaroo" to the children. Have them tell who the poem is about. Ask, "What sound do you hear at the beginning of *Katie*? Let's say the sound together." Ask children to tell how they form the /k/ sound in the back of their mouth. Read the poem again and ask children to listen for other words that begin with the /k/ sound.

> kangaroo   keeps   koalas

PLAY KATIE IN KINDERGARTEN Tell children that you will play a game. Explain that Katie can only do or have things that begin with the /k/ sound. For example, if you ask, "Can Katie go to kindergarten?" children are to reply, "Katie can." For words that do not begin with /k/,

children should say, "Katie cannot." As you pose questions, emphasize the initial /k/ sound.

- Can Katie have a kite?
- Can Katie be kind?
- Can Katie have a kitty?
- Can Katie have a key?

Objective: Review Initial /g/G,g

IDENTIFY INITIAL /g/ Ask children to listen as you read them the following sentence:

- Gary got a gorilla for his birthday.

Exaggerate the words with initial /g/ as you read. Have children tell you who the sentence is about. Ask, "What sound do you hear at the beginning of *Gary*? Let's say the word together." Have volunteers tell how they make their mouths form the /g/ sound.

EXTEND LEARNING Read the sentence again and ask children what Gary got for his birthday. Have them identify the initial sound of *gorilla*. Then tell children that you know some other animals that Gary got. Explain that you will give hints and the children should guess. Begin each hint by saying, "Gary got an animal that begins like /g/."

For example:

- It has feathers and rhymes with moose. (goose)
- It is a small fish that you keep for a pet. (goldfish, guppy)
- It lives on a farm and eats grass. (goat)

Read Together

From Phonemic Awareness to Phonics

Objective: Review Initial /b/B,b

RELATE THE SOUND AND LETTER Tell children that the letter *b* stands for the sound /b/. Display the Phonics Rhyme poem and point out the letter in the upper left corner. Explain that the letter is b, and say its sound.

READ THE POEM Read the poem and ask children to listen for words that begin with the /b/ sound. As children identify words, have the class repeat them. Then read the poem again and tap each word with a pointer. Emphasize the words that begin with b.

LOOK FOR THE LETTER Ask children to find words in the poem that begin with b. Remind children that the b's can be small or capital letters. Mention that many of the words beginning with b are names. Ask children to think of other names that begin with this letter.

Bb

Bounce the Ball

Billy, Billy, bounce the ball.
Bounce the ball
To Bob and Paul.
Bounce the ball
To Barb and Bea.
Billy, bounce the ball
To me.

Big Book of Phonics Rhymes and Poems, 10

OBJECTIVES

Children will:

- identify and discriminate among /k/K,k, /g/G,g, /b/B,b
- write and use *K,k, G,g, B,b*

....

MATERIALS

- letter cards from the Word Play Book

TEACHING TIP

INSTRUCTIONAL

Identify any children whose names begin with *K, G,* or *B*. Ask them to say their names, and write the names on the chalkboard under the headings *K, G, B*. As children repeat the names, have them trace the letter in the air with their fingers. Invite children to suggest other names that begin with these letters.

ALTERNATE TEACHING STRATEGY

....

INITIAL /k/k, /g/g, /b/b

For a different approach to teaching this skill, see pages T24, T28, and T32.

▶ **Visual/Auditory/ Kinesthetic**

Review Initial /k/k, /g/g, /b/b

TEACH

Discriminate Among /k/K,k, /g/G,g, /b/B,b

Tell children they will review the sounds /k/, /g/, and /b/ and write the letters *K,k, G,g,* and *B,b*. Ask them to say the sound of each letter with you as you write it on the chalkboard. Have volunteers point to the letter that each of the following words begins with: *give, kit, bat, got, bug, kid.*

Write and Use *K,k, G,g, B,b*

Write letters *K,k, G,g,* and *B,b,* at the top of three columns on the chalkboard. Ask children to write both forms of *k, g,* and *b* on one side of three index cards and to hold up a card when they recognize a word that begins with that letter. Write the following sentences on the chalkboard, and read them aloud as you track print with your hand: *Bob's best pal was Gary the goat. They were both good kids.* Explain the joke—that *kid* is the correct name for a young goat.

PRACTICE

Complete the Pupil Edition Page

Read the directions on page 294 to the children, and make sure they clearly understand what they are being asked to do. Identify each picture, and complete the first item together. Then work through the page with children, or have them complete the page independently.

ASSESS/CLOSE

Identify and Use *K,k, G,g, B,b*

Say the following words: *gas, kid, got, big, kit, but, gum.* Have children hold up the matching initial letter card and point to the column the word belongs in. Write the word, then have children name the first letter of the word and make the sound of that letter.

Kk Gg Bb   Name_____

girl
g

box
b

kangaroo
k

boy
b

key
k

goose
g

Say the name of each picture. • Then write the letter for the sound you hear at the beginning of the picture name.

McGraw-Hill School Division

Pupil Edition, page 294

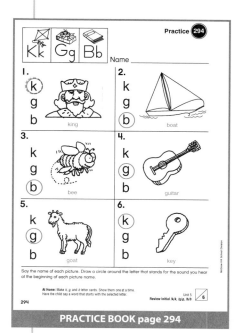

PRACTICE BOOK page 294

Meeting Individual Needs for Phonics

EASY	ON-LEVEL	CHALLENGE	LANGUAGE SUPPORT
Have children listen as you pack a grocery bag with imaginary items such as *kiwi fruit, ketchup, kidney beans, garbage bags, butter, beets, bananas.* Have them trace letter cards *k, g,* and *b* and hold up the one that shows which letter each word begins with.	**Ask** children to match pictures with a key picture of an object whose name begins with *k, g,* or *b,* for example: *key, kite, kitten, gum, goat, gate, boy, banana, bus.* For each match, have them write the first letter of the words.	**Say** a word, and ask children to choose among *k, g,* and *b* to find a letter they can use to make a word that rhymes, such as: *bite (kite), get (bet), Gus (bus), Ken (Ben).* Ask children to write the first letter of the rhyming word.	Some ESL children may have trouble distinguishing between initial sounds /k/ and /g/. Provide opportunities to sort *k, g* by sound and sight. Write these words, and ask children to repeat them as you read, emphasizing the first letter: *kid, get, got, kit.*

294

Children will:

- match letter cards with letters in the story
- use letters to recognize key words in the story
- review initial and final *n*

Read the Big Book

Before Reading

Develop Oral Language Read "The Alphabet Chant" with the children on pages 6-7 in the Big Book of Phonics Rhymes and Poems. Remind children about the two mice, Blink and Dee. Ask children to recount some of their adventures.

Set Purposes Explain that children will use letters to name key words. They will also match letter cards with the letters in the book. Distribute two or three upper-case and lowercase letters to each child. As you read the story, children holding the letter in the story stand up and name the letter. Tell children that they will also think about how the characters are feeling during the story.

Dee and Bink hide by the **fan**.
"We must **get** out of here!" said Bink.

Mice Mischief, an Alphabet Story, pages 10-11

During Reading

Read Together

- As you point to the letter, have children holding the letter cards stand up and identify them. Run your finger under each word in the story as you read. Have children repeat the words after you. *Concepts of Print*

- After you read page 6, ask children to describe the cat. Talk about how the cat might be feeling and why. Continue with other animals in the story. *Make Inferences*

- After you read pages 16-17, ask children to look around the kitchen and find something the man might use to catch the mice. *Use Illustration*

- Also after reading pages 16-17, remind students of the final *n* sound. Ask them to find objects in the kitchen with the final *n* sound. *(pan, spoon) Phonics*

Dee and Bink hide by the **fan**.
"We must **get** out of here!" said Bink.

Mice Mischief, an Alphabet Story, page 11

After Reading

Literary Response

Ask children to draw and write about the mice in one of the situations in the book.

ORAL RESPONSE Then ask:

- *How do you think the mice are feeling? Why?*

ABC Activity

Say the first three letters of the alphabet and stop. Then ask a volunteer to say the next letter. Continue, choosing beginning letters at random.

INFORMAL ASSESSMENT

LETTER RECOGNITION
HOW TO ASSESS
Use an index card to cover a letter on an alphabet chart. Ask a child to identify the letter by looking at the letter that comes before and the letter that comes after.

FOLLOW-UP Help children who experience difficulty by singing the ABC song.

CENTER Activity

Cross Curricular: Language Arts

PICK A LETTER Make game cards with 3-by-4 grids. Write letters of the alphabet at random in each square. Put alphabet cards in a box, and have one child take a letter out and name it. If a player has that letter on their card, he or she covers it with a counter. Children continue until a game card is covered.

▶ **Spatial**

OBJECTIVES

Children will:

- identify and describe naming words
- identify and describe action words

MATERIALS

- *Any Kind of Dog* Big Book

TEACHING TIP

MANAGEMENT You may wish to make a class wall chart of naming words and action words. Have children suggest words that name their favorite pets, clothing, and toys. Provide frequent opportunities for children to generate other common nouns to add to the *Naming Words* side of the chart. On the *Action Words* side of the chart, have children brainstorm actions that they, their pets, or their favorite storybook characters might do. Post the completed wall chart for children to use as a resource for speaking or writing.

Review Naming and Action Words

PREPARE

Play a Game Play a game of "I Spy." Say a naming word or an action word and invite children to say "Naming" or "Action" to tell which type of word you said. (Be careful to select words that cannot be used in both ways.) Then have volunteers take turns saying a word, and have the class respond with the correct identification.

TEACH

Identify Naming Words and Describe Actions Display the Big Book *Any Kind of Dog*, and have volunteers retell the story. Look at pages 2–3, and have children name the characters they see on the page. (Richard, or the boy; his dog) Then have them name the object that Richard is holding. (stick) Invite volunteers to choose one of these naming words and say an action word to describe what is shown in the illustrations. (Richard throws. Dog jumps.) You may wish to continue this activity on other pages, helping children identify naming words and action words shown in the story.

Naming Word or Action Word? Some children may mention that some words can be either naming words or action words. Explain that some words have more than one meaning and that children will usually be able to distinguish between a naming word and an action word by how it is used in the sentence.

PRACTICE

Distinguish Between Naming Words and Action Words Read the directions on page 295 to the children, and make sure they clearly understand what they are being asked to do. Help children read the words, if necessary. Complete the first item. Then work through the page with children, or have them complete the page independently.

ASSESS/CLOSE

Review the Page Check children's work on the Pupil Edition page. Note areas where children need extra help distinguishing naming words and action words.

Name _____

1. Tom (go) cap

2. (kick) cat (run)

3. (dig) Mom Nan

4. Dad den (sit)

Draw a circle around the word that describes an action. • Draw a line under the word that names a person, place or thing.

Unit 5 Review Naming and Action Words   **295**

Pupil Edition, page 295

ALTERNATE TEACHING
STRATEGY
....

NAMING AND ACTION
WORDS
For a different approach to
teaching this skill, see
pages T25 and T31.

▶ **Visual/Auditory/
Kinesthetic**

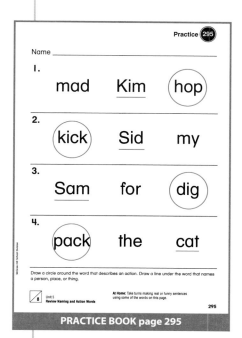

PRACTICE BOOK page 295

Meeting Individual Needs for Grammar

EASY	ON-LEVEL	CHALLENGE	LANGUAGE SUPPORT
Recall with children a favorite story. Help children list persons or things from the story. Then have them think of an appropriate or humorous action word for each one: *Goldilocks sleeps.*	**Play** a game of "Word Match." Have children say a naming word for a person. Then have a volunteer say an action word whose initial sound matches that of the naming word: *Danielle dances.* You may wish to encourage humorous responses.	**Have** pairs of children work together to write a poem. Each line will have two words: a naming word followed by an action word. Poems can be real or nonsense, rhyming or non-rhyming. For example: *Children play./Dogs stay.* Have children share their poems.	**Relate** the term *naming word* to *name* to help children distinguish between *naming* and *action*. Give examples as you remind children of naming words for a person, place, or thing. Help children pair each naming word with an action word, emphasizing the word *act* in *action*.

Develop Phonological Awareness

Listen

Miss Mary Mack
a poem

Little Pig
a poem

Miss Mary Mack,
   Mack, Mack,
All dressed in black,
   black, black,
With silver buttons,
   buttons, buttons,
All down her back,
   back, back.

Little Pig had lost his way
In a fog so thick and gray.

First Pig bumped into a log.
Next, he sat upon a frog.

"Oh," Pig said in a ho-hum way.
"I guess this is just not my day!"

Big Book of Phonics Rhymes and Poems, 30, 22

Objective: Review Final /k/ *ck*

IDENTIFY FINAL /k/ Review the title of the poem. Ask children what Miss Mary's last name is. Say, "What sound do you hear at the end of Miss Mary's last name-*M-a-k*?" Have children repeat the /k/ sound with you. Then tell them to listen for other words that end with this sound as you read the poem.

black   back

EXPAND THE POEM Make up additional verses using words in the *-ack* family. As you introduce each new verse, have children identify the final sound /k/. Teach children the verses so the class can say them in unison. Possible verses might be:

- All dressed in a sack, sack, sack
- Stepped on a tack, tack, tack
- Fell in a crack, crack, crack

Objective: Review Final /g/g

IDENTIFY THE SOUND Review the poem "Little Pig" with the class. Have children tell what sound they hear at the end of *pig*. Say, "Let's say this word together . . . *p-i-ggg*." Ask children to show how their mouths make the /g/ sound. Mention that the /g/ sound can be at the beginning or end of a word.

> final g = pig   initial g = guess

USE THE POEM Read the poem again and then give children practice in saying and hearing other words that end in /g/ by posing questions such as these:

- What was so thick and gray? (fog)
- What did Little Pig bump into? (log)
- What did he sit on? (frog)

Read Together

From Phonemic Awareness to Phonics

Objective: Review Final /b/b

NAME THE LETTER Review with children that the letter b stands for the sound /b/. Display the Phonics Rhyme poem "Tub Time" and point to the letter in the upper right corner. Remind children that this is the letter b and it sounds like /b/.

READ THE POEM Read the poem and draw children's attention to the sound of /b/ at the end of words like *rub* and *tub*. As you read, exaggerate the words with final /b/.

LOOK AT THE LETTERS Ask children to point out the letter *b* at the end of words in the poem. Have children repeat each word as you pronounce it.

COLLECT PICTURES Glue pictures of items such as a bib, crib, crab, tub, cub, and cab onto index cards. Label each picture with its name. Underline the letter *b* on each. Have children identify the pictures and point to the letter that makes the final sound in each word.

Tub Time

Rub-a-dub-dub,
Scrub-a-scrub-scrub,
I'm taking a bubble bath
In the tub.

Rub-a-dub-dub,
Scrub-a-scrub-scrub,
I'm pulling the plug out.
Blub, blub, blub.

Big Book of Phonics Rhymes and Poems, 11

OBJECTIVES

Children will:

- identify and discriminate among /k/*ck*, /g/*g*, and /b/*b*
- write and use letters *ck, g, b*

....

MATERIALS

- letter cards from the Word Play Book

TEACHING TIP

MANAGEMENT Some children may be aware that there are words that end in /k/*k* such as *book* and *week*. You may wish to keep track of these words in a Final /k/ envelope. Then when children mention a final /k/ word that doesn't end in *ck*, write it on a piece of paper and put it in the envelope for later reference.

ALTERNATE TEACHING STRATEGY

....

FINAL /k/*ck*, /g/*g*, /b/*b*

For a different approach to teaching this skill, see pages T28 and T32.

▶ **Visual/Auditory/ Kinesthetic**

Review Final /k/ck, /g/g, /b/b

TEACH

Discriminate Among /k/ck, /g/g, /b/b

Tell children they will review the sounds /k/, /g/, and /b/ at the end of words, and write letters *ck, g,* and *b*. Make word cards for the following words, and place them on the chalkboard ledge. Point to each one as you read it aloud, emphasizing the final sounds: *pack, luck, tuck, tug, log, rag, cab, rib, tub*. Rearrange the words, and ask children to say the final sound and to name the last letter or letters of each word as you point to it.

Form ck, g, b

Rearrange the above word cards on the chalkboard ledge once again, and ask children to write on letter strips the order of final sounds *ck, g,* and *b*. Invite volunteers to name the letters they wrote, and have the rest of the children check their work.

PRACTICE

Complete the Pupil Edition Page

Read the directions on page 296 to the children, and make sure they clearly understand what they are being asked to do. Identify each picture, and complete the first item together. Then work through the page with children, or have them complete the page independently.

ASSESS/CLOSE

Identify and Use ck, g, and b

Write the following sentences on the chalkboard and read them aloud: *Mack and Meg rode in a cab. They went to a lab. They met their friend Rob.*

You may want to read the sentence three times so that the children may listen for each of the ending sounds separately. Ask children to clap their hands each time they hear a word that ends with /k/, /g/, or /b/.

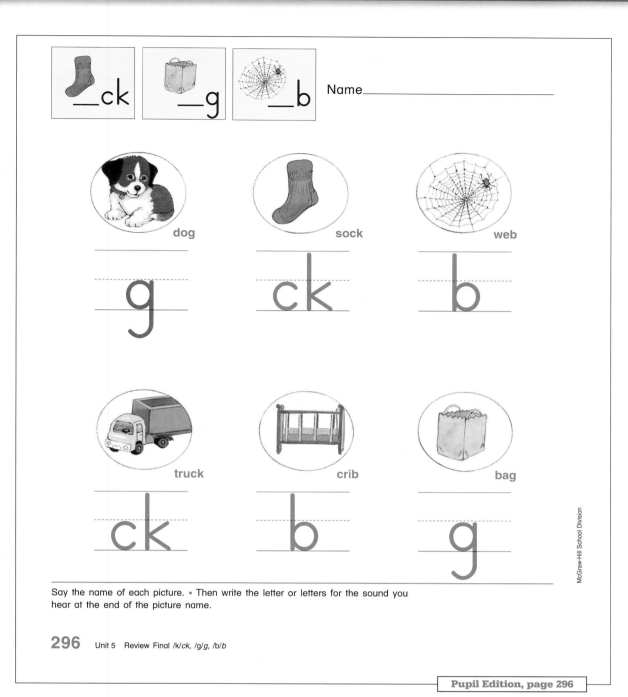

Name_____

_ck   _g   _b

dog

g

sock

ck

web

b

truck

ck

crib

b

bag

g

Say the name of each picture. • Then write the letter or letters for the sound you hear at the end of the picture name.

McGraw-Hill School Division

Pupil Edition, page 296

ADDITIONAL PHONICS RESOURCES

Practice Book *page 296*
Phonics Workbook

McGraw-Hill School
TECHNOLOGY

Phonics CD-ROM
Activities for practice with Initial Letters

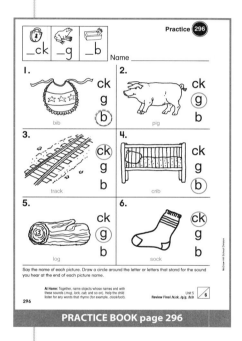

PRACTICE BOOK page 296

Meeting Individual Needs for Phonics

EASY	ON-LEVEL	CHALLENGE	LANGUAGE SUPPORT
Say the following words, and write them on the chalkboard: *tick, rib, dig, cub, tag, tug, duck, tub*. Have children repeat each word and make the sound the word ends with.	**Show** picture cards, such as: *duck, sock, tack, tub, cub, bib, log, pig, dig*. Have children write letters on self-stick labels and label these pictures with *ck, g,* or *b* to show how each picture name ends.	**Form** a circle with children and play "Sack Tag." One child in the center *picks* letter card *ck, g,* or *b* from a *sack* and *tags* someone to say a word that ends in that way. Then that child goes into the center, picks a letter card, and tags someone else.	**Reinforce** ESL children's familiarity with final *ck, g, b* by showing them how to pantomime such action words as: *tag, tuck, rub, pick, dig*. Write the ending letters on the chalkboard. Ask children to point to the letter each word ends with.

296

Children will:

- review words with final /k/*ck*
- review words with final /g/*g*
- describe story structure
- summarize a story

MATERIALS

- *Any Kind of Dog*

Read the Big Book

Before Reading

Develop Oral Language

SING A SONG Display letter cards to spell BINGO. Have children read the word. Have them recall the song they learned about Bingo, the dog. As children sing and clap along, remove the letter cards.

REVISIT THE LITERATURE When the last letter is removed, display *Any Kind of Dog*. Have children read the title. Ask what the story is about.

Set Purposes

Give children a chance to determine their purpose for rereading *Any Kind of Dog*. For example, they might read to see how the illustrations help tell the story.

So his mother gave him a dog.

The dog was very nice.
It looked exactly like a dog.

Just a Dog

The dog was a lot of trouble,

Any Kind of Dog, pages 22-23

During Reading

Read Together As you read *Any Kind of Dog*, you may wish to pause before the repetitive phrase, "Richard wanted a dog. His mother said a dog was too much trouble." Have children join you in saying the words.

- As you read, emphasize how to read (turn) the pages in order from front to back. *Concepts of Print*

- Have children point to words that have the final /g/*g*. *Phonemic Awareness*

- Since there are no /k/*ck* words in the story, you may want to have children think of names with final *ck*, such as Jack, to name the dogs in the story. *Phonemic Awareness*

- After reading the story, review the concept of story structure. Help children recall that a story has a pattern of words or actions. Have them name the word pattern (Richard wanted a dog) and action pattern (Mother keeps giving him bigger pets). *Story Structure*

- Have children summarize the story. *Summarize a Story*

Any Kind of Dog, page 1

After Reading

Return to Purposes Discuss the purposes children set before reading *Any Kind of Dog*. Ask how the illustrations helped tell the story. Revisit the Big Book as needed.

Literary Response **JOURNAL WRITING** Discuss with children those parts of the story they liked best. Have them write about or draw to record.

ORAL RESPONSE Have children share their journal entries with each other.

CENTER Activity

Cross Curricular: Social Studies/Science

ANIMAL HABITATS Have children paint land, sky, and water on a large sheet of paper. Then ask them to draw or cut from magazines a variety of animals. Have them paste the animals in the appropriate habitat.

▶ **Logical/Kinesthetic**

INQUIRY Ask children what else they would like to learn about the habitats of some of the animals in *Any Kind of Dog*.

*inter*NET **CONNECTION** Help children log on to **www.mhschool.com/reading,** where they can access links to various sites about many kinds of animals.

Children will:

- recognize a story structure to understand a story

....

MATERIALS

- *Any Kind of Dog*

TEACHING TIP

INSTRUCTIONAL Have children join you in singing a cumulative song such as "Old MacDonald Had a Farm." Point out that the song has a beginning, a middle, and an end.

Review Story Structure

PREPARE

Recall the Story

Review the story *Any Kind of Dog* with children. Direct children's attention to recalling the story by asking: *What happened in the beginning of the story?* Repeat with questions about the middle and the end of the story.

TEACH

Understanding Story Structure

Tell children that all books have beginnings, middles, and ends. Show a few pages from the beginning of the book and ask children how Richard got interested in dogs. (from reading a book) Then turn to the middle of the book and ask children what happened. (His mother kept giving him other kinds of animals.) Then turn to the end of the book and ask what happened. (His mother finally gave him a real dog.)

PRACTICE

Complete the Pupil Edition Page

Read the directions on page 297 to the children, and make sure they clearly understand what they are asked to do. Identify each picture, and complete the first item together. Then work through the page with children or have them complete the page independently.

ASSESS/CLOSE

Review the Page

Go over children's work and take note of children who are experiencing difficulty.

Name_____

1.

2.

3.

Look at the first picture. • Then look at the second picture. • Think about what is happening in the story. • In the last box, draw what you think will happen at the end of the story.

Pupil Edition, page 297

Meeting Individual Needs for Comprehension

EASY	ON-LEVEL	CHALLENGE	LANGUAGE SUPPORT
Invite children to act out the story *Any Kind of Dog*. Children can take turns being Richard and his mother while you act as the narrator. Point out which animals are in the beginning, middle, and end of the story.	**Have** children look carefully at the illustrations in *Any Kind of Dog*. Ask them to explain how the illustrations show the number of animals increasing from the beginning to the end. Talk about how the illustrations support the story structure.	**Have** children look at the story structure in other classroom books. For example, they might look at counting books such as *Warthogs in the Kitchen* or books that cover the seasons such as *The Apple Pie Tree*. Talk with children about the structure of these books.	**Use** the story to review the names of different animals. If possible, provide photographs of the animals in *Any Kind of Dog* and have children match the names to the photographs.

Develop Phonological Awareness

Listen

Katie's Kangaroo
a poem

Gobble, Gobble
a poem

Katie has a kangaroo.
She keeps it on her bed.
Katie has a kangaroo.
It sleeps on Katie's head.
Katie has a kangaroo
And five koalas, too.
She has so many animals,
Her room looks like a zoo!

A turkey is a funny bird,
His head goes wobble, wobble,
And he knows just one word,
Gobble, Gobble, Gobble.

Big Book of Phonics Rhymes and Poems, p. 29, p. 21

Objective: Listen and Clap Syllables

READ THE POEM Read the poem "Katie's Kangaroo" aloud, emphasizing each two-syllable word as you say it.

CLAP SYLLABLES Reread the poem, but this time clap two beats each time you say a two-syllable word. Then read the poem again and encourage children to clap the syllables of each two-syllable word.

CLAP THREE TIMES Repeat the activity, emphasizing the three-syllable words in the poem.

kangaroo   koalas   animals

SUBSTITUTE NAMES Help children substitute their names for *Katie* in the poem, clapping to show the number of syllables in their names.

David   Bobby   Helen   Mary   Greg   Caitlin

Objective: Listen for /k/, /g/, /b/

LISTEN AND THEN SAY /k/, /g/, /b/ Segment /k/ as you say the word *kangaroo*. Have children repeat the /k/ sound, then say *kangaroo* with you.

Repeat by having children listen for and segment /g/ in *gobble*, and /b/ in *bird*.

COUNT WORDS WITH /k/ Reread "Katie's Kangaroo," line by line, not including the title. Have children hold up a finger each time they hear /k/. Count to find out how many times /k/ was said.

Say the words from the poems with /k/ and have children put down a finger for each word you say.

> Katie   Kangaroo   keeps   Katie   Kangaroo
> Katie's   Katie   Kangaroo   koalas

Repeat by reading "Gobble, Gobble." Have children listen for /g/, then /b/, at the beginning of words.

CLAP FOR THE SOUND Say words aloud. Have children clap each time they hear a word that begins or ends with /k/.

> kite   track   sleep   kind   lick   keep   find

Repeat for words with initial or final /g/. Then repeat for words with initial or final /b/.

Read Together

From Phonemic Awareness to Phonics

Objective: Associate Sounds with Letters

IDENTIFY THE LETTER
Display pages 29 and 21 in the *Big Book of Phonics Rhymes and Poems*. On each page, point to the letters, identify them, and say the sound they stand for. Have children say each sound with you.

REREAD THE POEMS Read the poems again as you point to each word. Emphasize words with /k/. Repeat for /g/ and /b/.

FIND WORDS WITH *K, k, g, b*
Have children point to words in the poems that begin with the letters *K, k, g,* or *b*.

Katie's Kangaroo   Kk

Katie has a kangaroo
She keeps it on her bed.
Katie has a kangaroo.
It sleeps by Katie's head.

Katie has a kangaroo
And five koalas, too.
She has so many animals,
Her room looks like a zoo!

Gobble, Gobble

A turkey is a funny bird,
His head goes wobble, wobble,
And he knows just one word,
Gobble, Gobble, Gobble.

Big Book of Phonics Rhymes and Poems, pages 29, 21

OBJECTIVES

Children will:

- identify and discriminate among /k/k,*ck*, /g/G,*g*, /b/B,*b*

- write and use letters *K,k,ck, G,g, B,b*

....

MATERIALS

- picture cards from the *Word Building Book*

TECHNOLOGY TIP

INSTRUCTIONAL

Children will enjoy pantomiming action words such as *kick, pack; give, dig; bend, rub.* Invite children to think of other actions that begin and end with *k, ck, g,* and *b.*

ALTERNATE TEACHING STRATEGY

....

LETTERS /K/K,*k*; *ck*, /G/G,*g*, /B/B,*b*

For a different approach to teaching this skill, see page T24 and T28.

▶ **Visual/Auditory/ Kinesthetic**

Review /k/k, /k/ck, /g/g, /b/b

TEACH

Identify and Discriminate Among /k/K,k,ck, /g/G,g and /b/B,b
Tell children they will review the sounds /k/, /g/, /b/ at the beginning and the end of words and write letters *K,k,ck, G,g,* and *B,b*. Ask them to say the sound of each letter as you write it on the chalkboard. Remind children that they are reviewing /k/ words that begin in *k* and end in *ck*. Note that the /g/ and /b/ words to be reviewed begin and end the same way, with just one letter. Write words on the chalkboard and read them aloud. Have children name them as beginning or ending with the sound /k/, /g/, or /b/.

Write and Use K,k,ck, G,g, B,b
Write the following word cards and arrange them on the chalkboard ledge: *got, kid, get, bed, bit, kit*. Ask children to write the same arrangement of first letters on letter strips. Rearrange the word cards, and have children repeat the activity. Then write the following word cards and arrange them on the ledge: *cub, duck, dig, lock, tub, log*. This time, have children write the same arrangement of last letters on letter strips. Rearrange the word cards and repeat the activity.

PRACTICE

Complete the Pupil Edition Page
Read the directions on page 298 to the children, and make sure they clearly understand what they are being asked to do. Identify each picture, and complete the first item together. Then work through the page with children, or have them complete the page independently.

ASSESS/CLOSE

Identify and Use K,k, G,g, B,b
Have children make self-stick labels and place them in the right- or left-hand corner of pictures of objects whose names begin or end in *k, ck, g, b,* such as: *truck, goat, rug, bed, tub, key.*

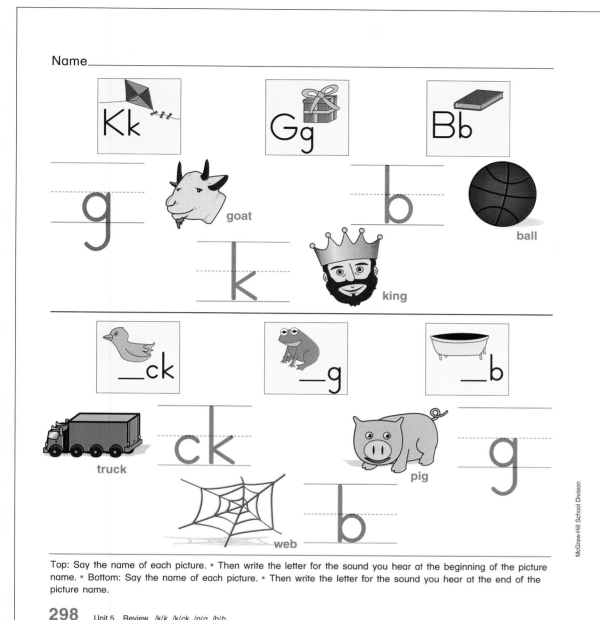

Name_____

Kk Gg Bb

g goat

b ball

k king

__ck _g _b

ck truck pig g

web b

Top: Say the name of each picture. • Then write the letter for the sound you hear at the beginning of the picture name. • Bottom: Say the name of each picture. • Then write the letter for the sound you hear at the end of the picture name.

McGraw-Hill School Division

298 Unit 5 Review /k/k, /k/ck, /g/g, /b/b

Pupil Edition, page 298

ADDITIONAL PHONICS RESOURCES

Practice Book, *page 298*
Phonics Workbook

McGraw-Hill School
TECHNOLOGY

Phonics CD-ROM
Activities for practice with Initial and Final Letters

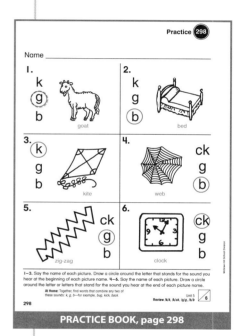

Practice 298

Name_____

1. k (g) b goat
2. k g (b) bed
3. (k) g b kite
4. ck g (b) web
5. ck (g) b zig-zag
6. (ck) g b clock

1–3. Say the name of each picture. Draw a circle around the letter that stands for the sound you hear at the beginning of each picture name. 4–6. Say the name of each picture. Draw a circle around the letter or letters that stand for the sound you hear at the end of each picture name.

At Home: Together, find words that combine any two of these sounds: *k, g, b*—for example, *bug, kick, back.*

298 Review /k/k, /k/ck, /g/g, /b/b Unit 5 6

PRACTICE BOOK, page 298

Meeting Individual Needs for Phonics

EASY	ON-LEVEL	CHALLENGE	LANGUAGE SUPPORT
Put pictures of objects whose names begin with *k, g,* or *b* in the hat. Children pass the hat as they sing a song. When you raise your hand, the person with the hat pulls out a picture and identifies it as beginning with *k, g,* or *b.* Suggested pictures: *kid, kitten, goat, girl, bear, bed, bat.*	**Have** children draw a picture of a scene that contains at least two objects that begin and end with *k, ck, g,* and *b.* (Suggestions: *kitten, kid, duck, rock; gift, goldfish, dig, rug; bat, boat, tub, cub.*)	**Ask** riddles for children to answer using initial or final *k, g, b,* such as: *It swims and quacks.* (duck) *You do this when you see a green light.* (go) *You take a bath in it.* (tub) Invite children to make up riddles. Children write the letter(s) of the initial or final sound for each answer.	**Reinforce** ESL children's fluency with final /g/ and /k/ by having them repeat such chants as the following: *tag-g-g-g, tack-ck-ck-ck, bag-g-g-g, back-ck-ck-ck, tug-g-g-g, tuck-ck-ck-ck, pig-g-g-g, pick-ck-ck-ck.* Be sure children know the word meanings.

Teacher Read Aloud

Listen

The Hare and the Tortoise

A fable by Aesop

T here once was a hare who was always boasting about how fast he could run. One day he said to the other animals, "I'm so fast that no one can beat me. I dare anyone here to a race."

The tortoise said quietly, "I will race you."

"You!" laughed the hare. "That's a joke! Why, I could run circles around you all the way."

"Save your boasting until you've won," said the tortoise. "Shall we race?"

So the race began. The hare darted almost out of sight at once, and very soon he was far ahead of the tortoise, who moved along at a steady, even pace.

The hare knew he was far ahead, so he stopped and said, "I think I'll take a little nap. When I wake up, I can zip ahead of the tortoise without even trying."

So the hare settled into a nice sleep. And he was still asleep when the tortoise passed by. And when the hare finally woke up, he looked ahead, and what did he see? The tortoise was just then crossing the finish line to win the race!

Continued on page T2

Oral Comprehension

LISTENING AND SPEAKING Review with children "The Hare and the Tortoise." Help them to recall how the tortoise won the race in the end.

Ask children what they learned from the story. What is boasting? What mistake did the hare make? Why did the tortoise offer to race him?

Activity Have children draw and color images of the hare and the tortoise. Then cut out the characters and make stick puppets of them. Using the puppets, children can retell the story. Encourage children to act out the personalities of the characters as they improvise the dialogue.

▶ **Kinesthetic/Linguistic**

Real-Life Reading

Can you help the families read the street signs?

33

Big Book of Real-Life Reading, pages 32–33

Objective: Read Environmental Print

READ THE PAGE Ask children to name different kinds of signs they recognize in their own neighborhood, such as traffic and crossing signs; store signs, such as "Sale," "Open," and "Closed"; and advertisements. Help them to be as specific as possible in recalling what they see on the signs.

FOLLOW-UP ACTIVITY Guide children to think of a sign they would like to make for their school or room at home. They can draw an image illustrating the sign's message, and write a word or two as a caption. Then have children act out the message in their signs without speaking. Other children guess what the child is trying to communicate.

Cross Curricular: Science

CLASSIFYING Discuss with children the difference between the hare and tortoise (appearance, speech, and so on). Have them:

- select any two animals
- make a two-column chart and put each

animal's name at the top of one of the columns

- list descriptive words under each animal, comparing how they move, how they look, and so on.

▶ Logical/Linguistic/Spatial

turtle	horse
has shell	has mane
moves slowly	can move very quickly

OBJECTIVES

Children will:

- review high-frequency words *for, he, she, has.*

MATERIALS

- word cards from the *Word Play* book
- *A Pup and a Cat*

TECHNOLOGY TIP

INSTRUCTIONAL Point out that the word *he* always refers to boys or males and the word *she* always refers to girls or females. Point to different children in the class and ask if the child is a *he* or a *she*.

Review for, he, she, has

PREPARE

Listen to Words   Tell children that they will be reviewing the words *for, he, she,* and *has*. Read each of the following sentences aloud and ask children to listen carefully:

1. The hare naps <u>for</u> a little while.

2. <u>He</u> stops, but <u>she</u> keeps going.

3. The hare <u>has</u> a lot to learn.

Explain that you will read the sentences again. This time children should raise their hands when they hear one of the high-frequency words.

TEACH

Model Reading the Word in Context   Distribute the word cards with the high-frequency words so that each child has a set. Hold up each card and pronounce the word. Ask children to listen for each high-frequency word as you reread the sentences. Have children raise their hands when they hear a word.

Identify the Words   Write the sentences on the chalkboard. Then read each sentence, tracking the print as you read. Have children hold up the correct word card when they hear each high-frequency word. Have volunteers come up and underline these words in the sentences.

PRACTICE

Complete the Pupil Edition Page   Read the directions on page 299 to the children, and make sure they clearly understand what they are asked to do. Complete the first item together. Then work through the page with children or have them complete the page independently.

ASSESS/CLOSE

Review the Page   Review children's pages and note any children who need additional support.

Name_____

1. (has)   she   for   he

2. she   (he)   for   has

3. he   has   she   (for)

4. for   (she)   he   has

Read the four words in each row. **1.** Draw a circle around the word *has*. **2.** Draw a circle around the word *he*. **3.** Draw a circle around the word *for*. **4.** Draw a circle around the word *she*.

Pupil Edition, page 299

ALTERNATE TEACHING STRATEGY

HIGH-FREQUENCY WORDS

For a different approach to teaching this skill, see page T27.

▶ **Visual/Auditory/ Kinesthetic**

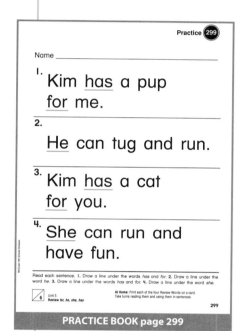

Practice 299

Name_____

1. Kim <u>has</u> a pup
<u>for</u> me.

2. <u>He</u> can tug and run.

3. Kim <u>has</u> a cat
<u>for</u> you.

4. <u>She</u> can run and
have fun.

Read each sentence. **1.** Draw a line under the words *has* and *for*. **2.** Draw a line under the word *he*. **3.** Draw a line under the words *has* and *for*. **4.** Draw a line under the word *she*.

Unit 5
Review *for, he, she, has*

At Home: Print each of the four Review Words on a card. Take turns reading them and using them in sentences.

299

PRACTICE BOOK page 299

Meeting Individual Needs for Vocabulary

EASY	ON-LEVEL	CHALLENGE	LANGUAGE SUPPORT
Tell children you will say a high-frequency word and they should hold up the card with that word. After a round or two, have children call out the words for the class to identify.	**Have** children draw a picture to illustrate the story "The Hare and the Tortoise." Then ask children to dictate a sentence about their picture using at least one of the words they have been learning. Read children's sentences aloud and ask the class to identify the high-frequency words.	**Give** children the following clues and have them hold up the correct word: 1. A word for a boy. *(he)* 2. The tortoise ___ a shell. *(has)* 3. It sounds like the number four. *(for)* 4. A word for a girl. *(she)*	**Give** children practice in subject/verb agreement using the pronouns *he* and *she* and the verbs *have* and *has*. Ask children to repeat these sentences with you paying attention to these words: *We have a ball. You have a ball. He has a ball. She has a ball.*

Develop Phonological Awareness

Listen

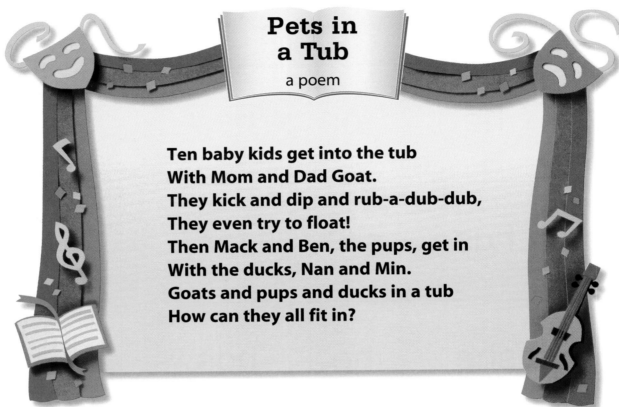

Pets in a Tub
a poem

Ten baby kids get into the tub
With Mom and Dad Goat.
They kick and dip and rub-a-dub-dub,
They even try to float!
Then Mack and Ben, the pups, get in
With the ducks, Nan and Min.
Goats and pups and ducks in a tub
How can they all fit in?

Objective: Focus on the Rhythm of the Chant

READ THE POEM Read the poem "Pets in a Tub." Help the children keep a steady rhythm as they recite the chant "rub-a-dub-dub" several times.

RECITE THE POEM Have children stand in a circle and join in saying lines 1 and 3. Suggest children clap to work with the chants rhythm.

PLAY A GAME To continue the game, say: *Rub-a-dub-dub, who's in the tub?* Name three children, and say: *Rub-a-dub-dub, get into the tub!* After the three children have moved to the center, invite children to chant: *Rub-a-dub-dub, get out of the tub!* Then have the three children in the middle rejoin the circle.

Be sure children understand they should respond to the chant by moving in or out of the circle when they hear their names called. Repeat until all children have responded to their names.

Phonemic
Awareness

Objective: Listen for Blending with Short *a, e, i, o, u*

LISTEN FOR BLENDING Tell children you are going to say one word in the poem differently. Read the poem, but substitute /k/-/i/-/k/, saying the sounds slowly, for *kick*. After reading the poem, have children say /k/-/i/-/k/ with you to discover the word. Repeat with short vowel words in the poem.

> **Mack   Ben   ducks**

WHAT IS IN THE BAG? Give children three blocks. Write words with short vowel sounds on index cards. Put index cards in a bag.

> **bag   back   beg   big   bog   bug**

Invite a volunteer to select a card and give it to you. Say the sounds in the word on the card, for example /b/-/a/-/g/. Have children place a block on their desks as they

say each sound with you. As children blend the sounds, have them move the blocks closer together.

Suggest children raise their hands when they know what the word on your card is. Repeat the activity with other words.

From Phonemic Awareness to Phonics

Objective: Relate *a, e, i, o, u* to Short Vowel Sounds

LISTEN FOR RHYMING WORDS Tell children you will say a list of words. Say *kick, kid, lick*. Ask children to name the words that rhyme.

> **kick   lick**

IDENTIFY THE LETTERS Say /k/-/i/-/k/. Write *kick* on chart paper as children say each sound. Identify the letters. Repeat with *lick*. Be sure to write *lick* under *kick*. Ask: *Which letters are the same in both words?*

MORE RHYMING WORDS Write *_ick* several times in list form under *kick* and *lick*.

Invite a volunteer to name a word that rhymes with kick and lick, such as *pick*. Emphasize /p/ as you write p next to –ick. Have children say /p/-/ick/, then blend the sounds to say pick. Repeat with other words that rhyme with kick.

Invite volunteers to highlight the letters that are the same in each word. Read the list aloud, emphasizing the –ick ending in each word.

kick   nick
pick   sick
lick   tick
Mick   wick

OBJECTIVES

Children will:

- identify/u/*u*
- blend and read short *a, e, i, o, u* words
- write short *a, e, i, o, u* words
- review /b/*b*, /g/*g*, /k/*k,ck*, /a/*a*, /e/*e*, /i/*i*, /o/*o*,

....

MATERIALS

- letter cards from the *Word Building Book*

TEACHING TIP

INSTRUCTIONAL. Display letter cards *b, g, c, ck* and ask children to identify the two cards that show the same sound. Show word cards that begin or end with /k/. Ask children to say which cards show /k/ at the beginning of a word and which show /k/ at the end of a word.

ALTERNATE TEACHING STRATEGY

....

BLENDING SHORT
a, e, i, o, u

For a different approach to teaching this skill, see Unit 1, page T32; Unit 2, page T32; Unit 3, page T30; Unit 4, page T32; Unit 5, page T30.

▶ **Visual/Auditory/ Kinesthetic**

Review Blending with short *a, e, i, o, u*

TEACH

Identify *a, e, i, o, u* as Symbols for /a/, /e/, /i/, /o/, /u/

Tell children they will continue to read words with *a, e, i, o, u.*

- Display the *a, e, i, o, u* letter cards and say /a/, /e/, /i/, /o/, /u/. Have children repeat the sounds as you point to the cards.

BLENDING Model and Guide Practice

- Place a *b* card before the *e* card. Blend the sounds together and have children repeat after you.

- Place a *d* letter card after the *b, e* cards. Blend and read *bed.*

Use the Word in Context

- Ask children to use *bed* in a sentence. Invite them to describe different coverings: *blanket, spread, quilt, sheet.*

Repeat the Procedure

- Use the following words to continue modeling and for guided practice with short *a, e, i, o, u: rag, kit, bug, got, tack, tub, Ken.*

PRACTICE

Complete the Pupil Edition Page

Read aloud the directions on page 300. Identify each picture, and complete the first item together. Work through the page, or have children complete the page independently.

ASSESS/CLOSE

Write Short *a, e, i, o, u* Words

Observe children as they complete page 300. Have them write words that have short *a, e, i, o,* or *u* and begin or end in: *b, g, k, ck.*

Name _____

1. K i m   Kim

2. s o c k   sock

3. t u b   tub

4. r u g   rug

Blend the sounds and say the word. • Write the word. • Draw a circle around the
picture that goes with the word.

300 Unit 5 Review Blending with Short *a, e, i, o, u*

McGraw-Hill School Division

ADDITIONAL PHONICS RESOURCES

Practice Book, *page 300*
Phonics Workbook

McGraw-Hill School
TECHNOLOGY

Phonics CD-ROM
**Activities for Practice with
Blending and Segmenting**

Practice **300**

Name _____

1. r o c k   rock

2. b a g   bag

3. b i g   big

4. l e g   leg

Blend the sounds and say the word. Write the word. Draw a line under the picture that
goes with the word.

At Home: Take turns writing a secret word on a scrap of
paper and hiding it in one hand. If the other person
chooses the hand with the word, he or she reads it.

300   Review Blending with Short *a, e, i, o, u*   Unit 5

PRACTICE BOOK page 300

Meeting Individual Needs for Phonics

EASY	ON-LEVEL	CHALLENGE	LANGUAGE SUPPORT
Show letter cards *a, e, i, o, u* on the chalkboard ledge and ask children to say each sound as you point to a letter and name it. Have them blend to read aloud, then sort these word cards by the middle letter: *fan, top, sit, men, rub, ten, rot, cat, dug, kid.*	**Give** children pictures of such objects as: *kid, bag (sack), tub, gum, bin, dog, lock, kit* and have them write labels for the pictures. Then ask them to sort the pictures to show /k/, /g/, /b/ sounds. Point out that some words can go in more than one group.	**Have** children form a circle and pass a sack that contains word cards that have medial *a, e, i, o, u* and begin or end with *b, g, k* or *ck*. Children select and read aloud their word cards, then use each word in a sentence.	**Write** the following list of words on the chalkboard: *kit, kid, sit, get, bad, fit, tug, hit, tab, lit.* Ask children to put a check mark next to the words that end in *-it*.

Guided Instruction

BEFORE READING

PREVIEW AND PREDICT Take a brief **picture walk** through the book, focusing on the illustrations.

- Who is this story about? Where does it take place?

- Do you think the story is realistic or make-believe? Why?

SET PURPOSES Discuss with children what they would like to find out about as they read the story. For example, they might want to know what the pup and cat are going to do.

TEACHING TIP

To put book together:

1. Tear out the story page.

2. Cut along dotted line.

3. Fold each section on fold line.

4. Assemble book.

INSTRUCTIONAL Talk about friendship, and how people and pets consider themselves friends. Talk about how "friendships" between people and animals may be different from friendships between people.

A Pup and a Cat

He is a big pup!

3

McGraw-Hill School Division

Kim has a pup.

2

McGraw-Hill School Division

The pup can sit up for Kim.

4

Guided Instruction

DURING READING

☑ **Concepts of Print**

☑ **High-Frequency Words:** *has, she, he, for*

☑ **Initial** *B, b*

☑ **Make Inferences**

① **CONCEPTS OF PRINT** Have children look at the title. Point to the capital *A* and then to the lowercase *a*. Remind children that the first word in a title always begins with a capital letter.

② **HIGH-FREQUENCY WORDS** After you read page 2, ask children to point to the word that begins with an *h*. (has) Model tracking print as you read the word together. Then have children reread the word and demonstrate how to track print.

③ **PHONICS** After you read the text on page 3, ask children which word begins with *b*. *(big)*

④ **MAKE INFERENCES** Ask children to look at page 4. Ask why Kim is holding out a dog treat.

LANGUAGE SUPPORT

ESL Some children may have difficulty with the phrase *sit up* on page 4. Use pantomime to show how the pup might *sit up* to beg for a bone.

Guided Instruction

DURING READING

⑤ CONCEPTS OF PRINT Ask children how many words are in the sentence on this page. (five) Ask which word has one letter. (a)

⑥ BLENDING WITH SHORT _i_ Point to the word _big_ on page 6. Have children blend the sounds of the letters together to read the word: _b, i, g, big._ Ask: _What other word in the sentence has the /i/ sound?_ (is)

⑦ PHONICS Ask children to read the two words on page 7 that end with _n._ (fun, Ben)

⑧ SUMMARIZE EVENTS After you read page 8, ask children to retell the story, focusing on how the story begins, what happens, and how the story ends.

INFORMAL ASSESSMENT

INITIAL _B, b_

HOW TO ASSESS Show children the following sentence: The big cat has a big bat. Ask them to point to the words that have the initial _b._ Have children track print as they read the sentence.

FOLLOW UP If children have trouble, ask them to look again at the story and find the words with initial _b._

Ben has a tan cat.

5

Kim and Ben have fun.

7

She is not a big cat.

6

The pup and the cat
have fun!

8

Guided Instruction

AFTER READING

RETURN TO PREDICTIONS AND PURPOSES Ask children to check to see if their predictions about the story were correct. Ask if they found out what the pup and the cat did.

RETELL THE STORY As a class, have children retell the story. Children can take turns retelling the parts of the story they remember. Have the children refer to the story to make sure that the sequence is correct.

LITERARY RESPONSE To help children respond to the story ask:

- Which pet in the story would you like to have?

  Why?

- Do you have a pet? How do you play together?

Invite children to draw and write about two friends in the story.

CENTER Activity

Cross Curricular: Social Studies

WE ARE FRIENDS Have children make a picture collage of things that friends do together. Children can draw or cut out pictures from magazines. Work together to make a poster that tells what it means to be a good friend.

▶ Interpersonal

301/302D

Children will:

- summarize events to understand a story

MATERIALS

- *A Pup and a Cat*

TEACHING TIP

INSTRUCTIONAL At the end of each day help children to practice summarizing by asking them to name the important things that happened that day.

Review Summarize

PREPARE

Recall the Story
Ask children to recall the story *A Pup and a Cat*. Talk about the important things the pup and the cat did together.

TEACH

List Parts of the Story to Summarize
Ask children to name the characters in the story, and ask how the story begins. Write children's ideas on chart paper. Encourage them to speak in complete sentences. Then ask what the animals did together, and write the responses. Finally, ask how the story ends. Read the sentences together, and explain that the sentences summarize the story by naming important parts.

PRACTICE

Complete the Pupil Edition Page
Read the directions on page 303 to the children, and make sure they clearly understand what they are asked to do. Identify each picture, and complete the first item together. Then work through the page with children or have them complete the page independently.

ASSESS/CLOSE

Review the Page
Review children's work, and note children who are experiencing difficulty.

Name _____

SUMMARIZE

For a different approach to teaching this skill, see page T29.

▶ **Visual/Auditory/ Kinesthetic**

(I)   ✕ 2   ✕ 3

Listen as I read three sentences. • One sentence will tell what the story "A Pup and a Cat" is about. • Circle the number of the sentence that tells what the story is about. • Cross out the number of each sentence that does not tell what the story is about.
     1. Kim and Ben play with their pets.
     2. Kim and her mom go shopping.
     3. Kim and Ben ride bikes together.
On the bottom, draw a picture of what "A Pup and a Cat" is about.

Unit 5 Review Summarize   **303**

PRACTICE BOOK page 303

Pupil Edition, page 303

Meeting Individual Needs for Comprehension

EASY	ON-LEVEL	CHALLENGE	LANGUAGE SUPPORT
Read a familiar nursery rhyme, such as "Humpty Dumpty." Give each child three index cards and ask them to draw pictures showing three important things that happened to Humpty Dumpty.	**Ask** children to draw three pictures that summarize the events in the story *A Pup and a Cat*. Have children describe each picture.	**Read** a new picture book to the children. Then ask them to summarize the events by asking: *How does the story begin? What happens during the story? How does the story end?* Children may draw pictures or write their responses.	**Ask** children to pantomime some of the important parts in the story. Point out illustrations in the book that may help them.

Develop Phonological Awareness

Listen

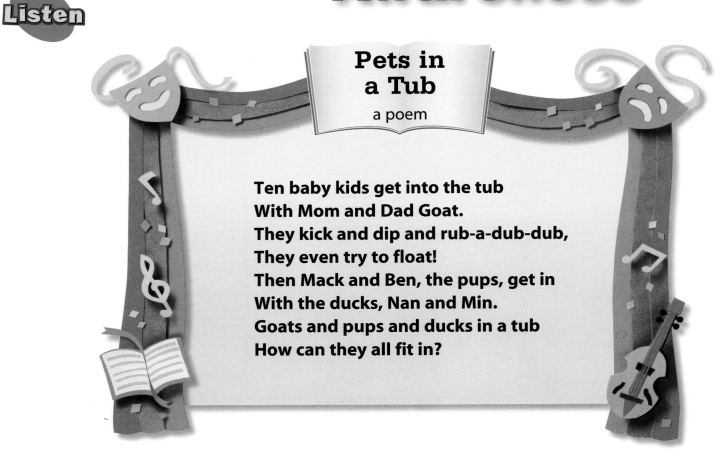

Pets in a Tub
a poem

Ten baby kids get into the tub
With Mom and Dad Goat.
They kick and dip and rub-a-dub-dub,
They even try to float!
Then Mack and Ben, the pups, get in
With the ducks, Nan and Min.
Goats and pups and ducks in a tub
How can they all fit in?

Objective: Listen to Sequences of Sounds

READ THE POEM Read the poem "Pets in a Tub." Ask: *Which animals are named in the poem?*

> kids   goats   pups   ducks

IDENTIFY ANIMAL SOUNDS Have children make a sound to associate with each animal named in the poem. Invite children to name other animals—and sounds associated with them.

> kitten-meow   cat-purr
> duck-quack   frog-croak   hog-squeal

COMPLETE A SEQUENCE OF SOUNDS Say a series of animal noises, omitting the final one in the series. For example: *Baah, baah, quack, baah, baah, quack, baah, baah, _____.* Pause, and have children fill in the missing animal sound. Repeat with other series of animal sounds.

Objective: Listen for Blending with Short *a, e, i, o, u*

LISTEN FOR BLENDING Read the title of the poem, but segment, then blend *tub* by saying /t/-/u/-/b/, tub. Have children segment, then blend the sounds in tub.

Tell children you are going to choose some words in the poem to say differently. After segmenting a word, pause at the end of the line that contains the word. Have the children repeat, then blend the sounds to determine what the word is.

> ten   Mom   kick   get   Nan   ducks   fit

MYSTERY WORDS Tell children you are thinking of a mystery word. Invite them to work in groups to figure out the word. Arrange children in groups of three, and assign each child in the group a number—1, 2, or 3. Assign /r/ to all children with 1, /u/ to children with 2, and /b/ to children with 3.

Have children say their sounds in number order. Encourage them to blend their sounds to discover the mystery word. Have one child in each group whisper the mystery word to you. Repeat with other words that contain short vowels.

> cat   red   pen   sick   log   gum

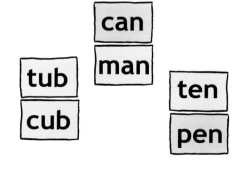

Read Together

From Phonemic Awareness to Phonics

Objective: Relate *a, e, i, o, u* to Short Vowel Sounds

LISTEN FOR RHYMING WORDS Read the first four lines of "Pets in a Tub." Ask children to name words that rhyme with tub.

> rub   dub

IDENTIFY THE LETTERS Say /t/-/u/-/b/. Write *tub* on the board as children say each sound. Identify the letters. Repeat by writing *rub* on the board directly under tub.

Invite a volunteer to circle the letters in the words that are the same. Then identify the letters. Ask children to say the sounds these letters stand for.

FIND RHYMING WORDS Write words on index cards, and give sets to small groups of children.

> tub   cub   can   ma
> ten   pen   dip
> lip   cot   dot

Have groups sort the cards into rhyming pairs.

Review Blending with short *a, e, i, o, u*

OBJECTIVES

Children will:

- identify /a/*a*, /e/*e*, /i/*i*, /o/*o*, /u/*u*
- blend and read short *a, e, i, o, u* words
- write short *a, e, i, o, u* words
- review /b/*b*, /g/*g*, /k/*k*,*ck*, /l/*l*, /p/*p*, /r/*r*, /f/*f*, /k/*c*, /t/*t*, /m/*m*, /s/*s*, /d/*d*, and /n/*n*

MATERIALS

- letter cards from the *Word Building Book*

TEACHING TIP

INSTRUCTIONAL When children are blending letters to read words aloud, ask them to first stop for a moment and look at the whole word, silently making the sound of each letter. If there is a letter they can't remember the sound of, encourage them to ask for a reminder.

ALTERNATE TEACHING STRATEGY

BLENDING SHORT
a, e, i, o, u

For a different approach to teaching this skill, see Unit 1, page T32; Unit 2, page T32; Unit 3, page T30; Unit 4, page T32; Unit 5, page T30.

▶ **Visual/Auditory/ Kinesthetic**

TEACH

Identify *a, e, i, o, u* as Symbols for /a/, /e/, /i/, /o/, /u/

Tell children they will continue to read words with *a, e, i, o, u*.

- Display the *a, e, i, o, u* letter cards and say /a/, /e/, /i/, /o/, /u/. Have children repeat the sounds as you point to the cards.

BLENDING Model and Guide Practice

- Place an *l* card before the *i* card. Blend the sounds together and have children repeat after you.

| l | i |
| l | i |

- Place a *t* letter card after the *l, i* cards. Blend the sounds to read *lit*.

| l | i | t |
| l | i | t |

Use the Word in Context

- Ask children to use *lit* in a sentence. Perhaps they can describe a home at night, or candles on a cake.

Repeat the Procedure

- Use the following words to continue modeling and for guided practice with short *a, e, i, o, u*: *pod, sun, kid, red, fit, cat, dog*.

PRACTICE

Complete the Pupil Edition Page

Read aloud the directions on page 304. Identify each picture, and complete the first item together. Work through the page, or have children complete the page independently.

ASSESS/CLOSE

Build Short *a, e, i, o, u* Words

Observe children as they complete page 304. Give them vowel letter cards. Write incomplete words on the chalkboard that children complete using a vowel card.

Name _____

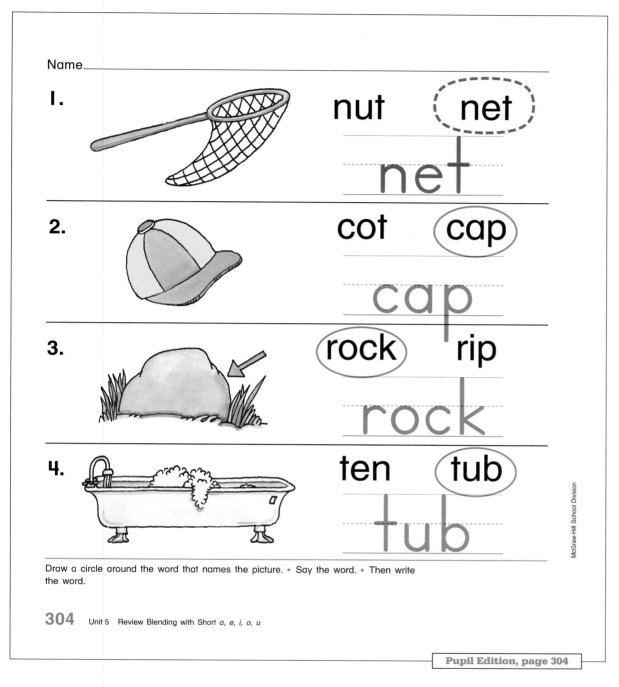

1. nut (net)

net

2. cot (cap)

cap

3. (rock) rip

rock

4. ten (tub)

tub

Draw a circle around the word that names the picture. • Say the word. • Then write the word.

McGraw-Hill School Division

304   Unit 5   Review Blending with Short *a, e, i, o, u*

Pupil Edition, page 304

ADDITIONAL PHONICS RESOURCES

Practice Book, *page 304*
Phonics Workbook

McGraw-Hill School
TECHNOLOGY

Phonics CD-ROM
Activities for Practice with Blending and Segmenting

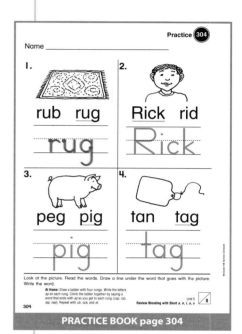

Name _____   Practice 304

1. rub rug   2. Rick rid

   rug   Rick

3. peg pig   4. tan tag

   pig   tag

Look at the picture. Read the words. Draw a line under the word that goes with the picture. Write the word.

At Home: Draw a ladder with four rungs. Write the letters *ap* on each rung. Climb the ladder together by saying a word that ends with *ap* as you get to each rung (*cap, rap, lap, nap*). Repeat with *ub, ock, and et.*

304

Unit 5
8

Review Blending with Short *a, e, i, o, u*

PRACTICE BOOK page 304

Meeting Individual Needs for Phonics

EASY	ON-LEVEL	CHALLENGE	LANGUAGE SUPPORT
Read aloud some of the words that children built in the Assess/Close activity. Ask children to hold up the card showing the letter sound they hear in the middle of each word, then show them the word card so they can check their work.	**Have** children build one word each with short *a, e, i, o, u* in the middle. Display their other letter choices: *l, p, r, f, c, t, m, s, d, n*. Ask them to use letter cards to build the word, then write the words and use them in sentences.	**On** the chalkboard write *a, e, i, o, u* on one side and *b, g, k, ck, l, p, r, f, c, t, m, s, d, n* on the other side. Invite children to write and read aloud ten words they have learned, using as many of the letters on the board as they can. Write the words the children make on the chalkboard.	**Reinforce** short vowel sounds *a, e, i, o, u,* by having children repeat as you blend and read words that rhyme, such as: *bet, get, let, pet, met, set, net*. Write words on the chalkboard and point to the medial vowel as you read each word.

Reread the Decodable Story

A Pup and a Cat

A Pup and a Cat

- ☑ **Initial and Final** *b, g*
- ☑ **High-Frequency Words:** *for, he, she, has*
- ☑ **Concepts of Print**
- ☑ **Summarize**

Guided Reading

SET PURPOSES Tell children that when they read the story again, they can find out more about what happened. Explain that you also want them to look for and read words that begin or end with *b,* or *g.* Remind them that they know the words *for, he, she,* and *has,* and will see them again in this story.

REREAD THE BOOK As you guide children through the story, address specific problems they may have had during the first read. Use the following prompts to guide the lesson:

- **CONCEPTS OF PRINT** Ask children to point to the exclamation mark on page 3, and tell why it's there. Have children reread the sentence with excitement.

- **SUMMARIZE** After you read the story, have children say three sentences that summarize what happened in the story.

RETURN TO PURPOSES Ask children if they found out more about what happened in the story. Ask if they found any words that begin or end with *b,* or *g.* Ask if anyone saw the words *for, he, she,* or *has.*

LITERARY RESPONSE Ask children to write what the pup or cat might say if they could talk. Have them dictate their ideas if necessary.

INFORMAL ASSESSMENT

INITIAL AND FINAL *b, g*
HOW TO ASSESS Invite children to look through the story to find the word that begins with *b* and ends with *g, (big).* How many times does this word appear in the story? (2) .

FOLLOW UP If children have difficulty, show them the letter cards *b, g.* Ask them to look at the card to help them find the *n* and *g.*

Read the  Patterned Book

Self-Selected Reading

Unit Skills Review

☑ **Phonics**

☑ **Comprehension**

☑ **High-Frequency Words**

Help children self-select a Patterned Book to read and apply phonics and comprehension skills.

Guided Reading

SET PURPOSES Have children select a patterned book and read it to find the pattern in the story.

READ THE BOOK Remind the children to run their fingers under each word in the story as they read. You may wish to stop and use the following prompts as they read.

• Name words that have *k, ck, g,* or *b* in them. Which words can you find that show short *a* blended with other letters? Short *e*? *(Answers will vary.) Phonics and Decoding*

• Where does the story take place? *(Answers will vary.) Story Structure*

• Summarize, or tell what happens, on this page. *(Answers will vary.) Summarize*

• Make up a sentence about the picture using as many of these words as you can: *for, he, she, has. (Answers will vary.) High-Frequency Words*

• Name the action words on this page. Name the naming words. *(Answers will vary.) Concepts of Print*

RETURN TO PURPOSES Have children share the patterns in their stories. Use these prompts.

• How many words were in your pattern? Was your pattern made up of statements and/or questions?

• Can you make a new sentence with your pattern?

LITERARY RESPONSE Have children who read different books work in pairs to compare their books. Have them think about these questions.

• How was the setting the same or different in each story?

• How were the characters the same or different in each story?

Have children discuss what they have learned from making comparisons about their books.

☑ **Phonics and Decoding**
• Initial /k/*k*, /g/*g*, e/*e*, /b/*b*
• Final /k/*ck*, /g/*g*, /b/*b*
• Medial /e/*e*
• Blending with Short *a, e, i, o, u*

☑ **Comprehension**
• Story Structure
• Summarize

☑ **Vocabulary**
• High-Frequency Words: *for, he, she, has*

CENTER **Activity**

Cross Curricular: Social Studies

LET'S TALK IT OUT
Discuss with children a class problem such as too much noise or messy cubbies. Have children suggest ways to solve the problem as you list ideas on a chart. Then point to each idea and have children act out the solution.

▶ **Logical/ Interpersonal**

OBJECTIVES

Children will:

- review high-frequency words *for, he, she, has.*

MATERIALS

- word cards from the *Word Play* book
- *A Pup and a Cat*

TEACHING TIP
INSTRUCTIONAL

Mention to children that the high-frequency word *for* is not the same as the word for the numeral four. Point out that although the words sound the same, they look different when you read them because they are spelled in different ways.

Review for, he, she, has

PREPARE

Listen to Words
Say aloud the following sentences emphasizing the underlined high-frequency words. Use the suggested motions given in parentheses. Ask children to listen to the sentences and then repeat each high-frequency word with you after the sentence is finished.

1. <u>She</u> <u>has</u> brown hair. *(point to a girl with brown hair)*

2. <u>He</u> <u>has</u> blonde hair. *(point to a boy with blonde hair)*

3. Will you get a book <u>for</u> me? *(point to a child)*

TEACH

Model Reading the Word in Context
Read aloud the decodable story "A Pup and a Cat." Ask children to listen for and identify the high-frequency words.

Identify the Words
Provide each child with a set of the high-frequency words on the cards from the *Word Play* Book. Identify each of the words and then read aloud sentences from the story that include the words. Ask children to hold up the correct word card as you read. Read the sentences again and have children place a different colored stick-on note (yellow for *he*, pink for *she*, and so on) under the word in their decodable books.

Review the High-Frequency Words
Pronounce each high-frequency word from the lesson and have children hold up the correct word card. Include words such as *and, we,* and *the* from earlier lessons.

PRACTICE

Complete the Pupil Edition Page
Read the directions on page 305 to the children, and make sure they clearly understand what they are asked to do. Complete the first item together. Then work through the page with children or have them complete the page independently.

ASSESS/CLOSE

Review the Page
Look over children's work on page 305 and note any children who need additional support.

Name_____

1.
she	he said (she) has

2.
for	my (for) are you

3.
he	(he) she the me

4.
has	have said that (has)

Say the first word in the row. • Draw a circle around the word where you see it in the same row.

Unit 5 Review *for, he, she, has* **305**

Pupil Edition, page 305

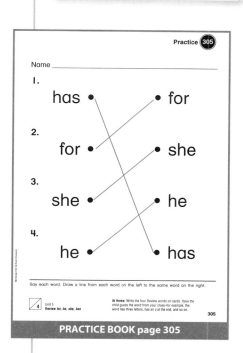

Practice 305

Name _____

1.
has •   • for

2.
for •   • she

3.
she •   • he

4.
he •   • has

Say each word. Draw a line from each word on the left to the same word on the right.

4 | Unit 5
Review *for, he, she, has*

At Home: Write the four Review words on cards. Have the child guess the word from your clues—for example, the word has three letters, has an *s* at the end, and so on.

305

PRACTICE BOOK page 305

Meeting Individual Needs for Vocabulary

EASY	ON-LEVEL	CHALLENGE	LANGUAGE SUPPORT
Place some classroom objects on a table. Choose a child to hold up one of the objects. Ask: *What does (he/she) have?* Have children display the appropriate word card for *he* or *she*. Then have a volunteer answer the question. *(He.She) has a (block)*.	**Write** the high-frequency words from this lesson and several from earlier lessons on the chalkboard. Point to a word and call on a volunteer to match a word to that word. Then have the child use the word in a sentence.	**Provide** children with pictures of common objects such as a glass, bed, or dog. Then give children word cards for the high-frequency words they have learned so far. Model how to use the cards and pictures to create rebus sentences. Ask children to make up their own sentences.	**Give** children practice in using the pronouns he and she to replace nouns. Have them repeat sentence pairs such as the following after you. *John runs fast. He runs fast.* *Pia draws a picture. She draws a picture.*

Interactive Writing

Write Dialogue

Prewrite

LOOK AT THE STORY PATTERN
Reread the story *Mice Mischief: An Alphabet Story*. Emphasize the pattern of the story: Each page has a letter of the alphabet. A word on that page starts with that letter. Then talk about the characters, and how they might have been feeling during different parts of the story. Make a list of children's responses.

Draft

WRITE DIALOGUE Discuss the end of the story, talking about what the characters might have been feeling.

• Invite children to dictate their ideas. Write the dialogue, using quotation marks. Explain the use of the marks.

• Write all of the ideas, having children help you write as appropriate.

Publish

RECORD DIALOGUE Have children choose one of the ideas, and write it on a strip of writing paper. Make sure they include quotation marks.

Presentation Ideas

MAKE FINGER PUPPETS Cut fingers from old gloves, and have pairs of children make finger puppets for Dan and Bink. Children can use markers to draw details.

► **Representing/Viewing**

SAY THE DIALOGUE Have partners act out the ending of the story, using the dialogue that they wrote. Children may wish to have you read the dialogue, or they may wish to say it themselves.

► **Speaking/Representing**

COMMUNICATION TIPS

• **Listening** Remind children to listen attentively as their classmates speak and perform. Encourage them to offer helpful comments.

TECHNOLOGY TIP

Have children write part of the dialogue on the computer.

LANGUAGE SUPPORT

ESL Say common phrases, such as *Good morning,* or *How are you?* Write them on the chalkboard, using quotation marks. Explain that the marks show someone is speaking. Have children repeat the phrases.

Meeting Individual Needs for Writing

EASY	ON-LEVEL	CHALLENGE
Draw a Picture Invite children to draw a picture of one of the characters in the story. Help them label their characters.	**Use Quotation Marks** Ask children to write a simple phrase that they would say to a friend. Help them to use quotation marks correctly.	**Write Dialogue** Invite partners to write dialogue for a different part of the story. Have them read the dialogue to others.

306B

Wrap Up
the Theme

Let's Work It Out

Working as part of a team can help me find a way to solve problems.

REVIEW THE THEME Read the theme statement to children. Pose a problem such as "How can we move the big box to the other side of the room?" Invite groups of children to show how they would solve the problem. Then read the poem.

HELPING

Agatha Fry, she made a pie,
And Christopher John helped bake it.
Christopher John, he mowed the lawn,
And Agatha Fry helped rake it.
Zachary Zugg took out the rug,
And Jennifer Joy helped shake it.
And Jennifer Joy, she made a toy,
And Zachary Zugg helped break it.

And some kind of help
Is the kind of help
That helping's all about.
And some kind of help
Is the kind of help
We all can do without.

Shel Silverstein

AUDIO

Student Listening Library

DISCUSS THE POEM Discuss ways in which the friends in "Helping" helped each other. Ask children to describe the help that was not good help. Invite them to suggest other ways that Zachary Zugg could have helped Jennifer Joy with the toy she made.

LOOKING AT GENRE: FOLKTALES The Literature Big Book *The Enormous Carrot* and the Read Aloud selection *It Could Always Be Worse* are examples of folktales. Explain how folktales are stories that were handed down from generation to generation.

The Enormous Carrot is a type of folktale called a cumulative tale, in which the repetition of the pulling of the carrot builds until the climax of the story. Reread the story and allow children to chime in on the repetitive lines.

Research *and Inquiry*

Theme Project: "How To Care for a Pet" Book

GROUP **Give the Presentation** Assign a group of children to complete the *How To Care for a Pet* book by binding the drawings and writings together and making a cover. As you look through the book with the class, invite each group to tell about the pages they created.

Draw Conclusions Children should be able to conclude that pet care is a daily task. Lead them to see that caring for any pet is a large responsibility.

Ask More Questions Ask children if there is anything else they would like to know about caring for the pet they chose. Make a list of their questions. As children conduct additional research to find answers, they can add more pages with this new information to the *How To Care for a Pet* book.

HIGH-FREQUENCY WORDS

GROUP Write the following words in a row on the chalkboard: *for, he, she, has.* Ask a child to come up and choose a word card from your hand and then place the card under the matching word written on the chalkboard.

Unit Review

Tom Is Sick
for

Pug
he

A Pet for Ken
she

A Big Bug
has

A Pup and a Cat
review: *for, he, she, has*

☑ SKILLS & STRATEGIES

Phonics and Decoding
☑ Initial /k/*k*, /g/*g*, /e/*e*, /b/*b*
☑ Final /k/*ck*, /g/*g*, /b/*b*
☑ Medial /e/*e*
☑ Blending with Short *a, e, i, o, u*

Comprehension
☑ Story Structure
☑ Summarize

Vocabulary
☑ High-Frequency Words: *for, he, she, has*

Beginning Reading Concepts
☑ Naming Words
☑ Action Words

UNIT 5 ASSESSMENT

Assessment
Follow-Up

Use the results of the informal and formal assessment opportunities in the unit to help you make decisions about future instruction.

SKILLS AND STRATEGIES	Alternate Teaching Strategies
Phonics and Decoding	
Initial /k/k, /g/g, /e/e, /b/b,	T24, T28, T30, T32
Final /k/ck, /g/g, /b/b, Medial /e/e	T24, T28, T30, T32
Blending with Short a, e, i, o ,u	Unit 1 T32, Unit 2 T32, Unit 3 T30, Unit 4 T32, T30
Comprehension	
Story Structure	T26
Summarize	T29
Vocabulary	
High-Frequency Words: for, he, she, has, for, you, me, is	T27
Beginning Reading Concepts	
Naming Words	T25
Action Words	T31

McGraw-Hill School
TECHNOLOGY

 CD-ROM Provides extra phonics support.

 Research & Inquiry Ideas. *Visit www.mhschool.com*

Cover Illustration: Mary Jane Begin

The publisher gratefully acknowledges permission to reprint the following copyrighted material:

"Aekyung's Dream" by Min Paek. Copyright © 1978, 1988 by Children's Book Press.

"Amazing Grace" by Mary Hoffman. Text copyright © 1991 by Mary Hoffman. Illustrations copyright © 1991 by Caroline Binch. Used by permission of Dial Books for Young Readers.

"Annie's Pet" by Barbara Brenner. Text copyright © 1989 by Bank Street College of Education. Used by permission of Bantam Books, a division of Bantam Doubleday Dell Publishing Group, Inc.

ANY KIND OF DOG by Lynn Whisnant Reiser. Copyright © 1992 by Lynn Whisnant Reiser. Reprinted by permission of William Morrow & Company.

THE APPLE PIE TREE by Zoe Hall. Text copyright ©1996 by Zoe Hall. Illustrations copyright ©1996 by Shari Halpern. Reproduced by permission of Scholastic Inc.

"Beehive" from A CHILDREN'S SEASONAL TREASURY compiled by Betty Jones. Copyright © 1971 by Dover Publishing, Inc. Reprinted by permission of Dover Publishing, Inc.

THE CHICK AND THE DUCKLING by Mirra Ginsburg. Text copyright © 1972 by Mirra Ginsburg. Illustration copyright © 1972 by Jose Aruego. Reprinted by permission of Simon & Schuster Children's Publishing Division.

"Cinderella" is primarily based on the version by Charles Perrault, in THE BLUE FAIRY BOOK, edited by A. Lang (1889) and incorporates elements of the Brothers Grimm version, translated by L. Crane (1886), as well as details from the retelling by F. Baker and A. Thorndike in EVERYDAY CLASSICS: THIRD READERS (1920).

"Clay" from A SONG I SANG TO YOU by Myra Cohn Livingston. Copyright © 1958, 1959, 1965, 1967, 1969, 1984 by Myra Cohn Livingston. Used by permission of Marian Reiner for the author.

"The Clever Turtle" retold by Margaret H. Lippert from CHILDREN'S ANTHOLOGY. Copyright © 1988 by Macmillan Publishing Company, a division of Macmillan Inc.

THE EARTH AND I by Frank Asch. Copyright © 1994 by Frank Asch. Reprinted by permission of Harcourt Brace & Company.

THE ENORMOUS CARROT by Vladimir Vagin. Copyright © 1998 by Vladimir Vagin. Reproduced by permission of Scholastic Inc.

"Every Time I Climb a Tree" from FAR AND FEW by David McCord. Copyright © 1929, 1931, 1952 by David McCord. Reprinted by permission of Little, Brown & Company.

"50 Simple Things Kids Can Do to Save the Earth" from 50 SIMPLE THINGS KIDS CAN DO TO SAVE THE EARTH by The EarthWorks Group. Copyright © 1990 by John Javna.

"Five Little Seeds" from THIS LITTLE PUFFIN compiled by Elizabeth Matterson. Copyright © 1969 by Puffin Books. Reproduced by permission of Penguin Books. Reprinted by permission.

FLOWER GARDEN by Eve Bunting. Text copyright ©1994 by Eve Bunting, illustrations copyright ©1994 by Kathryn Hewitt. Reprinted by permission of Harcourt Brace & Company.

"The Hare and the Tortoise" from THE FABLES OF AESOP by Aesop, retold by Joseph Jacobs (c. 1900).

"Helping" from WHERE THE SIDEWALK ENDS by Shel Silverstein. Copyright © 1974 by Evil Eye Music, Inc. Reprinted by permission of HarperCollins Publishers.

"Hill of Fire" from HILL OF FIRE by Thomas P. Lewis. Text copyright © 1971 by Thomas P. Lewis. Used by permission of Harper & Row Publishers, Inc.

"How Many Spots Does a Leopard Have?" from HOW MANY SPOTS DOES A LEOPARD HAVE AND OTHER STORIES by Julius Lester. Copyright © 1989 by Julius Lester. Reprinted by permission of Scholastic Inc.

"It Could Always Be Worse" by Margot Zemach. Copyright © 1976 by Margot Zemach. Reprinted by permission of Farrar, Straus & Giroux, Inc.

"A Kite" from READ-ALOUD RHYMES FOR THE VERY YOUNG. Copyright © 1986 by Alfred A. Knopf, Inc.

"Learning" from POETRY PLACE ANTHOLOGY by M. Lucille Ford. Copyright © 1983 by Instructor Publications, Inc.

"The Legend of the Bluebonnet" by Tomie dePaola. Copyright © 1983 by Tomie dePaola. Used by permission of The Putnam Publishing Group.

"Little Brown Rabbit" from THIS LITTLE PUFFIN compiled by Elizabeth Matterson. Copyright © 1969 by Puffin Books. Reprinted by permission of Penguin Books Ltd.

"The Little Engine That Could" by Watty Piper. Copyright © 1930, 1945, 1954, 1961, 1976 by Platt & Munk, Publishers. Used by permission of Platt & Munk, Publishers, a division of Grosset & Dunlap, Inc., which is a member of the Putnam & Grosset Group, New York.

"The Little Red Hen" from WHAT YOUR KINDERGARTNER NEEDS TO KNOW edited by E. D. Hirsch, Jr., and John Holdren. Copyright © 1996 by The Core Knowledge Foundation. Used by permission of Delta Books, a division of Bantam Doubleday Dell Publishing Group, Inc.

"The Little Turtle" from COLLECTED POEMS by Vachel Lindsay. Copyright © 1920 by Macmillan Publishing Co., Inc., renewed 1948 by Elizabeth C. Lindsay.

"Making Friends" from NATHANIEL TALKING by Eloise Greenfield. Text copyright © 1988 by Eloise Greenfield. Illustrations copyright © by Jan Spivey Gilchrist. Used by permission of Writers and Readers Publishing, Inc., for Black Butterfly Children's Books.

"Mary Had a Little Lamb" from WHAT YOUR KINDERGARTNER NEEDS TO KNOW edited by E. D. Hirsch, Jr., and John Holdren. Copyright © 1996 by The Core Knowledge Foundation. Used by permission of Delta Books, a division of Bantam Doubleday Dell Publishing Group, Inc.

"Morning Verse" from THE KINDERGARTEN SERIES. Copyright ©1983 by Wynstone Press. Reprinted by permission of Wynstone Press.

NATURE SPY by Shelley Rotner and Ken Kreisler. Text copyright © 1992 by Shelley Rotner and Ken Kreisler. Illustrations copyright © 1992 by Shelley Rotner. Reprinted by permission of Simon & Schuster Children's Publishing Division.

PEANUT BUTTER AND JELLY by Nadine Bernard Westcott. Copyright ©1987 by Nadine Bernard Westcott. Reprinted by permission of Dutton Children's Books, a division of Penguin Books USA Inc.

PRETEND YOU'RE A CAT by Jean Marzollo, illustrated by Jerry Pinkney. Text copyright © 1990 by Jean Marzollo. Paintings copyright © 1990 by Jerry Pinkney. Reprinted by permission of Dial Books for Young Readers, a division of Penguin Putnam Inc.

"Shell" from WORLDS I KNOW AND OTHER POEMS by Myra Cohn Livingston. Copyright © 1985 by Myra Cohn Livingston. Reprinted by permission of Margaret K. McElderry Books, an imprint of Simon & Schuster Children's Publishing Division.

SHOW AND TELL DAY by Anne Rockwell. Text copyright © 1997 by Anne Rockwell. Illustrations copyright © 1997 by Lizzy Rockwell. Reprinted by permission of HarperCollins Publishers.

"The Squeaky Old Bed" from CROCODILE! CROCODILE! STORIES TOLD AROUND THE WORLD by Barbara Baumgartner. Text copyright © 1994 by Barbara Baumgartner. Illustrations copyright © by Judith Moffatt. Used by permission of Dorling Kindersley.

"The Three Little Pigs" by Joseph Jacobs from TOMIE DEPAOLA'S FAVORITE NURSERY TALES. Illustrations copyright © 1986 by Tomie dePaola. Used by permission of the Putnam Publishing Group.

"Tommy" from BRONZEVILLE BOYS AND GIRLS by Gwendolyn Brooks. Copyright © 1956 by Gwendolyn Brooks Blakely.

"The Town Mouse and the Country Mouse" retold and illustrated by Lorinda Bryan Cauley. Copyright © 1984 by Lorinda Bryan Cauley. Used by permission of G.P. Putnam's Sons.

Untitled from JUNE IS A TUNE THAT JUMPS ON A STAIR by Sarah Wilson. Copyright © 1992 by Sarah Wilson. Used by permission of Simon & Schuster Books for Young Readers.

"The Velveteen Rabbit; or, How Toys Become Real" from WHAT YOUR KINDERGARTNER NEEDS TO KNOW edited by E. D. Hirsch, Jr., and John Holdren. Copyright © 1996 by The Core Knowledge Foundation. Used by permission of Delta Books, a division of Bantam Doubleday Dell Publishing Group, Inc.

WARTHOGS IN THE KITCHEN by Pamela Duncan Edwards. Text ©1998 by Pamela Duncan Edwards. Illustrations ©1998 by Henry Cole. Reprinted by Hyperion Books for Children.

"Whistling" from RAINY RAINY SATURDAY by Jack Prelutsky. Copyright © 1980 by Jack Prelutsky. Used by permission of William Morrow & Company.

WHITE RABBIT'S COLOR BOOK by Alan Baker. Copyright © 1994 by Alan Baker. Reprinted by permission of Larousse Kingfisher Chambers, Inc.

"Winnie the Pooh" from WINNIE-THE-POOH by A. A. Milne. Copyright © 1926 by E.P. Dutton, renewed 1954 by A. A. Milne.

"Winter Days in the Big Woods" from LITTLE HOUSE IN THE BIG WOODS by Laura Ingalls Wilder. Copyright © 1932 by Laura Ingalls Wilder, renewed 1959 by Roger L. MacBride. Illustrations copyright © 1994 by Reneé Graef. Used by permission of HarperCollins Publishers.

"Wonderful World" from POETRY PLACE ANTHOLOGY by Eva Grant. Copyright © 1983 by Instructor Publications, Inc.

"Yesterday's Paper" by Mabel Watts from READ-ALOUD RHYMES FOR THE VERY YOUNG. Copyright © 1986 by Alfred A. Knopf, Inc.

Backmatter Contents

The Hare and the Tortoise

There once was a hare who was always boasting about how fast he could run. One day he said to the other animals, "I'm so fast that no one can beat me. I dare anyone here to a race."

The tortoise said quietly, "I will race you."

"You!" laughed the hare. "That's a joke! Why, I could run circles around you all the way."

"Save your boasting until you've won," said the tortoise. "Shall we race?"

So the race began. The hare darted almost out of sight at once, and very soon he was far ahead of the tortoise, who moved along at a steady, even pace.

The hare knew he was far ahead, so he stopped and said, "I think I'll take a little nap. When I wake up, I can zip ahead of the tortoise without even trying."

So the hare settled into a nice sleep. And he was still asleep when the tortoise passed by. And when the hare finally woke up, he looked ahead, and what did he see? The tortoise was just then crossing the finish line to win the race!

It Could Always Be Worse
a Yiddish folk tale retold by Margot Zemach

Once upon a time in a small village a poor unfortunate man lived with his mother, his wife, and his six children in a little one-room hut. Because they were so crowded, the man and his wife often argued. The children were noisy, and they fought. In winter, when the nights were long and the days were cold, life was especially hard. The hut was full of crying and quarreling. One day, when the poor unfortunate man couldn't stand it any more, he ran to the Rabbi for advice.

"Holy Rabbi," he cried, "things are in a bad way with me, and getting worse. We are so poor that my mother, my wife, my six children, and I all live together in one small hut. We are too crowded, and there's so much noise. Help me, Rabbi. I'll do whatever you say."

The Rabbi thought and pulled on his beard. At last he said, "Tell me, my poor man, do you have any animals, perhaps a chicken or two?"

"Yes," said the man. "I do have a few chickens, also a rooster and a goose."

"Ah, fine," said the Rabbi. "Now go home and take the chickens, the rooster, and the goose into your hut to live with you."

"Yes indeed, Rabbi," said the man, though he was a bit surprised.

The poor unfortunate man hurried home and took the chickens, the rooster, and the goose out of the shed and into his little hut.

When some days or a week had gone by, life in the hut was worse than before. Now with the quarreling and crying there was honking, crowing, and clucking. There were feathers in the soup. The hut stayed just as small and the children grew bigger. When the poor unfortunate man couldn't stand it any longer, he again ran to the Rabbi for help.

"Holy Rabbi," he cried, "see what a misfortune has befallen me. Now with the crying and quarreling, with the honking, clucking, and crowing, there are feathers in the soup. Rabbi, it couldn't be worse. Help me, please."

The Rabbi listened and thought. At last he said, "Tell me, do you happen to have a goat?"

"Oh, yes, I do have an old goat, but he's not worth much."

"Excellent," said the Rabbi. "Now go home and take the old goat into your hut to live with you."

"Ah, no! Do you really mean it, Rabbi?" cried the man.

"Come, come now, my good man, and do as I say at once," said the Rabbi.

The poor unfortunate man tramped back home with his head hanging down and took the old goat into his hut.

When some days or a week had gone by, life in the little hut was much worse. Now, with the crying, quarreling, clucking, honking, and crowing, the goat went wild, pushing and butting everyone with his horns. The hut seemed smaller, the children grew bigger.

When the poor unfortunate man couldn't stand it another minute, he again ran to the Rabbi.

"Holy Rabbi, help me!" he screamed. "Now the goat is running wild. My life is a nightmare."

The Rabbi listened and thought. At last he said, "Tell me, my poor man. Is it possible that you have a cow? Young or old doesn't matter."

"Yes, Rabbi, it's true I have a cow," said the poor man fearfully.

"Go home then," said the Rabbi, "and take the cow into your hut."

"Oh, no, surely not, Rabbi!" cried the man.

"Do it at once," said the Rabbi.

The poor unfortunate man trudged home with a heavy heart and took the cow into his hut. Is the Rabbi crazy? he thought.

When some days or a week had gone by, life in the hut was very much worse than before. Everyone quarreled, even the chickens. The goat ran wild. The cow trampled everything. The poor man could hardly believe his misfortune. At last, when he could stand it no longer, he ran to the Rabbi for help.

"Holy Rabbi," he shrieked, "help me, save me, the end of the world has come! The cow is trampling everything. There is no room even to breathe. It's worse than a nightmare!"

The Rabbi listened and thought. At last he said, "Go home now, my poor unfortunate man, and let the animals out of your hut."

"I will, I will, I'll do it right away," said the man.

The poor unfortunate man hurried home and let the cow, the goat, the chickens, the goose, and the rooster out of his little hut.

That night the poor man and all his family slept peacefully. There was no crowing, no clucking, no honking. There was plenty of room to breathe.

The very next day the poor man ran back to the Rabbi.

"Holy Rabbi," he cried, "you have made life sweet for me. With just my family in the hut, it's so quiet, so roomy, so peaceful . . . What a pleasure!"

Winter Days in the Big Woods
by Laura Ingalls Wilder

Once upon a time, a little girl named Laura lived in the Big Woods of Wisconsin in a little house made of logs.

Laura lived in the little house with her Pa, her Ma, her big sister Mary, her baby sister Carrie, and their good old bulldog Jack.

Winter was coming to the Big Woods. Soon the little house would be covered with snow. Pa went hunting every day so that they would have meat during the long, cold winter.

Ma, Laura, and Mary gathered potatoes and carrots, beets and turnips, cabbages and onions, and peppers and pumpkins from the garden next to the little house.

By the time winter came, the little house was full of good things to eat. Laura and Mary thought the attic was a lovely place to play. They played house by using the round orange pumpkins as tables and chairs, and everything was snug and cozy.

Soon the first snow came, and it was very cold. In the mornings the windows were covered with beautiful frost pictures of trees and flowers and fairies. Ma said that Jack Frost came in the night and made the pictures while everyone was asleep. Laura and Mary were allowed to use Ma's thimble to make pretty patterns of circles in the frost.

In the mornings Laura and Mary helped Ma wash the dishes and make the beds. After this was done, Ma began the work that belonged to that day. Each day had its own proper work. Ma would say:

"Wash on Monday,

Iron on Tuesday,

Mend on Wednesday,

Churn on Thursday,

Clean on Friday,

Bake on Saturday,

Rest on Sunday."

Laura liked the churning and baking days best of all. Ma had to churn the cream for a long time until it turned into butter. Mary could sometimes churn while Ma rested, but Laura was too little.

On Saturdays, when Ma made the bread, Laura and Mary each had a little piece of dough to make into a little loaf. Ma even gave them a bit of cookie dough to make little cookies.

After the day's work was done, Ma would sometimes cut out paper dolls for Laura and Mary. She drew their faces on with a pencil, and cut dresses, hats, and ribbons out of colored paper so that Mary and Laura could dress their dolls beautifully.

But the best time of all was at night, when Pa came home. He would throw off his fur cap and coat and mittens and call, "Where's my little half-pint of sweet cider half drunk up?" That was Laura, because she was so small.

Sometimes Pa would take down his fiddle and sing. Pa would keep time with his foot. Laura and Mary would clap their hands to the music when he sang:

"Yankee Doodle went to town,

He wore his striped trousies,

He swore he couldn't see the town,

There was so many houses."

Other times Pa would tell stories. When Laura and Mary begged him for a story, he would take them on his knees and tickle their faces with his long whiskers until they laughed out loud. His eyes were blue and merry.

Outside it was cold and snowy, but the little log cabin was snug and cozy. Pa, Ma, Laura, Mary, and Baby Carrie were comfortable and happy in their little house in the Big Woods.

Winnie the Pooh Gets Stuck

Pooh always liked a little something at eleven o'clock in the morning, and he was very glad to see Rabbit getting out the plates and mugs; and when Rabbit said, "Honey or condensed milk with your bread?" he was so excited that he said, "Both," and then, so as not to seem greedy, he added, "But don't bother about the bread, please." And for a long time after that he said nothing . . . until at last, humming to himself in a rather sticky voice, he got up, shook Rabbit lovingly by the paw, and said that he must be going on.

"Must you," said Rabbit politely.

"Well," said Pooh, "I could stay a little longer if it—if you—" and he tried very hard to look in the direction of the larder.

"As a matter of fact," said Rabbit, "I was going out myself directly."

"Oh, well, then, I'll be going on. Good-bye."

"Well, good-bye, if you're sure you won't have any more."

"Is there any more?" asked Pooh quickly.

Rabbit took the covers off the dishes, and said no, there wasn't.

"I thought not," said Pooh, nodding to himself. "Well, good-bye. I must be going on."

So he started to climb out of the hole. He pulled with his front paws, and pushed with his back paws, and in a little while his nose was out in the open again . . . and then his ears . . . and then his front paws . . . and then his shoulders . . . and then—

"Oh, help!" said Pooh. "I'd better go back."

"Oh, bother!" said Pooh. "I shall have to go on."

"I can't do either!" said Pooh. "Oh, help and bother!"

Now by this time Rabbit wanted to go for a walk too, and finding the front door full, he went out by the back door, and came round to Pooh, and looked at him.

"Hallo, are you stuck?" he asked.

"N-no," said Pooh carelessly. "Just resting and thinking and humming to myself."

"Here, give us a paw."

Pooh Bear stretched out a paw, and Rabbit pulled and pulled and pulled . . . .

"Ow!" cried Pooh. "You're hurting me!"

"The fact is," said Rabbit, "you're stuck."

"It all comes," said Rabbit sternly, "of eating too much. I thought at the time," said Rabbit, "only I didn't like to say anything," said Rabbit, "that one of us was eating too much," said Rabbit, "and I knew it wasn't me," he said. "Well, well, I shall go and fetch Christopher Robin."

Christopher Robin lived at the other end of the Forest, and when he came back with Rabbit, and saw the front half of Pooh, he said, "Silly old Bear," in such a loving voice that everybody felt quite hopeful again.

"I was just beginning to think," said Bear, sniffing slightly, "that Rabbit might never be able to use his front door again. And I should hate that," he said.

"So should I," said Rabbit.

"Use his front door again?" said Christopher Robin. "Of course he'll use his front door again."

"Good," said Rabbit.

"If we can't pull you out, Pooh, we might push you back."

Rabbit scratched his whiskers thoughtfully, and pointed out that, when once Pooh was pushed back, he was back, and of course nobody was more glad to see Pooh than he was, still there it was, some lived in trees, and some lived underground, and—

"You mean I'd never get out?" said Pooh.

"I mean," said Rabbit, "that having got so far, it seems a pity to waste it."

Christopher Robin nodded.

"Then there's only one thing to be done," he said. "We shall have to wait for you to get thin again."

"How long does getting thin take?" asked Pooh anxiously.

"About a week, I should think."

"But I can't stay here for a week!"

"You can stay here all right, silly old Bear. It's getting you out which is so difficult."

"We'll read to you," said Rabbit cheerfully. "And I hope it won't snow," he added. "And I say, old fellow, you're taking up a good deal of room in my house—do you mind if I use your back legs as a towel-horse? Because, I mean, there they are—doing nothing—and it would be very convenient just to hang the towels on them."

"A week!" said Pooh gloomily. "What about meals?"

"I'm afraid no meals," said Christopher Robin, "because of getting thin quicker. But we will read to you."

Bear began to sigh, and then found he couldn't because he was so tightly stuck; and a tear rolled down his eye, as he said:

"Then would you read a Sustaining Book, such as would help and comfort a Wedged Bear in Great Tightness?"

So for a week Christopher Robin read that sort of book at the North end of Pooh, and Rabbit hung his washing on the South end . . . and in between Bear felt himself getting slenderer and slenderer. And at the end of the week Christopher Robin said, "Now!"

So he took hold of Pooh's front paws and Rabbit took hold of Christopher Robin, and all Rabbit's friends and relations took hold of Rabbit, and they pulled together . . . .

And for a long time Pooh only said "Ow!" . . .

And "Oh!" . . .

And then, all of a sudden, he said "Pop!" just as if a cork were coming out of a bottle.

And Christopher Robin and Rabbit and all Rabbit's friends and relations went head-over-heels backwards . . . and on the top of them came Winnie-the-Pooh-free!

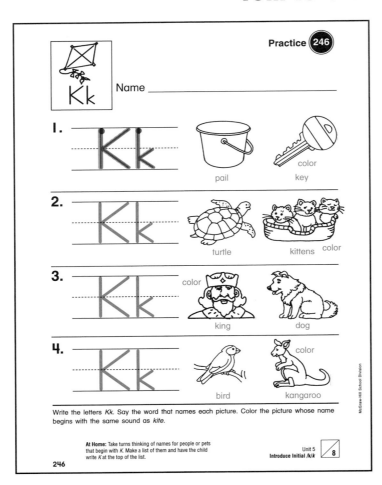

Practice 246

Name _____

1. Kk — pail / key (color)

2. Kk — turtle / kittens (color)

3. Kk — king (color) / dog

4. Kk — bird / kangaroo (color)

Write the letters *Kk*. Say the word that names each picture. Color the picture whose name begins with the same sound as *kite*.

At Home: Take turns thinking of names for people or pets that begin with *K*. Make a list of them and have the child write *K* at the top of the list.

Unit 5
Introduce Initial /k/k 8

246

Practice 247

Name _____

1. (color)

2. (color)

3. (color)

Look at the pictures in each row. Draw a circle around the person in each row. Color the place in each row. Draw a line under the thing in each row.

9 Unit 4
Introduce Naming Words

At Home: Have the child draw a picture of a favorite place to visit. Ask the child to point to the people and things in the picture. Then discuss the place.

247

Practice 248

_ck
Name _____

1. duck (color) / lion — ck

2. sock (color) / shoe — ck

3. doll / clock (color) — ck

Say the name of each picture. Color the picture whose name has the same ending sound as *lock*. Write the letters *ck*.

At Home: Talk about and write "sound" words that end with *ck*. You say the words and the child repeats them: *click, tick tock, clickety clack, yackity yack.*

Unit 5
Introduce Final /k/ck 6

248

Practice 249

Name _____

1. 3   1   2

2. 2   3   1

3. 2   3   1

Look at the pictures. Write *1* on the line under the picture that shows the beginning of the story. Write *2* on the line that shows the middle of the story. Write *3* on the line that shows the end of the story.

9 Unit 5
Introduce Story Structure

At Home: Read a story with the child. Afterwards, have the child tell what happened in the beginning, middle, and end of the story.

249

Annotated Workbooks

Kk _ck Name _____

1. kangaroo (k) ck

2. k duck (ck)

3. kettle (k) ck

4. (k) king ck

5. block k (ck)

6. (k) kittens ck

Say the name of the picture. Where do you hear the sound /k/k or /k/ck ? Draw a circle around the first *k* if it is the beginning sound (as in *kite*). Draw a circle around *ck* if it is the ending sound (as in *lock*).

At Home: Play "Mystery Word." Take turns giving clues for words that begin or end with /k/—for example, *I'm thinking of a word that is an animal that has a pouch and jumps (kangaroo)*.

250

Unit 5
Review /k/k, /k/ck   6

Name _____

1. "Is the cap <u>for</u> me?" said Tom.

2. "The cap is <u>for</u> you," said Kim.

3. "Is the pup <u>for</u> me?" said Pam.

4. "The pup is <u>for</u> you," said Mom.

Read the sentence. Draw a line under the word *for* in the sentence.

Unit 5
Introduce High-Frequency Words: *for*

At Home: Help the child find the word *for* in a magazine or newspaper article.

251

Name _____

1. n a p
nap

2. d u ck
duck

3. s o ck
sock

4. T i m
Tim

Blend the sounds and say the word. Write the word. Draw a line under the picture that goes with the word.

At Home: Give a set of clues: "It begins with *s*. It ends with *ck*. It has a short *o* in the middle. Name that word!" Continue with other words.

252

Unit 5
Review Blending with Short *a, i, o, u*   8

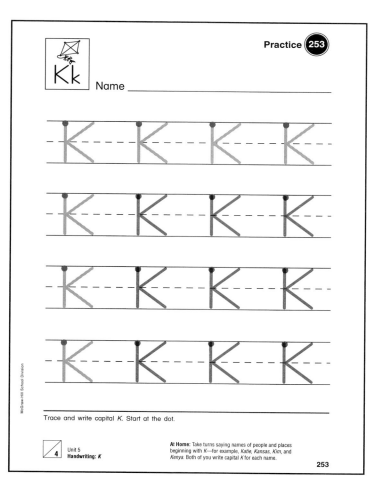

Kk Name _____

K K K K

K K K K

K K K K

K K K K

Trace and write capital *K*. Start at the dot.

Unit 5
Handwriting: *K*

At Home: Take turns saying names of people and places beginning with *K*—for example, *Katie, Kansas, Kim,* and *Kenya*. Both of you write capital *K* for each name.

253

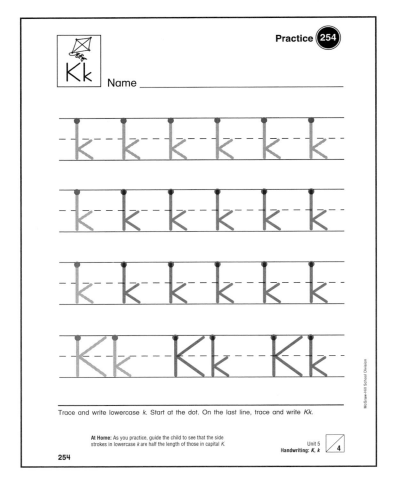

Kk

Name _____

Trace and write lowercase k. Start at the dot. On the last line, trace and write Kk.

At Home: As you practice, guide the child to see that the side strokes in lowercase k are half the length of those in capital K.

Unit 5
Handwriting: K, k | 4

254

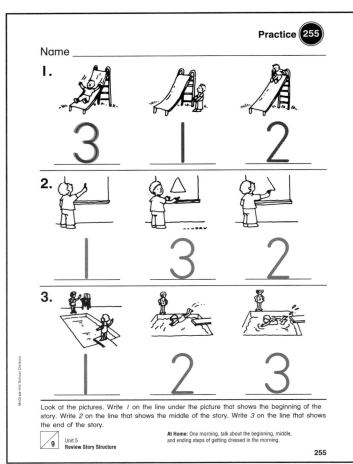

Name _____

1.

3   1   2

2.

1   3   2

3.

1   2   3

Look at the pictures. Write 1 on the line under the picture that shows the beginning of the story. Write 2 on the line that shows the middle of the story. Write 3 on the line that shows the end of the story.

9 | Unit 5
Review Story Structure

At Home: One morning, talk about the beginning, middle, and ending steps of getting dressed in the morning.

255

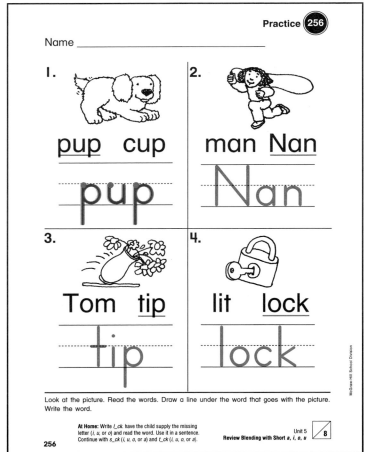

Name _____

1.

pup   cup

pup

2.

man   Nan

Nan

3.

Tom   tip

tip

4.

lit   lock

lock

Look at the picture. Read the words. Draw a line under the word that goes with the picture. Write the word.

At Home: Write l_ck. have the child supply the missing letter (i, u, o, or o) and read the word. Use it in a sentence. Continue with s_ck (i, u, o, or a) and t_ck (i, u, o, or a).

Unit 5
Review Blending with Short a, i, o, u | 8

256

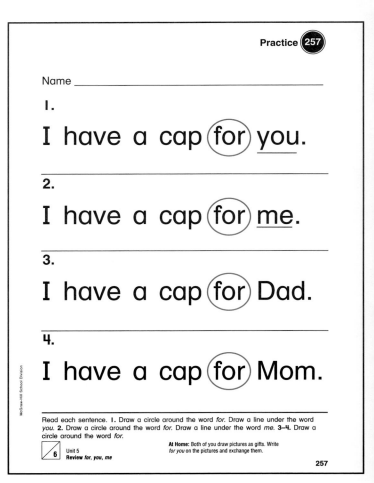

Name _____

1.

I have a cap (for) you.

2.

I have a cap (for) me.

3.

I have a cap (for) Dad.

4.

I have a cap (for) Mom.

Read each sentence. 1. Draw a circle around the word for. Draw a line under the word you. 2. Draw a circle around the word for. Draw a line under the word me. 3–4. Draw a circle around the word for.

6 | Unit 5
Review for, you, me

At Home: Both of you draw pictures as gifts. Write for you on the pictures and exchange them.

257

Pug • PRACTICE

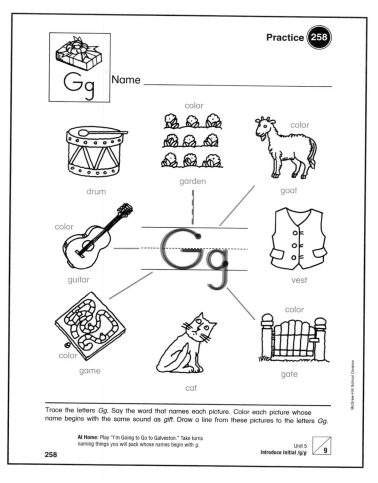

Name _____

color
drum
garden
color
goat
color
guitar
vest
color
game
cat
color
gate

Gg

Trace the letters *Gg*. Say the word that names each picture. Color each picture whose name begins with the same sound as *gift*. Draw a line from these pictures to the letters *Gg*.

At Home: Play "I'm Going to Go to Galveston." Take turns naming things you will pack whose names begin with *g*.

258

Unit 5
Introduce Initial /g/g **9**

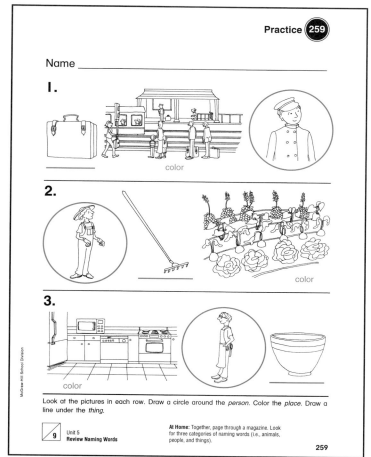

Name _____

1.

color

2.

color

3.

color

Look at the pictures in each row. Draw a circle around the *person*. Color the *place*. Draw a line under the *thing*.

9 Unit 5
Review Naming Words

At Home: Together, page through a magazine. Look for three categories of naming words (i.e., animals, people, and things).

259

Name _____

-g

bag   fan   tag

g   g

hen   rug   dog

g   g

Say the name of each picture. Write the letter *g* under each picture that has the same ending sound as *frog*.

At Home: Take a walk to find words that end with *g*. Look at street signs, store windows, everywhere. *Jog* when you find one.

260

Unit 5
Introduce Final /g/g **6**

Name _____

1.

2.

3.

4.

Look at the pictures in each row. Draw a circle around the picture that shows something that happened in "Any Kind of Dog." Then use the pictures you circled to retell the story.

4 Unit 5
Introduce Summarize

At Home: Take turns with the child in telling family members about a story he or she likes.

261

Pug • PRACTICE

Gg   –g   Name _____

1. goose   g   g
2. dig   g   g
3. log   g   g
4. gate   g   g
5. pig   g   g
6. g   goat   g

Say the name of the picture. Where do you hear the sound /g/g? Draw a circle around the first g if it is the beginning sound (as in gift). Draw a circle around the second g if it is the ending sound (as in frog).

At Home: Have the child say "good" every time you say a word that begins with the same sound as gift.

Unit 5
Review /g/g   6

262

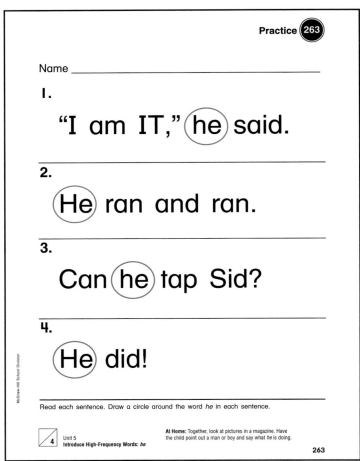

Name _____

1. "I am IT," he said.

2. He ran and ran.

3. Can he tap Sid?

4. He did!

Read each sentence. Draw a circle around the word he in each sentence.

4   Unit 5
Introduce High-Frequency Words: he

At Home: Together, look at pictures in a magazine. Have the child point out a man or boy and say what he is doing.

263

Name _____

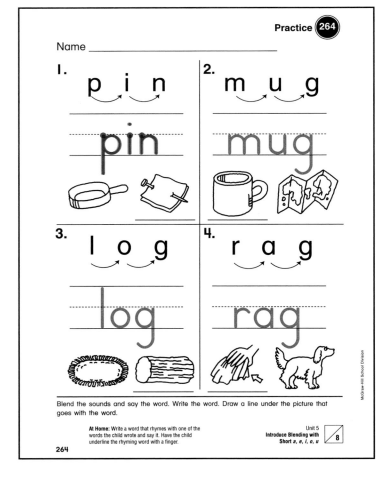

1. p i n
   pin

2. m u g
   mug

3. l o g
   log

4. r a g
   rag

Blend the sounds and say the word. Write the word. Draw a line under the picture that goes with the word.

At Home: Write a word that rhymes with one of the words the child wrote and say it. Have the child underline the rhyming word with a finger.

Unit 5
Introduce Blending with
Short a, e, i, o, u   8

264

Gg   Name _____

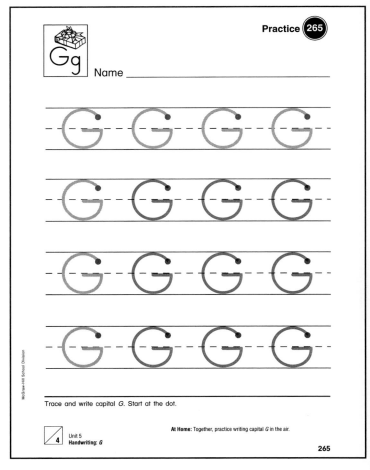

G G G G
G G G G
G G G G
G G G G

Trace and write capital G. Start at the dot.

4   Unit 5
Handwriting: G

At Home: Together, practice writing capital G in the air.

265

Pug • PRACTICE

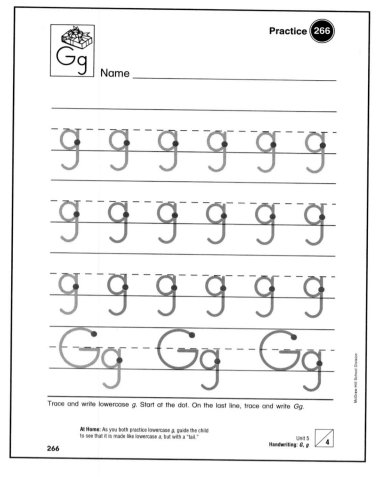

Gg

Name _____

g g g g g g

g g g g g g

g g g g g g

Gg Gg Gg

Trace and write lowercase g. Start at the dot. On the last line, trace and write Gg.

At Home: As you both practice lowercase g, guide the child to see that it is made like lowercase a, but with a "tail."

266

Unit 5
Handwriting: G, g 4

Name _____

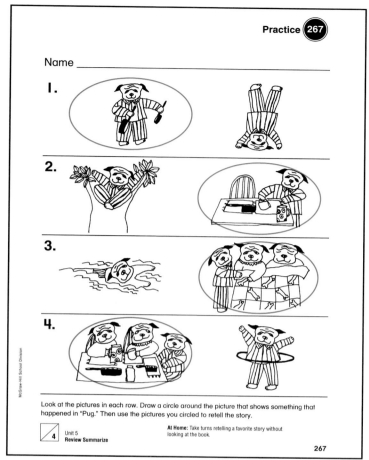

1.

2.

3.

4.

Look at the pictures in each row. Draw a circle around the picture that shows something that happened in "Pug." Then use the pictures you circled to retell the story.

Unit 5
Review Summarize 4

At Home: Take turns retelling a favorite story without looking at the book.

267

Name _____

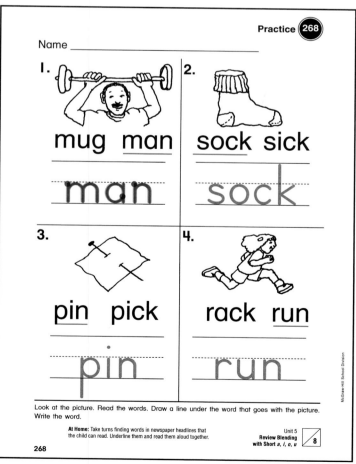

1.

mug man

man

2.

sock sick

sock

3.

pin pick

pin

4.

rack run

run

Look at the picture. Read the words. Draw a line under the word that goes with the picture. Write the word.

At Home: Take turns finding words in newspaper headlines that the child can read. Underline them and read them aloud together.

268

Unit 5
Review Blending
with Short a, i, o, u 8

Name _____

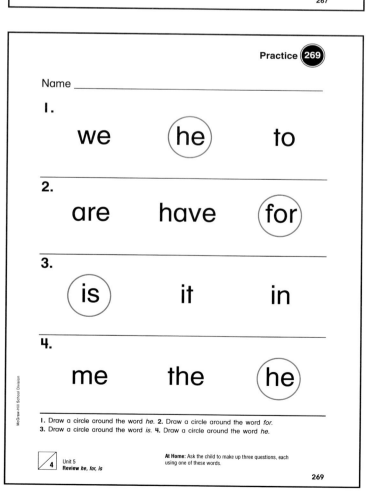

1.

we   (he)   to

2.

are   have   (for)

3.

(is)   it   in

4.

me   the   (he)

1. Draw a circle around the word he. 2. Draw a circle around the word for.
3. Draw a circle around the word is. 4. Draw a circle around the word he.

Unit 5
Review he, for, is 4

At Home: Ask the child to make up three questions, each using one of these words.

269

T13

A Pet for Ken • PRACTICE

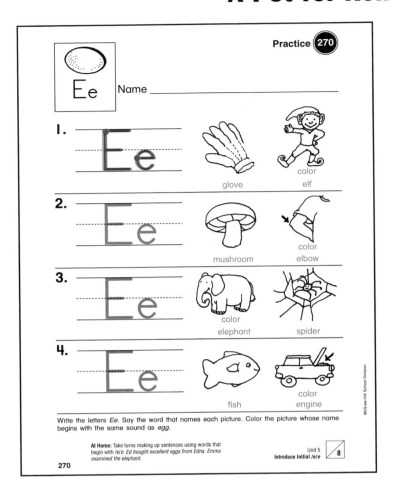

Practice **270**

Ee Name _____

1. Ee — glove — color elf

2. Ee — mushroom — color elbow

3. Ee — color elephant — spider

4. Ee — fish — color engine

Write the letters *Ee*. Say the word that names each picture. Color the picture whose name begins with the same sound as *egg*.

At Home: Take turns making up sentences using words that begin with /e/e: *Ed bought excellent eggs from Edna. Emma examined the elephant.*

Unit 5
Introduce Initial /e/e   8

270

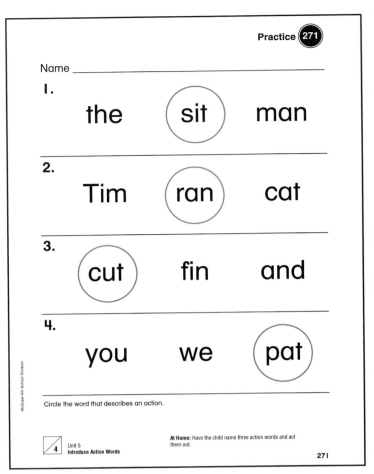

Practice **271**

Name _____

1. the (sit) man

2. Tim (ran) cat

3. (cut) fin and

4. you we (pat)

Circle the word that describes an action.

Unit 5
Introduce Action Words   4

At Home: Have the child name three action words and act them out.

271

Practice **272**

_e_ Name _____

e e

color web — color bed — fish

dog — pig — color pen

sock — color nest

Write the letter *e*. Say the word that names each picture. Listen for the sound in the middle of the word. Color each picture whose name has the same middle sound as *net*.

At Home: Take turns saying other words that have the /e/ sound as in *red, peg, set,* and so on. Help the child find at least two of these words that rhyme (for example, *bed/red*).

Unit 5
Introduce Medial /e/e   9

272

Practice **273**

Name _____

1. 3 2 1

2. 3 2 1

3. 2 1 3

Look at the pictures. Write *1* on the line under the picture that shows the beginning of the story. Write *2* on the line that shows the middle of the story. Write *3* on the line that shows the end of the story.

Unit 5
Review Story Structure   9

At Home: Ask about the child's day at school. Fold a piece of paper into three sections. Have the child draw what happened in the beginning, the middle, and the end of the day.

273

T14 *Annotated Workbooks*

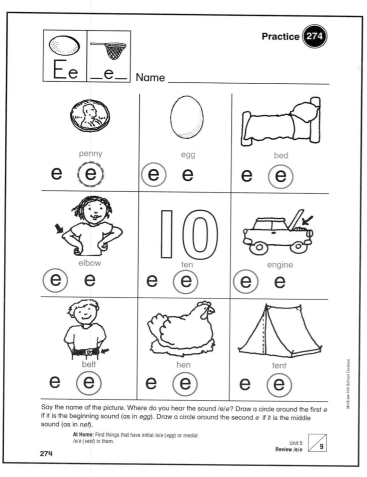

Ee __e__ Name _____

penny · egg · bed

e (e) · (e) e · e (e)

elbow · ten · engine

(e) e · e (e) · (e) e

belt · hen · tent

e (e) · e (e) · e (e)

Say the name of the picture. Where do you hear the sound /e/e? Draw a circle around the first *e* if it is the beginning sound (as in *egg*). Draw a circle around the second *e* if it is the middle sound (as in *net*).

At Home: Find things that have initial /e/e (*egg*) or medial /e/e (*vest*) in them.

274 · Unit 5 · Review /e/e · 9

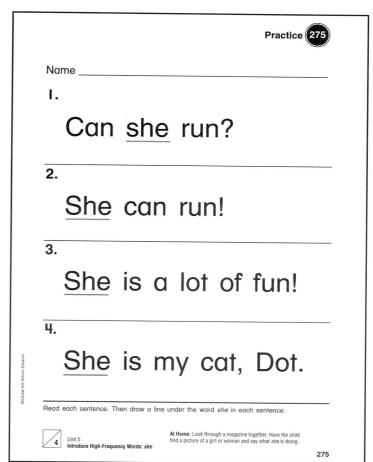

Name _____

1.

Can she run?

2.

She can run!

3.

She is a lot of fun!

4.

She is my cat, Dot.

Read each sentence. Then draw a line under the word *she* in each sentence.

4 · Unit 5 · Introduce High-Frequency Words: *she*

At Home: Look through a magazine together. Have the child find a picture of a girl or woman and say what *she* is doing.

275

Name _____

1. n e t
net

2. t e n
ten

3. p e n
pen

4. m e n
men

Blend the sounds and say the word. Write the word. Draw a line under the picture that goes with the word.

At Home: Write p_n three times. Have the child make words by adding *a*, *i*, and *e* on the blanks. Say each word and use it in a sentence.

276 · Unit 5 · Introduce Blending with Short *e* · 8

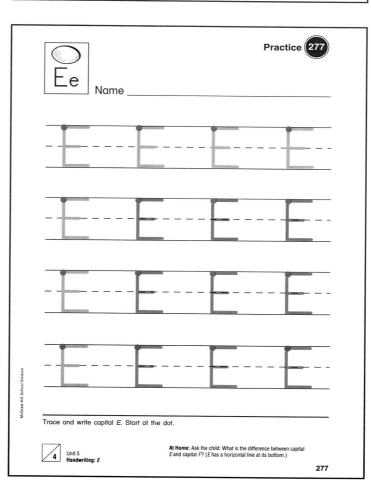

Ee Name _____

E E E E

E E E E

E E E E

E E E E

Trace and write capital E. Start at the dot.

4 · Unit 5 · Handwriting: *E*

At Home: Ask the child: What is the difference between capital *E* and capital *F*? (*E* has a horizontal line at its bottom.)

277

Practice 278

Ee

Name _____

e e e e e e

e e e e e e

e e e e e e

Ee Ee Ee

Trace and write lowercase *e*. Start at the dot. On the last line, trace and write *Ee*.

At Home: Together, practice writing *Ee*. As you write, talk about how the two forms of the letter are the same and how they are different.

Unit 5
Handwriting: E, e 4

278

Practice 279

Name _____

1.

2 1 3

2.

2 3 1

3.

3 2 1

Look at the pictures. Write *1* on the line under the picture that shows the beginning of the story. Write *2* on the line that shows the middle of the story. Write *3* on the line that shows the end of the story.

At Home: Take turns telling the beginning, middle, and end of each other's favorite stories.

Unit 5
Review Story Structure 9

279

Practice 280

Name _____

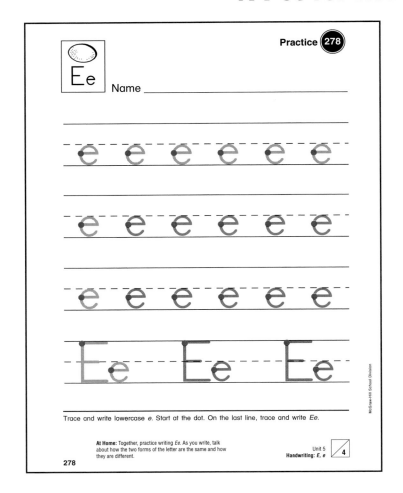

1. leg let

leg

2. rug red

rug

3. pet pen

pet

4. fin fed

fed

Look at the picture. Read the words. Draw a line under the word that goes with the picture. Write the word.

At Home: Take turns rhyming words with these short *e* and short *u* words: *red, leg, let, mug, fun, up.*

Unit 5
Review Blending with Short e, u 8

280

Practice 281

Name _____

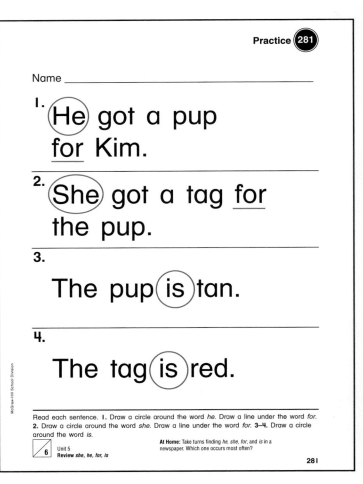

1. (He) got a pup for Kim.

2. (She) got a tag for the pup.

3. The pup (is) tan.

4. The tag (is) red.

Read each sentence. 1. Draw a circle around the word *he*. Draw a line under the word *for*. 2. Draw a circle around the word *she*. Draw a line under the word *for*. 3–4. Draw a circle around the word *is*.

At Home: Take turns finding *he, she, for,* and *is* in a newspaper. Which one occurs most often?

Unit 5
Review she, he, for, is 6

281

A Big Bug • PRACTICE

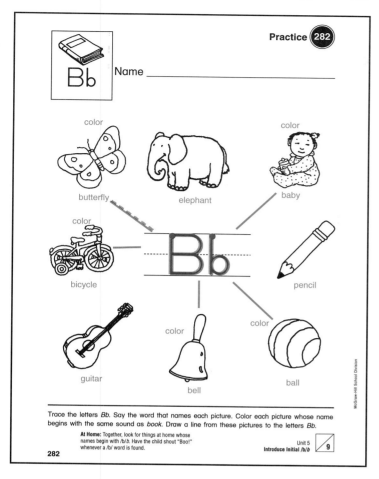

Bb

Name _____

color — butterfly

elephant

color — baby

color — bicycle

Bb

pencil

guitar

color — bell

color — ball

Trace the letters *Bb*. Say the word that names each picture. Color each picture whose name begins with the same sound as *book*. Draw a line from these pictures to the letters *Bb*.

At Home: Together, look for things at home whose names begin with /b/b. Have the child shout "Boo!" whenever a /b/ word is found.

282

Unit 5
Introduce Initial /b/b 9

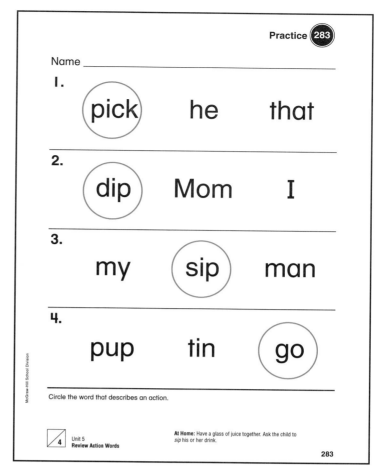

Name _____

1. (pick)   he   that

2. (dip)   Mom   I

3. my   (sip)   man

4. pup   tin   (go)

Circle the word that describes an action.

4 | Unit 5
Review Action Words

At Home: Have a glass of juice together. Ask the child to *sip* his or her drink.

283

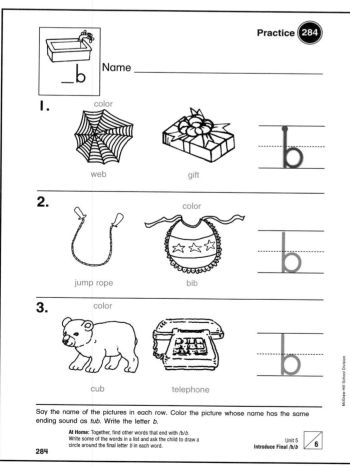

_b

Name _____

1. color — web   gift   b

2. jump rope   color — bib   b

3. color — cub   telephone   b

Say the name of the pictures in each row. Color the picture whose name has the same ending sound as *tub*. Write the letter *b*.

At Home: Together, find other words that end with /b/b. Write some of the words in a list and ask the child to draw a circle around the final letter *b* in each word.

284

Unit 5
Introduce Final /b/b 6

Name _____

1.

2.

3.

4.

Look at the pictures in each row. Draw a circle around the picture that shows something that happened in "The Enormous Carrot." Then use the pictures you circled to retell the story.

4 | Unit 5
Review Summarize

At Home: Take turns telling each other what a favorite movie was about.

285

A Big Bug • PRACTICE

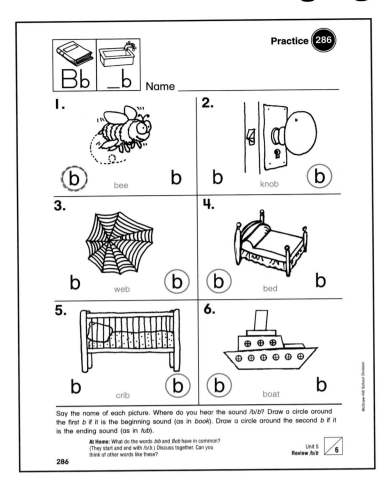

Bb _b Name _____

1.
bee   b   b

2.
b   knob   b

3.
b   web   b

4.
b   bed   b

5.
b   crib   b

6.
b   boat   b

Say the name of each picture. Where do you hear the sound /b/b? Draw a circle around the first *b* if it is the beginning sound (as in *book*). Draw a circle around the second *b* if it is the ending sound (as in *tub*).

At Home: What do the words *bib* and *Bob* have in common? (They start and end with /b/b.) Discuss together. Can you think of other words like these?

Unit 5
Review /b/b 6

286

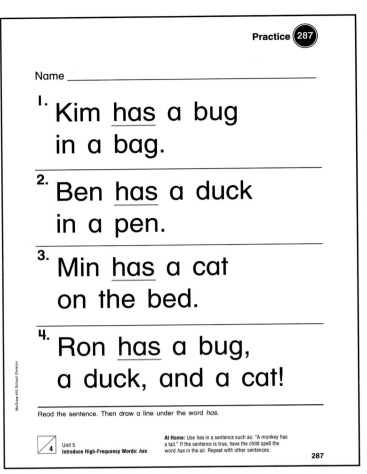

Name _____

1. Kim <u>has</u> a bug in a bag.

2. Ben <u>has</u> a duck in a pen.

3. Min <u>has</u> a cat on the bed.

4. Ron <u>has</u> a bug, a duck, and a cat!

Read the sentence. Then draw a line under the word *has*.

Unit 5
Introduce High-Frequency Words: *has*

At Home: Use *has* in a sentence such as: "A monkey has a tail." If the sentence is true, have the child spell the word *has* in the air. Repeat with other sentences.

287

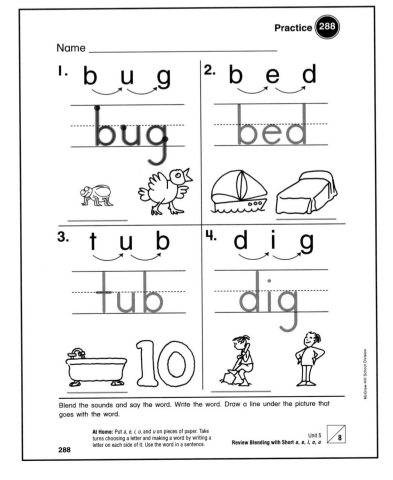

Name _____

1. b u g
bug

2. b e d
bed

3. t u b
tub
10

4. d i g
dig

Blend the sounds and say the word. Write the word. Draw a line under the picture that goes with the word.

At Home: Put *a, e, i, o,* and *u* on pieces of paper. Take turns choosing a letter and making a word by writing a letter on each side of it. Use the word in a sentence.

Unit 5
Review Blending with Short *a, e, i, o, u* 8

288

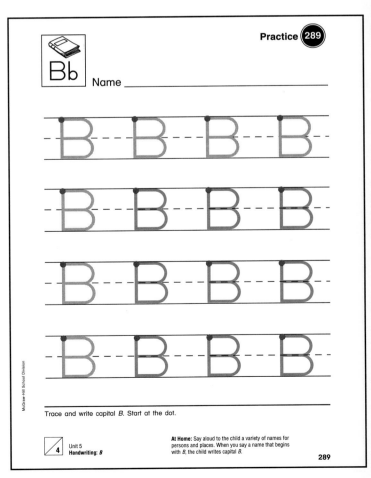

Bb Name _____

B B B B

B B B B

B B B B

B B B B

Trace and write capital *B*. Start at the dot.

Unit 5
Handwriting: *B*

At Home: Say aloud to the child a variety of names for persons and places. When you say a name that begins with *B*, the child writes capital *B*.

289

Practice 290

Bb

Name _____

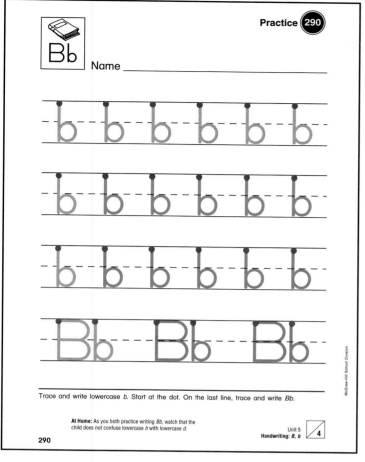

Trace and write lowercase *b*. Start at the dot. On the last line, trace and write *Bb*.

At Home: As you both practice writing *Bb*, watch that the child does not confuse lowercase *b* with lowercase *d*.

290

Unit 5
Handwriting: B, b 4

Practice 291

Name _____

1.

2.

3.

4.

Look at the pictures in each row. Draw a circle around the picture that shows something that happened in "A Big Bug." Then use the pictures you circled to retell the story.

4 Unit 5
Review Summarize

At Home: Take turns retelling a favorite fairy tale or folk tale.

291

Practice 292

Name _____

1. rub <u>cub</u>

cub

2. <u>pen</u> ten

pen

3. but <u>bat</u>

bat

4. log fog

log

Look at the picture. Read the words. Draw a line under the word that goes with the picture. Write the word.

At Home: Write *p_g*. Take turns adding *a, e, i, o,* and *u*. If you decide the word you've made is a real word, circle it. Continue with *b_t*.

292

Unit 5
Review Blending with Short *a, e, i, o, u* 8

Practice 293

Name _____

1. "Is it for <u>me</u>?"
<u>he</u> said.

2. "It is <u>for</u> you,"
<u>she</u> said.

3. Mom <u>has</u> a cap
for me!

Read each sentence. 1. Draw a line under the words *me* and *he*. 2. Draw a line under the words *for* and *she*. 3. Draw a line under the word *has*.

5 Unit 5
Review *has, he, she, me, for*

At Home: Make letter cards for the letters *a, e, f, h, m, o, r,* and *s*. Have the child make the words *has, he, she, me,* and *for*.

293

A Pup and a Cat • PRACTICE

Kk   Gg   Bb

Name _____

1. (k) g b king

2. k g (b) boat

3. k g (b) bee

4. k (g) b guitar

5. k (g) b goat

6. (k) g b key

Say the name of each picture. Draw a circle around the letter that stands for the sound you hear at the beginning of each picture name.

At Home: Make *k*, *g*, and *b* letter cards. Show them one at a time. Have the child say a word that starts with the selected letter.

Unit 5
Review Initial /k/k, /g/g, /b/b   6

294

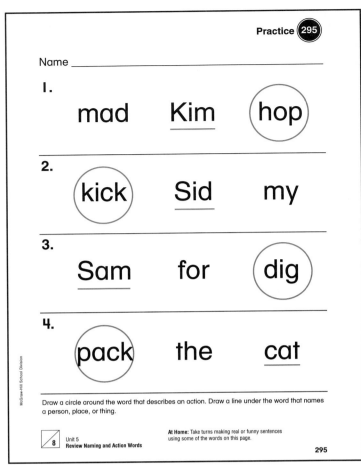

Name _____

1. mad   Kim   (hop)

2. (kick)   Sid   my

3. Sam   for   (dig)

4. (pack)   the   cat

Draw a circle around the word that describes an action. Draw a line under the word that names a person, place, or thing.

8 Unit 5
Review Naming and Action Words

At Home: Take turns making real or funny sentences using some of the words on this page.

295

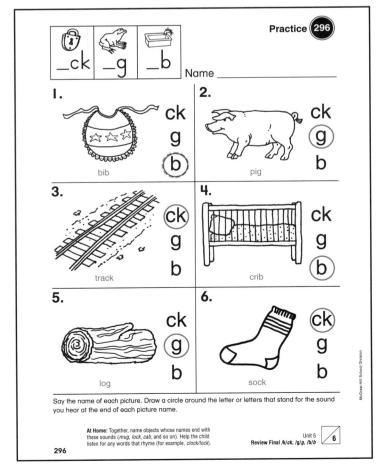

_ck   _g   _b

Name _____

1. ck g (b) bib

2. ck (g) b pig

3. (ck) g b track

4. ck g (b) crib

5. ck (g) b log

6. (ck) g b sock

Say the name of each picture. Draw a circle around the letter or letters that stand for the sound you hear at the end of each picture name.

At Home: Together, name objects whose names end with these sounds (*mug, lock, cab*, and so on). Help the child listen for any words that rhyme (for example, *clock/lock*).

Unit 5
Review Final /k/ck, /g/g, /b/b   6

296

Name _____

1. 3   1   2

2. 3   2   1

3. 2   3   1

Look at the pictures. Write *1* on the line under the picture that shows the beginning of the story. Write *2* on the line that shows the middle of the story. Write *3* on the line that shows the end of the story.

9 Unit 5
Review Story Structure

At Home: After a familiar activity, briefly review the first part, middle part, and last part and then number them 1, 2, 3. For example: 1. Cook supper. 2. Eat supper. 3. Do the dishes.

297

A Pup and a Cat • PRACTICE

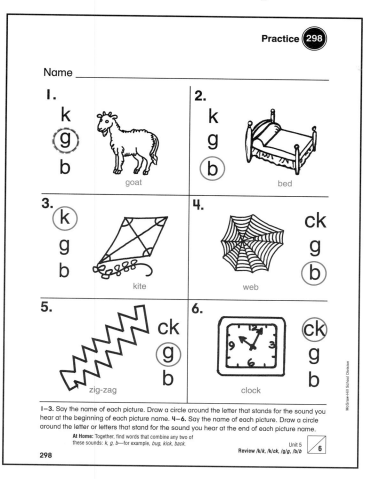

Name _____

1. k (g) b — goat

2. k g (b) — bed

3. (k) g b — kite

4. ck g (b) — web

5. ck (g) b — zig-zag

6. (ck) g b — clock

1–3. Say the name of each picture. Draw a circle around the letter that stands for the sound you hear at the beginning of each picture name. 4–6. Say the name of each picture. Draw a circle around the letter or letters that stand for the sound you hear at the end of each picture name.

At Home: Together, find words that combine any two of these sounds: *k, g, b*—for example, *bug, kick, back.*

298

Unit 5
Review /k/k, /k/ck, /g/g, /b/b   6

Name _____

1. Kim <u>has</u> a pup <u>for</u> me.

2. <u>He</u> can tug and run.

3. Kim <u>has</u> a cat <u>for</u> you.

4. <u>She</u> can run and have fun.

Read each sentence. 1. Draw a line under the words *has* and *for*. 2. Draw a line under the word *he*. 3. Draw a line under the words *has* and *for*. 4. Draw a line under the word *she*.

6 Unit 5
Review *for, he, she, has*

At Home: Print each of the four Review Words on a card. Take turns reading them and using them in sentences.

299

Name _____

1. r o ck — rock

2. b a g — bag

3. b i g — big

4. l e g — leg

Blend the sounds and say the word. Write the word. Draw a line under the picture that goes with the word.

At Home: Take turns writing a secret word on a scrap of paper and hiding it in one hand. If the other person chooses the hand with the word, he or she reads it.

300

Unit 5
Review Blending with Short *a, e, i, o, u*   8

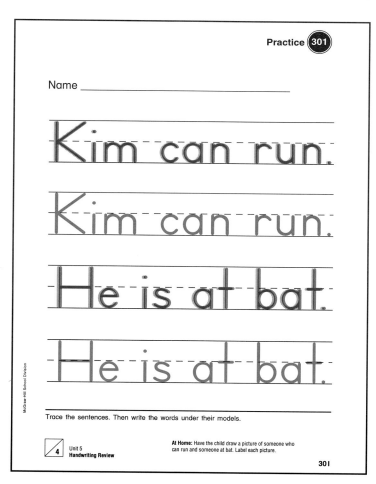

Name _____

Kim can run.

Kim can run.

He is at bat.

He is at bat.

Trace the sentences. Then write the words under their models.

4 Unit 5
Handwriting Review

At Home: Have the child draw a picture of someone who can run and someone at bat. Label each picture.

301

A Pup and a Cat • PRACTICE

Name _____

I fed a duck.

I fed a duck.

A bug bit me.

A bug bit me.

Trace the sentences. Then write the words under their models.

At Home: Have the child draw his or her favorite animal.
Help the child label it: *I have a ____.*

Unit 5
Handwriting Review 4

302

Name _____

Look at the pictures in each row. Draw a circle around the picture that shows something that happened in "A Pup and a Cat." Then use the pictures you circled to retell the story.

4 Unit 5
Review Summarize

At Home: Take turns telling about a funny event you both experienced.

303

Name _____

1. rub <u>rug</u>

rug

2. <u>Rick</u> rid

Rick

3. peg <u>pig</u>

pig

4. tan <u>tag</u>

tag

Look at the picture. Read the words. Draw a line under the word that goes with the picture. Write the word.

At Home: Draw a ladder with four rungs. Write the letters *ap* on each rung. Climb the ladder together by saying a word that ends with *ap* as you get to each rung (*cap, rap, lap, nap*). Repeat with *ub, ock,* and *et.*

Unit 5
Review Blending with Short *a, e, i, o, u* 8

304

Name _____

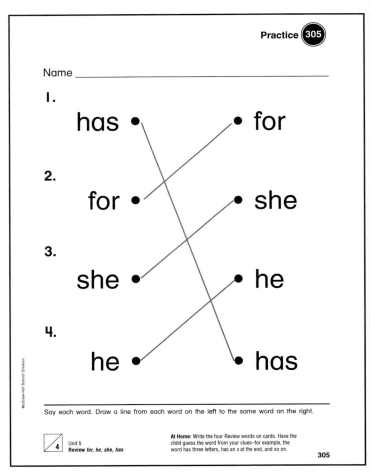

1. has •   • for

2. for •   • she

3. she •   • he

4. he •   • has

Say each word. Draw a line from each word on the left to the same word on the right.

4 Unit 5
Review for, he, she, has

At Home: Write the four Review words on cards. Have the child guess the word from your clues–for example, the word *has* has three letters, has an *s* at the end, and so on.

305

Initial /k/ *k;* Final /k/ *ck*

OBJECTIVES Children will apply letter/sound associations for /k/ *k, ck.* They will identify words that begin or end with /k/.

Alternate Activities

Visual

SHAPE BOOKS

Materials: kite-shaped, blank book for each child; crayons or markers

Children will draw and label objects whose names begin or end with /k/.

- For each child, create a blank, kite-shaped book by cutting pages in the shape of a kite and stapling them together.

- Help children brainstorm a list of words that begin the same as *kite.* Point out that *k* stands for the beginning sound.

- Explain that /k/ can also come at the end of words, and that the letters *ck* stand for the sound in that position. Brainstorm words that end with /k/, such as *lock, rock,* and *chick.*

Have children label their kite books *k.* On the inside pages, have them draw pictures whose names begin or end with /k/. Help children label their drawings. ▶**Intrapersonal**

Kinesthetic

UNLOCK WITH A KEY

Materials: old keys, pictures of objects whose names begin or end with /k/, pictures of objects whose names begin and end with other sounds

Children will pretend to "unlock" pictures whose names begin or end with /k/.

- Point out that the word *key* begins with /k/ and that the letter *k* stands for that sound.

- Ask children what keys are used to do. (unlock doors) Point out that *unlock* ends with /k/, and that the letters *ck* stand for the sound at the end of the word.

- Display a variety of pictures. Have pairs of children take turns trying to "unlock" the pictures. Explain that the keys will only unlock pictures whose names begin or end with /k/. Have children sort the pictures. ▶**Linguistic**

Auditory

KANGAROO

Children will respond with different actions to words that begin or end with /k/.

- Ask children what they know about kangaroos. (kangaroos hop) Point out that *kangaroo* begins with /k/. Have children pretend to hop as a kangaroo does.

- Explain that *unlock* ends with /k/. Have children pretend to use a key to unlock a lock.

- Read the following list of words. Have children hop like a kangaroo if the word begins with /k/, or pretend to unlock a lock if the word ends with /k/.

| king | pick | kite | pack |
| sock | kiss | kitten | luck |

▶**Bodily/Kinesthetic**

 **CD-ROM**

Naming Words

Alternate Activities

Kinesthetic

NAMING WALK

GROUP **Materials:** art paper, crayons or markers

Children will go on a walk to notice things around them. They will use naming words to draw a picture of a place they saw.

- Take children on a walk around the school. Have them identify things they see.

- When back in the classroom, help each child plan a drawing of a place you saw on the walk, such as the playground, garden area, or lunchroom. Ask children to name things that belong in the place.

- Have children include in their drawing each object they named.

- When children have finished drawing, label the objects in each picture so that children can see the naming words and try to blend and read them. ▶**Spatial**

Visual

NURSERY RHYME NAMING WORDS

PARTNERS **Materials:** illustrated nursery rhymes

Children will use illustrations to identify naming words in nursery rhymes.

- Share a familiar nursery rhyme with children, leaving out the naming words. Have children point to details in the illustration and say the naming word that completes each line.

- Have partners take turns saying the rhyme, pointing to the pictures, and supplying the naming words. ▶**Interpersonal**

Auditory

LISTS OF NAMING WORDS

GROUP **Materials:** chart paper, markers

Children will suggest naming words for different categories.

- On separate pages of chart paper, write various headings, such as *toys, clothes, foods, games, places to have fun,* and *names* of *people in a family.* Remind children that naming words can identify people, places, or things.

- Have children suggest naming words for each category. Record children's responses. You may wish to have children illustrate each word.

- Invite children to think of additional categories and suggest naming words for these categories as well. ▶**Logical/Mathematical**

Story Structure

 OBJECTIVES Children will identify the three parts of a story—*beginning, middle,* and *end.*

Alternate Activities

Visual

ACCORDION BOOKS

 Materials: strips of paper, crayons or markers

Children will draw a story in three panels to represent the beginning, the middle, and the end.

- Remind children that every story has a beginning, a middle, and an end.

- Invite children to tell a story related to a current topic of study, an upcoming holiday, or a traditional tale. Have each child tell his or her story to a partner.

- Fold a strip of paper into thirds for each child to make an accordion book. Show children the three sections. Explain that the sections represent the beginning, middle, and end of their story. Then have children draw a picture in each section, illustrating the story in its three parts.

- Invite children to share their books with classmates. ▶**Spatial**

Auditory

STORY IN A SONG

 Children will identify the beginning, middle, and end of a story as told through a song.

- Lead children in singing a song that tells a story in sequence, such as "Oats, Peas, Beans and Barley Grow," or "There Was an Old Lady Who Swallowed a Fly."

- Ask children what happened at the beginning, middle, and end of the story. ▶**Musical**

Kinesthetic

RETELL THE STORY

Materials: photocopies of illustrations from stories to represent *beginning, middle,* and *end*

Children will work in groups to arrange story events in order.

- Photocopy three illustrations each from familiar stories to represent the beginning, middle, and end of each story.

- Organize children into groups of three. Give each group a set of illustrations in mixed order.

- Have each child hold one of the illustrations. Have children in each group arrange themselves so that the pictures retell the story. ▶**Bodily/Kinesthetic**

High-Frequency Words
for, he, she, has

OBJECTIVES Children will read fluently the high-frequency words *for, he, she,* and *has.*

Alternate Activities

Visual

SPIN A WORD

PARTNERS **Materials:** paper plates, construction paper, scissors, brads, markers

Children will make a spinner to practice reading high-frequency words.

- For each child, draw lines to divide a paper plate into four sections. Attach a construction-paper arrow with a brad.

- **WRITING** On the chalkboard, write the words *for, he, she, has.* Read them with children. Have children copy the words from the chalkboard, one onto each section of their spinner.

- Have partners use the spinner to practice reading words. As children read each word, encourage them to use it in an oral sentence. ▶**Linguistic**

Kinesthetic

BOUNCE A WORD

GROUP **Materials:** large plastic ball, masking tape, marker

Children will bounce a ball labeled with high-frequency words. They will read the word their right index finger is on or nearest to.

- Write the high-frequency words *for, he, she,* and *has* on separate strips of masking tape. Attach the tape to a plastic ball.

- Have groups of children take turns bouncing the ball to one another. Have them read the word their right index finger is touching or is nearest to when they catch the ball. Ask them to use the word in an oral sentence. ▶**Bodily/Kinesthetic**

Auditory

SING A WORD

PARTNERS **Materials:** index cards, marker

Children will identify high-frequency words as they sing a song.

- **WRITING** Have each child make a set of individual word cards for *for, he, she,* and *has.* Help children read the words.

- Lead children in singing the following pattern to the tune of "For He's a Jolly Good Fellow."

  He has a ___ for ____. (repeat twice more)

  And he has a wonderful time!

- Have children supply words to complete the pattern, such as *He has a* bike *for* riding. Sing the verse, and have children point to high-frequency word cards as those words are sung.

- Repeat the verse, replacing *he* with *she.* ▶**Musical**

Initial and Final *g*

OBJECTIVES Children will apply letter/sound associations for *g*. They will identify words that begin or end with *g*.

Alternate Activities

Kinesthetic

GALLOP FOR *G*!

Children will gallop when they hear words that begin with *g*.

- Ask children to demonstrate a gallop. Point out that *gallop* begins with *g* and that the letter *g* stands for that sound. Explain that *g* can also come at the end of words, as in *bug*.

- Have children suggest words that begin or end with *g*. Tell children you will say some words. If they begin or end with *g*, then children should gallop. If the words do not begin or end with *g*, children should stand still. ▶**Bodily/Kinesthetic**

Auditory

TIC-TAC-TOE

Materials: masking tape, pictures of objects whose names begin or end with *g*

Partners will play *tic-tac-toe* using pictures of objects whose names begin or end with *g*.

- Use masking tape to make a tic-tac-toe grid on the floor.

- Supply pairs with five pictures of objects whose names begin with *g* and five pictures of objects whose names end with *g*. The pictures will serve as X's and O's.

- Have each child take one stack of pictures, either those beginning or those ending with *g*. Have them play the game by taking turns naming their picture and placing it on the grid. Players should try to get three pictures in a row across, down, or diagonally. Continue playing until each pair has had a chance to play. ▶**Interpersonal**

Visual

GUM PACK OF WORDS

Materials: sentence strips, marker, scissors, empty food box, construction paper, tape

Children will blend sounds to read words that begin or end with *g*.

- Cover a long empty food box, such as one pasta comes in, with construction paper. Label the box *gum* to simulate a gum wrapper.

- Cut sentence strips to fit inside the box and serve as sticks of sugar-free gum. On the strips, write words that begin or end with *g*, such as *gum, gas, got, mug, rag, dig*. Put the strips inside the box.

- Have children use the strips to practice blending the sounds to read the words. ▶**Linguistic**

 **CD-ROM**

Summarize

OBJECTIVES Children will summarize familiar stories and stories depicted in pictures.

Kinesthetic

PUPPET TELLS A STORY

ONE **Materials:** paper bags, crayons or markers

Children will use a puppet to pretend to be a main character summarizing story events.

- Have each child select a story to summarize.

- Ask children to use a paper bag to create a puppet of a main character in the story.

- Have children pretend to be the character. Encourage them to summarize the story, briefly retelling it as if they were the character.
  ▶Linguistic

Visual

COMIC SUMMARIES

PARTNERS **Materials:** comic strips

Pairs of children will look at comic strips and summarize what they see depicted.

- Provide each pair of children with a comic strip. Use as many strips from the same series as possible. Have children talk about what they see and summarize the strip.

- Have several pairs mix up their strips. Have one pair summarize a strip as the other pairs identify it. ▶Logical/Mathematical

Auditory

SUMMARY RIDDLES

ONE Children will give clues about a familiar story to help classmates guess the title.

- Model giving summary clues about a story by summarizing a familiar tale in a couple of sentences. For example, *A little girl isn't supposed to talk to strangers, but she stops and talks to a wolf. Because she does, the wolf tricks the little girl and tries to eat her. A woodcutter saves the girl.*

- Tell children to raise their hand when they know the title of the story.

- Have children summarize other familiar tales and provide clues for classmates to guess.
  ▶Interpersonal

Initial and Medial Short *e*

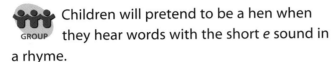

OBJECTIVES Children will apply letter/sound associations for short *e*. They will identify words that have the short *e* sound in the initial and medial positions.

Alternate Activities

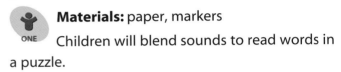

Auditory

HEN PECKS

Children will pretend to be a hen when they hear words with the short *e* sound in a rhyme.

- Share the following rhyme with children. Ask them to pretend to walk like a hen when they hear words that have the short *e* sound.

  Mrs. Hen pecks the ground.

  Mrs. Hen checks around.

  Where are her ten chicks?

  Some are in the pen, and the rest near Mrs. Hen!
  ▶**Bodily/Kinesthetic**

Kinesthetic

YES! CARDS

Materials: index cards, markers, pictures of objects whose names contain the short *e* sound, pictures of objects whose names contain other short vowel sounds

Children will hold up a *yes* card when they see a picture whose name has the short *e* sound in the initial or medial positions.

- On the chalkboard, write *yes* and read it to children. Point out that the word has the short *e* sound.

  Have children write the word *yes* on an index card.

- Show a variety of pictures, some of whose objects contain the short *e* sound and some of whose objects do not. Have children stand up and show their *yes* cards if the name has short *e*. Lead children to notice whether the short *e* sound comes at the beginning or in the middle of the word. ▶**Logical/Mathematical**

Visual

BLENDING PUZZLES

Materials: paper, markers

Children will blend sounds to read words in a puzzle.

- Create simple crossword puzzles that have intersecting boxes—three going down and three going across. In the puzzles, write words with the short *e* sound, such as *net/pet, beg/leg, bet/set, fed/led, men/pen*. Add directional arrows to show which way to read the words.

- Show children how to blend the sounds to read the words. Have them practice blending and reading.

- Have children use each pair of rhyming words in a silly sentence, such as *Is there a pet in that net?*
  ▶**Linguistic**

 **CD-ROM**

Action Words

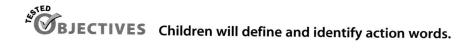

Visual

I CAN DO IT! BOOK

 Materials: paper, stapler, crayons or markers, pencils

Children will use action words to create a book about things they can do.

- Assemble a blank book for each child.

- Tell children that action words tell about doing things. Help children brainstorm things they can do, such as run, draw, sing, and jump.

- Have children draw on each page of the book a different picture of themselves doing something. Record for children what each drawing depicts. Point out the action words.

 On the cover of the book, write the title *I Can Do It!* Also write *by* and have children write their names.

- Invite children to share their books.
▶Intrapersonal

Auditory

ACTION INNOVATIONS

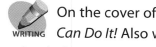 Children will suggest new action words to create innovations on favorite songs.

- Lead children in singing "Ten in the Bed." Help children identify the action words. Have children explain what an action word is; lead them to explain that it is a word that tells about doing something.

- Tell children that you want to sing a new version of the song that uses new action words in place of *roll.* Invite them to suggest other action words and sing them in the verse. ▶Musical

Kinesthetic

TAKING ACTION

 Materials: photos or illustrations of various settings

Children will dramatize various actions that commonly take place in particular settings.

- Gather pictures of various settings, such as a garden, a playground, or a kitchen.

- Share the pictures, and have children pantomime actions someone would likely do in the place, such as digging, pulling weeds, or picking flowers in a garden.

- Invite children to name their actions. Point out that these are action words that tell about doing something. List children's suggestions on the chalkboard. ▶Bodily/Kinesthetic

Initial and Final *b*

OBJECTIVES Children will apply letter/sound associations for *b*. They will identify words that have *b* in the initial and final positions.

Alternate Activities

Visual

B IS FOR BOX

 Materials: refrigerator carton or other large box, crayons or markers

Children will label a large box with pictures and words that begin or end with *b*.

- Find a large box. Cut windows and doors in it. Share the box with children. Point out that *box* begins with *b* and that the letter *b* stands for the sound. Explain that *b* can also come at the end of words, as in *tub*.

Invite children to draw and label on the box. Have them draw objects whose names begin with *b* on the outside of the box. Have them draw objects whose names end with *b* on the inside of the box. Help children label their drawings.
▶**Spatial**

Kinesthetic

BAT THE BALLOON

Materials: a balloon

Partners will take turns supplying words that begin or end with *b* as they bat a balloon back and forth.

- Show children an inflated balloon. Point out that *balloon* begins with *b*.

- Demonstrate how to bat the balloon back and forth softly with a partner. As each person bats the balloon, he or she says a word that begins or ends with *b*. ▶**Bodily/Kinesthetic**

Auditory

OVER THE MOUNTAIN

 Children will innovate on a familiar tune as they supply examples of words that begin or end with *b*.

- Lead children in singing "The Bear Went Over the Mountain." Point out that *bear* begins with *b*.

- Help children brainstorm additional words that begin or end with b to replace *bear,* such as b*ug,* *bat,* or *cab*.

- Guide children as they sing the new verses. ▶**Musical**

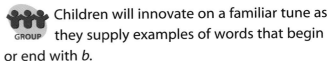 **CD-ROM**

Writing Readiness

Before children begin to write, fine motor skills need to be developed. Here are examples of activities that can be used:

- **Simon Says** Play Simon Says using just finger positions.
- **Finger Plays and Songs** Sing songs such as "Where Is Thumbkin" or "The Eensie, Weensie, Spider" or songs that use Signed English or American Sign Language.
- **Mazes** Use or create mazes, especially ones that require moving the writing instruments from left to right.

The Mechanics of Writing

POSTURE

- Chair height should allow for the feet to rest flat on the floor.
- Desk height should be two inches above the elbows.
- There should be an inch between the child and the desk.
- Children sit erect with the elbows resting on the desk.
- Letter models should be on the desk or at eye level.

PAPER POSITION

- **Right-handed children** should turn the paper so that the lower left-hand corner of the paper points to the abdomen.

- **Left-handed children** should turn the paper so that the lower right-hand corner of the paper points to the abdomen.

- The nondominant hand should anchor the paper near the top so that the paper doesn't slide.
- The paper should be moved up as the child nears the bottom of the paper. Many children won't think of this.

The Writing Instrument Grasp

For handwriting to be functional, the writing instrument must be held in a way that allows for fluid dynamic movement.

FUNCTIONAL GRASP PATTERNS

- **Tripod Grasp** The writing instrument is held with the tip of the thumb and the index finger and rests against the side of the third finger. The thumb and index finger form a circle.

- **Quadrupod Grasp** The writing instrument is held with the tip of the thumb and index finger and rests against the fourth finger. The thumb and index finger form a circle.

INCORRECT GRASP PATTERNS

- **Fisted Grasp** The writing instrument is held in a fisted hand.

- **Pronated Grasp** The instrument is held diagonally within the hand with the tips of the thumb and index finger but with no support from other fingers.

- **Five-Finger Grasp** The writing instrument is held with the tips of all five fingers.

- **Flexed or Hooked Wrist** Flexed or bent wrist is typically seen with left-handed writers but is also present in some right-handed writers.

- To correct wrist position, have children check their writing posture and paper placement.

TO CORRECT GRASPS

- Have children play counting games with an eye dropper and water.
- Have children pick up small objects with a tweezer.
- Do counting games with children picking up small coins using just the thumb and index finger.

Evaluation Checklist

Formation and Strokes

- ☑ Does the child begin letters at the top?
- ☑ Do circles close?
- ☑ Are the horizontal lines straight?
- ☑ Do circular shapes and extender and descender lines touch?
- ☑ Are the heights of all upper-case letters equal?
- ☑ Are the heights of all lower-case letters equal?
- ☑ Are the lengths of the extenders and descenders the same for all letters?

Directionality

- ☑ Do the children form letters starting at the top and moving to the bottom?
- ☑ Are letters formed from left to right?

Spacing

- ☑ Are the spaces between letters equidistant?
- ☑ Are the spaces between words equidistant?
- ☑ Do the letters rest on the line?
- ☑ Are the top, bottom and side margins on the paper even?

Write the Alphabet

Trace and write the letters.

Trace and write the letters.

C C C

c c c

D D D

d d d

Trace and write the letters.

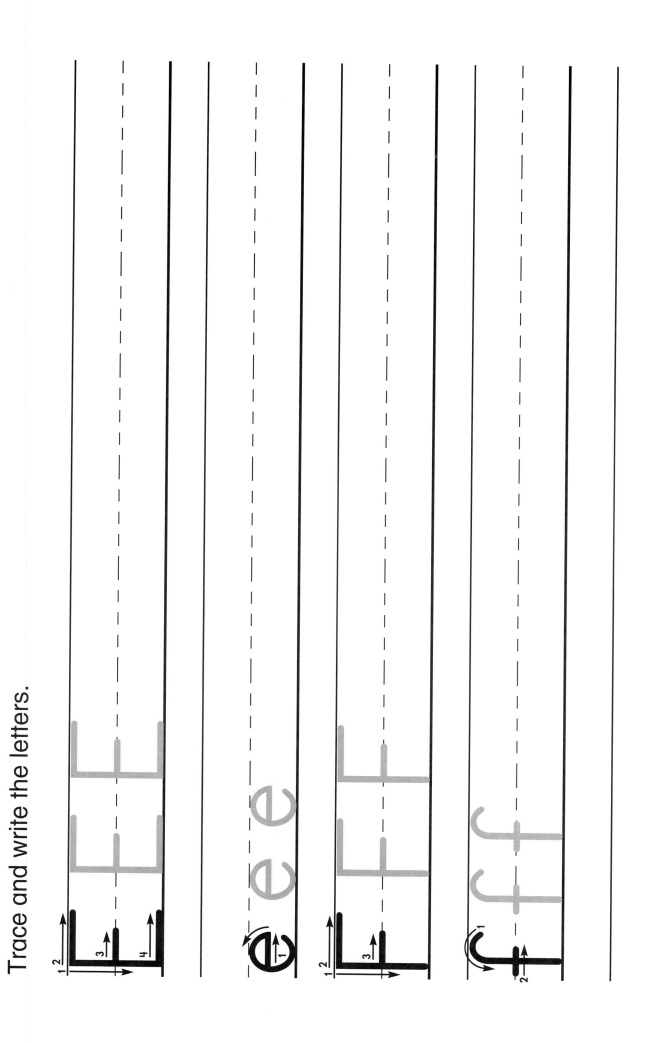

Trace and write the letters.

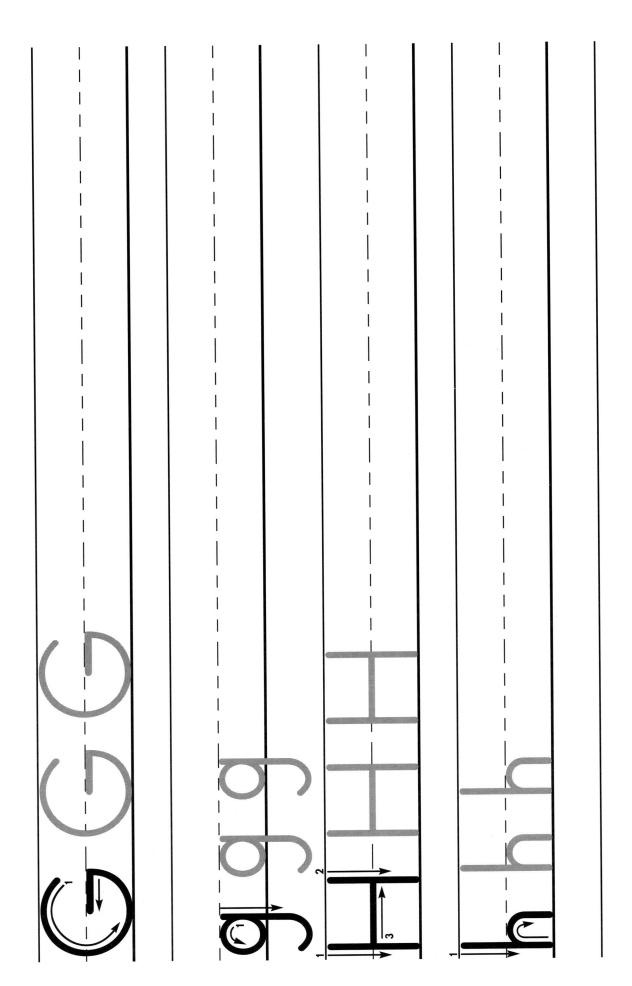

Trace and write the letters.

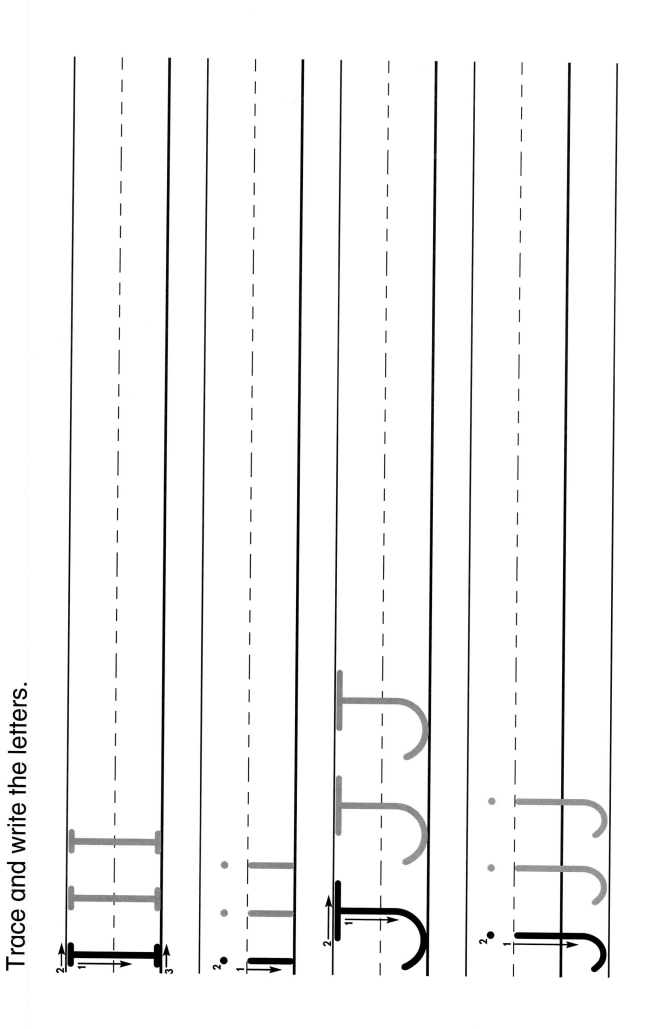

Trace and write the letters.

Trace and write the letters.

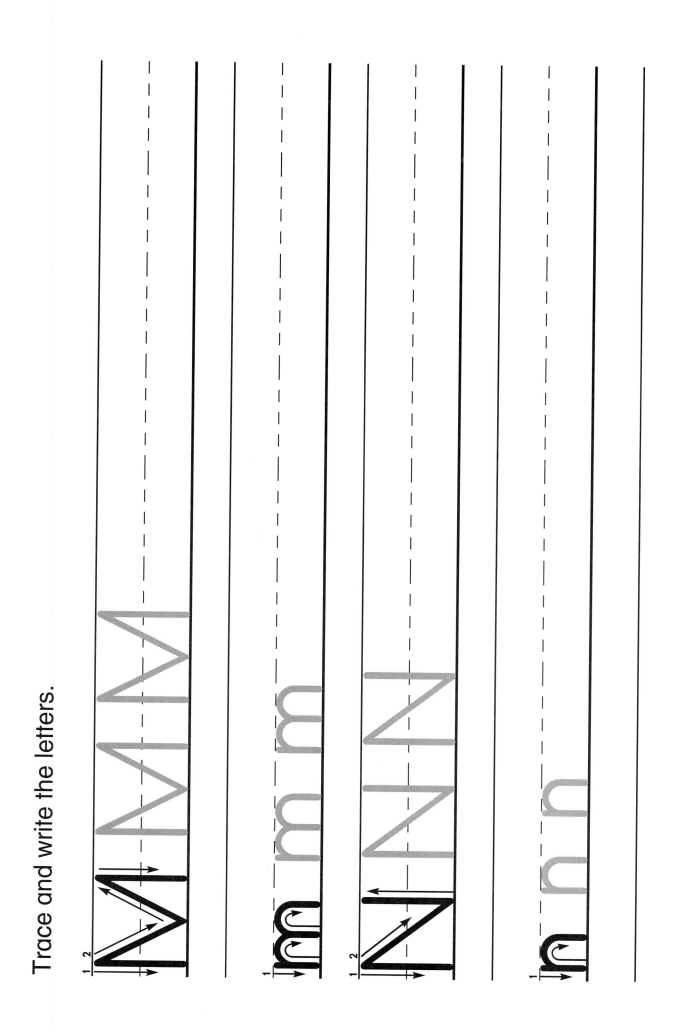

Trace and write the letters.

Trace and write the letters.

Q Q Q

q q q

R R R

r r r

Trace and write the letters.

S S S

s s s

T T T

t t t

Trace and write the letters.

Trace and write the letters.

Trace and write the letters.

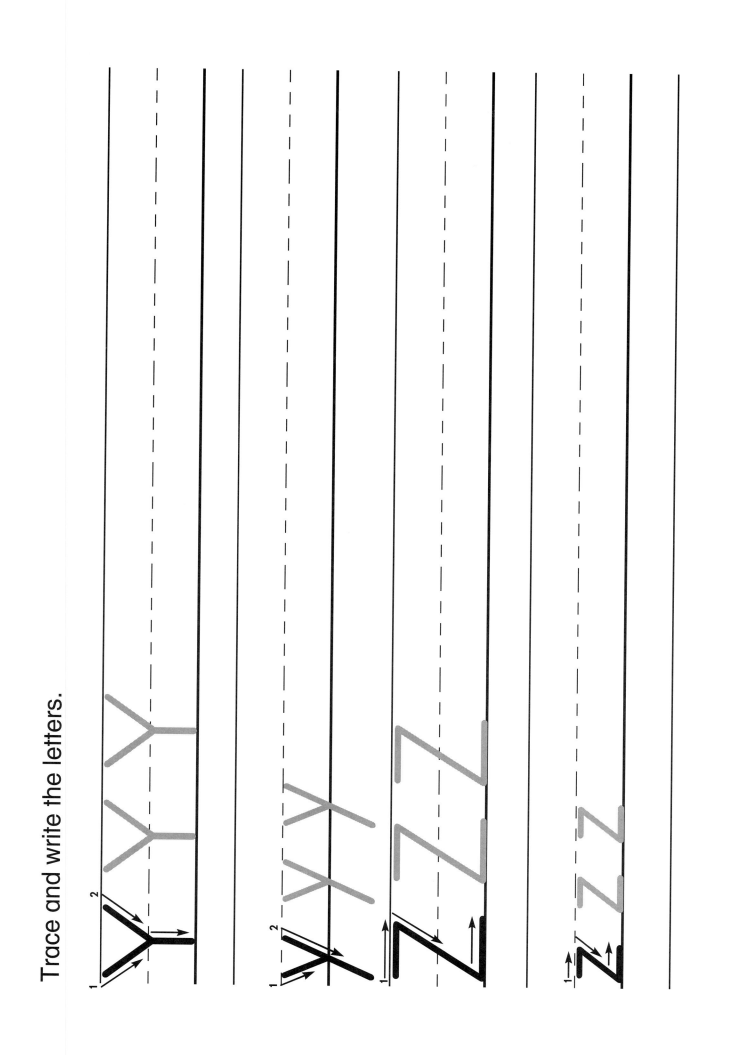

for Dick, Chris, and Mort, who love dogs

Richard wanted a dog, any kind of dog.

But his mother said
a dog was
too much trouble,

5

so she gave him a caterpillar.

6

The caterpillar was very nice.
It looked a little like a dog,

Lhasa Apso

but it was not a dog.
Richard wanted a dog.
His mother said
a dog was too much trouble,

7

so she gave him a mouse.

8

The mouse was very nice.
It looked a little like a dog,

Chihuahua

but it was not a dog.
Richard wanted a dog.
His mother said
a dog was too much trouble,

9

so she gave him a baby alligator.

10

The baby alligator was very nice.
It looked a little like a dog,

Dachshund

but it was not a dog.
Richard wanted a dog.
His mother said
a dog was too much trouble,

11

so she gave him a lamb.

12

The lamb was very nice.
It looked a little like a dog,

Bedlington
Terrier

but it was not a dog.
Richard wanted a dog.
His mother said
a dog was too much trouble,

13

so she gave him a pony.

14

The pony was very nice.
It looked a little like a dog,

Great Dane

but it was not a dog.
Richard wanted a dog.
His mother said
a dog was too much trouble,

15

so she gave him a lion.

16

The lion was very nice.
It looked a little like a dog,

Chow Chow

but it was not a dog.
Richard wanted a dog.
His mother said
a dog was too much trouble,

17

so she gave him a bear.

18

The bear was very nice.
It looked a little like a dog,

Newfoundland

but it was not a dog.

19

All of the animals were very nice,

but Richard still wanted a dog.

20

21

So his mother gave him a dog.

The dog was very nice.
It looked exactly like a dog.

Just a Dog

The dog was a lot of trouble,

22

23

but
it was
worth it.

24

THE ENORMOUS CARROT

BY VLADIMIR VAGIN

McGraw Hill

THE ENORMOUS CARROT

McGraw-Hill School Division
New York   Farmington

Early one spring, Daisy and Floyd planted seeds in their garden.

5

Each day, they watered and weeded.

Everything grew exactly as they had planned.

6

7

Then one morning . . .

Daisy and Floyd discovered an enormous carrot
growing in the middle of their garden.

8

9

"This carrot is ready to pick," said Floyd.
So Floyd tried to pull the carrot out of the ground.
But the carrot stayed put.
It wouldn't come out.

"I'll pull it out," said Daisy.
Daisy tried to pull the carrot out of the ground.
But the carrot stayed put.
It wouldn't come out.

10

11

Then Daisy and Floyd tried together
to pull the carrot out of the ground.

They tugged and they lugged.
But the carrot stayed put. It wouldn't come out.

12

13

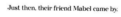

Just then, their friend Mabel came by.

"Will you help us pull this carrot out?" asked Daisy.
"Naturally," said Mabel.

14

15

So Daisy, Floyd, and Mabel tried together
to pull the enormous carrot out of the ground.
They heaved and they ho'd.
But the carrot stayed put. It wouldn't come out.

Just then, their friend Henry came by.
"Will you help us pull this carrot out?" asked Mabel.
"Glad to," said Henry.

16

17

So Daisy, Floyd, Mabel, and Henry tried together
to pull the enormous carrot out of the ground.
They grunted and they groaned.
But the carrot stayed put. It wouldn't come out.

18

Just then, their friend Gloria came by.
"Will you help us pull this carrot out?" asked Henry.
"Absolutely," said Gloria.

19

So Daisy, Floyd, Mabel, Henry, and Gloria
tried together to pull the enormous carrot out of the ground.
They teamed and they towed.
But the carrot stayed put. It wouldn't come out.

20

Just then, their friend Buster came by.
"Will you help us pull this carrot out?" asked Gloria.
"Sure thing," said Buster.

21

So Daisy, Floyd, Mabel, Henry, Gloria, and Buster
tried together to pull the enormous carrot out of the ground.
They stretched and they swayed.
But the carrot stayed put. It wouldn't come out.

22

Just then, their friend Claire came by.
"Will you help us pull this carrot out?" asked Buster.
"I'd be delighted," said Claire.

23

So Daisy, Floyd, Mabel, Henry, Gloria, Buster, and Claire
tried together to pull the enormous carrot out of the ground.
They hollered and they hauled.
But the carrot stayed put. It wouldn't come out.

24

Just then, their friend Lester came by.
"May I help you pull that carrot out?" asked Lester.
"You're much too small!" said Claire.
"Let me try," said Lester.

25

So Daisy, Floyd, Mabel, Henry, Gloria, Buster, Claire, and Lester
tried together to pull the enormous carrot out of the ground.
They tugged and they lugged,
they heaved and they ho'd,
they grunted and they groaned.

26

they teamed and they towed,
they stretched and they swayed,
they hollered and they hauled,
and all at once . . .

27

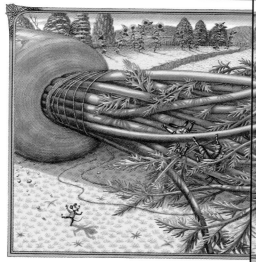

the enormous carrot... CAME OUT!

28

29

Then Daisy, Floyd, Mabel, Henry, Gloria, Buster, Claire, Lester, and all   their friends ate every bit of that enormous carrot until it was all gone.

30

31

That afternoon, Daisy said, "I can't wait to see what comes up tomorrow."
"Neither can I," said Floyd. "But first it's time for an ENORMOUS REST."

32

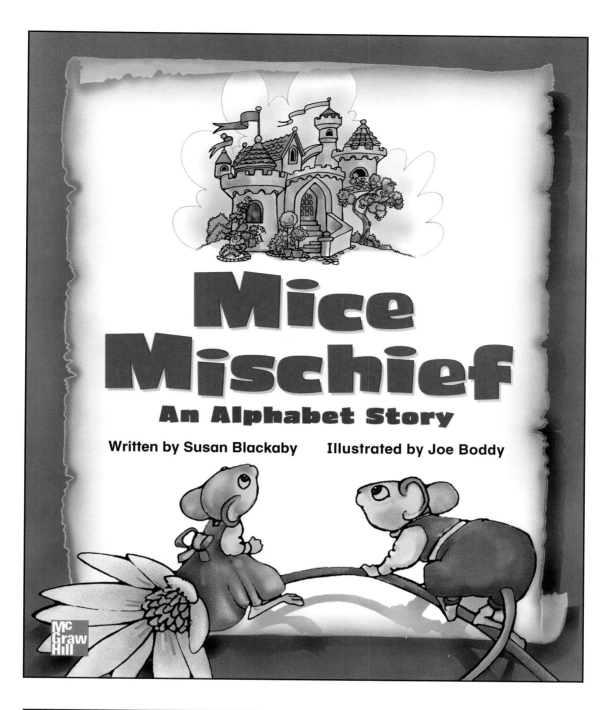

Mice Mischief
An Alphabet Story

Written by Susan Blackaby   Illustrated by Joe Boddy

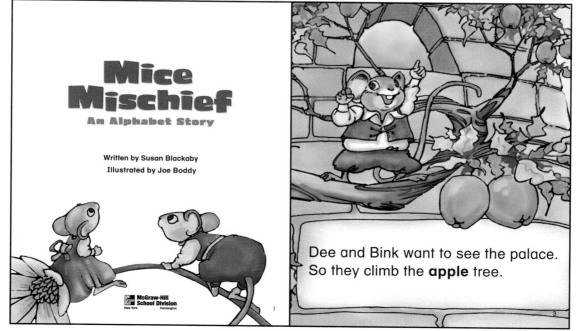

Dee and Bink want to see the palace.
So they climb the **apple** tree.

"Look at the **bed**," said Dee.

"Look at that **cat**!" said Bink.

"Run to the **desk**!" said Dee.

Bink gets stuck on the **edge**.

Dee and Bink hide by the **fan**.
"We must **get** out of here!" said Bink.

Dee gets in the **hat**.
Bink cannot get **in**.

Bink hides behind the **jar**.

The mice run past the **king**.

They run up a **ladder**.

16

17

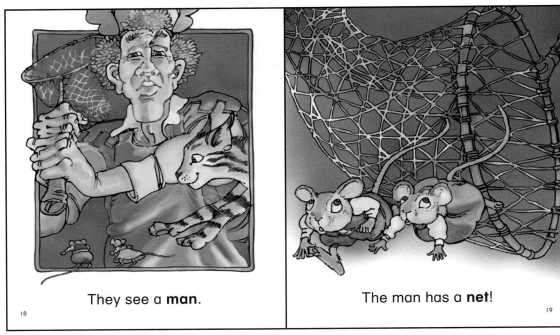

They see a **man**.

18

The man has a **net**!

19

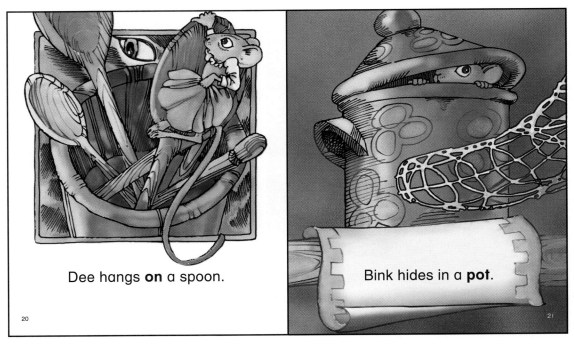

Dee hangs **on** a spoon.

20

Bink hides in a **pot**.

21

They tiptoe **quietly** past the dog.

22

They run under the **rug**.

23

Dee hides by the **salt**.

24

Bink runs across the **table**.

25

Bink hides **under** a napkin.

26

Then Bink tears his **vest**!

27

"Let's try the **window**!" said Dee.

28

29

"I found an **exit**!" said Dee.

30

The mice run across the **yard**.

31

And they **zig-zag** all the way home!

32

Selection Titles

Honors, Prizes, and Awards

 SHOW AND TELL DAY
by **Anne Rockwell**

Author/Ilustrator Anne Rockwell, winner of American Booksellers' Award Pick of the List for *Boats* (1985) and *Cars* (1986); National Science Teachers Association Award for Outstanding Science Trade Book for Children (1988) for *Trains*

CHICK AND THE DUCKLING
by **Mirra Ginsburg**
Illustrated by **Jose Aruego and Ariane Dewey**

Illustrators: Jose Aruego and Ariane Dewey, winners of Boston Globe-Horn Book Honor (1974) for *Herman the Helper*

 FLOWER GARDEN
by **Eve Bunting**
Illustrated by **Kathryn Hewitt**

Author: Eve Bunting, winner of ALA Notable Book (1990), IRA-CBC Children's Choice, IRA-Teachers' Choice, School Library Journal Best Book (1989) for *The Wednesday Surprise;* Mark Twain Award (1989) for *Sixth Grade Sleepover;* ALA Notable (1990) for *Wall;* ALA Notable (1992) for *Fly Away Home;* Edgar Allen Poe Juvenile Award (1993) for *Coffin on a Case;* ALA Notable, Caldecott Medal (1995) for *Smoky Night;* Booklist Editors' Choice (1995) for *Spying on Miss Müller;* ALA Notable, Booklist Editors' Choice (1997) for *Train to Somewhere;* National Council for Social Studies Notable Children's Book Award (1998) for *Moonstick,* and *I Am the Mummy Heb-Nefert,* and *On Call Back Mountain;* Young Reader's Choice Award (1997) for *Nasty Stinky Sneakers*
Illustrator: Kathryn Hewitt, winner of Association of Booksellers for Children, Children's Choice Award (1998) for *Lives of the Athletes: Thrills, Spills (And What the Neighbors Thought);* ALA Notable (1994) Boston Globe-Horn Book Honor (1993) for *Lives of the Musicians: Good Times, Bad Times (and What the Neighbors Thought)*

 PRETEND YOU'RE A CAT
by **Jean Marzolla**
Illustrated by **Jerry Pinkney**

Author: Jean Marzolla, winner of 1998 Association of Booksellers for Children, Children's Choice Award for *I Spy Little Book*
Illustrator: Jerry Pinkney, winner of Coretta Scott King Award, ALA Notable, Christopher Award (1986) for *Patchwork Quilt;* Newbery Medal, Boston Globe-Horn Book Honor (1977) for *Roll of Thunder, Hear My Cry;* Boston Globe-Horn Book Honor (1980) *Childtimes: A Three Generation Memoir;* Coretta Scott King Award (1987) for *Half a Moon and One Whole Star;* ALA Notable (1988) for

Selection Titles	Honors, Prizes, and Awards
 **PRETEND YOU'RE A CAT (CONTINUED)** by ***Jean Marzolla*** Illustrated by ***Jerry Pinkney***	*Tales of Uncle Remus: The Adventures of Brer Rabbit;* ALA Notable, Caldecott Honor, Coretta Scott King Award (1989) for *Mirandy and Brother Wind;* ALA Notable, Caldecott Honor, Coretta Scott King Honor (1990) for *Talking Eggs: A Folktale for the American South;* Golden Kite Award Book (1990) for *Home Place;* ALA Notable (1991) for *Further Tales of Uncle Remus: The Misadventures of Brer Rabbit, Brer Fox ...;* ALA Notable (1993) for *Back Home;* ALA Notable, Boston Globe-Horn Book Award, Caldecott Honor (1995) for *John Henry;* ALA Notable, Blue Ribbon, Booklist Editors' Choice (1997) for *Sam and the Tigers;* ALA Notable, Christopher Award, Coretta Scott King Award, Golden Kite Honor Book (1997) for *Minty: A Story of Young Harriet Tubman;* Aesop Prize (1997) for *The Hired Hand;* National Council for Social Studies Notable Children's Book Award (1998) for *The Hired Hand* and *Rikki-Tikki-Tavi* (also Children's Choice Award, Association of Booksellers for Children, and Booklist Editors' Choice, 1998); Rip Van Winkle Award (1998); 1998 Hans Christian Andersen nominee
 **ANY KIND OF DOG** by ***Lynn Reiser***	**Author/Illustrator: *Lynn Reiser,*** winner of ALA Notable (1995) for *The Surprise Family*
 **THE EARTH AND I** by ***Frank Asch***	**Author/Illustrator: *Frank Asch,*** winner of American Book Award Pick of the List Award (1997) for *Barnyard Animals*

Trade Books

Additional fiction and nonfiction trade books related to each selection can be shared with children throughout the unit.

At the Fire Station
Carol Greene, illustrated by Phil Martin (Child's World, 1997)

Photographs and text show firefighters at work together.

Goodnight, Owl
Pat Hutchins (Macmillan, 1972)

When all the other animals keep Owl awake with their noise, he waits for a chance to take his revenge.

Hummingbird's Gift
Stefan Czernecki (Hyperion Books, 1994)

When Consuelo saves the hummingbirds' lives, they show her how to save her family from drought.

Elephant in a Well
Marie Hall Ets (Viking, 1972)

Several animals cannot pull an elephant from a well until a mouse adds his strength.

Great Big Enormous Turnip
Aleksey N. Tolstoy (Watts, 1968)

After several characters attempt to pull up a turnip, a mouse adds just the right weight to complete the job.

What's the Matter, Habibi?
Betsy Lewin (Clarion, 1997)

When Habibi, the camel, gets loose, Ahmen follows him, trying to figure out what is wrong.

Technology

Multimedia resources can be used to enhance children's understanding of the selections.

The Pigeon Race (BFA Educational Media) Video, 11 min. A group of dolls work together to free a prize race pigeon when it becomes entangled in a telephone wire.

The Wednesday Surprise (Coronet/MTI) Video, 14 min. A seven-year-old girl teaches her grandmother how to read.

The Little Engine That Could (Coronet/MTI) Video, 10 min. The classic story of the little engine that refused to give up.

Rufus M. Try Again (BFA Educational Media) Video, 13 min. Rufus wants to learn to write, no matter how many obstacles he must first overcome.

Mr. Gumpy's Motor Car
John Burningham (Crowell, 1976)

Mr. Gumpy's car passengers join together to help when the vehicle gets stuck.

The Supermarket Mice
Margaret Gordon (Dutton, 1984)

A group of supermarket mice find a way to deal with a new cat in the store.

Roxaboxen
Alice McLerran, illustrated by Barbara Cooney (Lothrop, 1991)

Marian, her sister, and their friends create an imaginary town with rocks and wooden boxes.

The Rag-Tag Champs (Pied Piper) Video, 48 min. A little league captain beats the odds when he gets his team to work together and act as a team.

The Lion and the Mouse (Encyclopedia Britannica Educational Corporation) Video, 13 min. A small mouse helps out a large lion.

Abdo & Daughters
4940 Viking Drive, Suite 622
Edina, MN 55435
(800) 458-8399 • www.abdopub.com

Aladdin Paperbacks
(Imprint of Simon & Schuster Children's
Publishing)

Atheneum
(Imprint of Simon & Schuster Children's
Publishing)

**Bantam Doubleday Dell Books for
Young Readers**
(Imprint of Random House)

Blackbirch Press
1 Bradley Road, Suite 205
Woodbridge, CT 06525
(203) 387-7525 • (800) 831-9183

Blue Sky Press
(Imprint of Scholastic)

Boyds Mills Press
815 Church Street
Honesdale, PA 18431
(570) 253-1164 • Fax (570) 251-0179 •
(800) 949-7777

Bradbury Press
(Imprint of Simon & Schuster Children's
Publishing)

BridgeWater Books
(Distributed by Penguin Putnam)

Candlewick Press
2067 Masssachusetts Avenue
Cambridge, MA 02140
(617) 661-3330 • Fax (617) 661-0565

Carolrhoda Books
(Division of Lerner Publications Co.)

Charles Scribners's Sons
(Imprint of Simon & Schuster Children's
Publishing)

Children's Press (Division of Grolier, Inc.)
P.O. Box 1796
Danbury, CT 06813-1333
(800) 621-1115 • www.grolier.com

Child's World
P.O. Box 326
Chanhassen, MN 55317-0326
(612) 906-3939 • (800) 599-READ •
www.childsworld.com

Chronicle Books
85 Second Street, Sixth Floor
San Francisco, CA 94105
(415) 537-3730 • (415) 537-4460 • (800)
722-6657 • www.chroniclebooks.com

Clarion Books
(Imprint of Houghton Mifflin, Inc.)
215 Park Avenue South
New York, NY 10003
(212) 420-5800 • (800) 726-0600 •
www.hmco.com/trade/childrens/
shelves.html

Crowell (Imprint of HarperCollins)

Crown Publishing Group
(Imprint of Random House)

Dial Books
(Imprint of Penguin Putnam Inc.)

Dorling Kindersley (DK Publishing)
95 Madison Avenue
New York, NY 10016
(212) 213-4800 • Fax (800) 774-6733 •
(888) 342-5357 • www.dk.com

Doubleday (Imprint of Random House)

E. P. Dutton Children's Books
(Imprint of Penguin Putnam Inc.)

Farrar Straus & Giroux
19 Union Square West
New York, NY 10003
(212) 741-6900 • Fax (212) 633-2427 •
(888) 330-8477

Four Winds Press
(Imprint of Macmillan, see Simon &
Schuster Children's Publishing)

Greenwillow Books
(Imprint of William Morrow & Co, Inc.)

Grosset & Dunlap
(Imprint of Penguin Putnam, Inc.)

Harcourt Brace & Co.
525 "B" Street
San Diego, CA 92101
(619) 231-6616 • (800) 543-1918 •
www.harcourtbooks.com

Harper & Row (Imprint of HarperCollins)

HarperCollins Children's Books
10 East 53rd Street
New York, NY 10022
(212) 207-7000 • Fax (212) 202-7044 •
(800) 242-7737 •
www.harperchildrens.com

Henry Holt and Company
115 West 18th Street
New York, NY 10011
(212) 886-9200 • (212) 633-0748 • (888)
330-8477 • www.henryholt.com/byr/

Holiday House
425 Madison Avenue
New York, NY 10017
(212) 688-0085 • Fax (212) 421-6134

Houghton Mifflin
222 Berkeley Street
Boston, MA 02116
(617) 351-5000 • Fax (617) 351-1125 •
(800) 225-3362 • www.hmco.com/trade

Hyperion Books
(Imprint of Buena Vista Publishing Co.)
114 Fifth Avenue
New York, NY 10011
(212) 633-4400 • (800) 759-0190 •
www.disney.com

Ideals Children's Books
(Imprint of Hambleton-Hill Publishing, Inc.)
1501 County Hospital Road
Nashville, TN 37218
(615) 254-2480 • (800) 336-6438

Joy Street Books
(Imprint of Little, Brown & Co.)

Just Us Books
356 Glenwood Avenue
E. Orange, NJ 07017
(973) 672-0304 • Fax (973) 677-7570

Alfred A. Knopf
(Imprint of Random House)

Lee & Low Books
95 Madison Avenue
New York, NY 10016
(212) 779-4400 • Fax (212) 683-1894

Lerner Publications Co.
241 First Avenue North
Minneapolis, MN 55401
(612) 332-3344 • Fax (612) 332-7615 •
(800) 328-4929 • www.lernerbooks.com

Little, Brown & Co.
3 Center Plaza
Boston, MA 02108
(617) 227-0730 • Fax (617) 263-2864 •
(800) 343-9204 • www.littlebrown.com

Lothrop Lee & Shepard
(Imprint of William Morrow & Co.)

Macmillan
(Imprint of Simon & Schuster
Children's Publishing)

Marshall Cavendish
99 White Plains Road
Tarrytown, NY 10591
(914) 332-8888 • Fax (914) 332-1082 •
(800) 821-9881 •
www.marshallcavendish.com

William Morrow & Co.
1350 Avenue of the Americas
New York, NY 10019
(212) 261-6500 • Fax (212) 261-6619 •
(800) 843-9389 •
www.williammorrow.com

Morrow Junior Books
(Imprint of William Morrow & Co.)

Mulberry Books
(Imprint of William Morrow & Co.)

National Geographic Society
1145 17th Street, NW
Washington, DC 20036
(202) 828-5667 • (800) 368-2728 •
www.nationalgeographic.com

Northland Publishing
(Division of Justin Industries)
P.O. Box 62
Flagstaff, AZ 86002
(520) 774-5251 • Fax (800) 257-9082 •
(800) 346-3257 • www.northlandpub.com

North-South Books
1123 Broadway, Suite 800
New York, NY 10010
(212) 463-9736 • Fax (212) 633-1004 •
(800) 722-6657 • www.northsouth.com

Orchard Books (A Grolier Company)
95 Madison Avenue
New York, NY 10016
(212) 951-2600 • Fax (212) 213-6435 •
(800) 621-1115 • www.grolier.com

Owlet (Imprint of Henry Holt & Co.)

Willa Perlman Books
(Imprint of Simon & Schuster
Children's Publishing)

Philomel Books
(Imprint of Putnam Penguin, Inc.)

Puffin Books
(Imprint of Penguin Putnam, Inc.)

G.P. Putnam's Sons Publishing
(Imprint of Penguin Putnam, Inc.)

Penguin Putnam, Inc.
345 Hudson Street
New York, NY 10014
(212) 366-2000 • Fax (212) 366-2666 •
(800) 631-8571 •
www.penguinputnam.com

Random House
201 East 50th Street
New York, NY 10022
(212) 751-2600 • Fax (212) 572-2593 •
(800) 726-0600 • www.randomhouse/kids

Rourke Corporation
P.O. Box 3328
Vero Beach, FL 32964
(561) 234-6001 • (800) 394-7055 •
www.rourkepublishing.com

Scholastic
555 Broadway
New York, NY 10012
(212) 343-6100 • Fax (212) 343-6930 •
(800) SCHOLASTIC • www.scholastic.com

Sierra Junior Club
85 Second Street, Second Floor
San Francisco, CA 94105-3441
(415) 977-5500 • Fax (415) 977-5799 •
(800) 935-1056 • www.sierraclub.org

Simon & Schuster Children's Books
1230 Avenue of the Americas
New York, NY 10020
(212) 698-7200 • (800) 223-2336 •
www.simonsays.com/kidzone

Smith & Kraus
4 Lower Mill Road
N. Stratford, NH 03590
(603) 643-6431 • Fax (603) 643-1831 •
(800) 895-4331 • www.smithkraus.com

Teacher Ideas Press
(Division of Libraries Unlimited)
P.O. Box 6633
Englewood, CO 80155-6633
(303) 770-1220 • Fax (303) 220-8843 •
(800) 237-6124 • www.lu.com

Ticknor & Fields
(Imprint of Houghton Mifflin, Inc.)

Usborne (Imprint of EDC Publishing)
10302 E. 55th Place, Suite B
Tulsa, OK 74146-6515
(918) 622-4522 • (800) 475-4522 •
www.edcpub.com

Viking Children's Books
(Imprint of Penguin Putnam Inc.)

Watts Publishing
(Imprint of Grolier Publishing;
see Children's Press)

Walker & Co.
435 Hudson Street
New York, NY 10014
(212) 727-8300 • (212) 727-0984 • (800)
AT-WALKER

Whispering Coyote Press
300 Crescent Court, Suite 860
Dallas, TX 75201
(800) 929-6104 • Fax (214) 319-7298

Albert Whitman
6340 Oakton Street
Morton Grove, IL 60053-2723
(847) 581-0033 • Fax (847) 581-0039 •
(800) 255-7675 • www.awhitmanco.com

Workman Publishing Co., Inc.
708 Broadway
New York, NY 10003
(212) 254-5900 • Fax (800) 521-1832 •
(800) 722-7202 • www.workman.com

Multimedia Resources

AGC/United Learning
6633 West Howard Street
Niles, IL 60714-3389
(800) 424-0362 • www.unitedlearning.com

AIMS Multimedia
9710 DeSoto Avenue
Chatsworth, CA 91311-4409
(800) 367-2467 •
www.AIMS-multimedia.com

BFA Educational Media
(see Phoenix Learning Group)

Broderbund
(Parsons Technology;
also see The Learning Company)
500 Redwood Blvd
Novato, CA 94997
(800) 521-6263 • Fax (800) 474-8840 •
www.broderbund.com

Carousel Film and Video
260 Fifth Avenue, Suite 705
New York, NY 10001
(212) 683-1660 • e-mail:
carousel@pipeline.com

Cloud 9 Interactive
(888) 662-5683 • www.cloud9int.com

Computer Plus (see ESI)

Coronet/MTI
(see Phoenix Learning Group)

Davidson (see Knowledge Adventure)

Direct Cinema, Ltd.
P.O. Box 10003
Santa Monica, CA 90410-1003
(800) 525-0000

Disney Interactive
(800) 900-9234 •
www.disneyinteractive.com

DK Multimedia (Dorling Kindersley)
95 Madison Avenue
New York, NY 10016
(212) 213-4800 • Fax: (800) 774-6733 •
(888) 342-5357 • www.dk.com

Edmark Corp.
P.O. Box 97021
Redmond, CA 98073-9721
(800) 362-2890 • www.edmark.com

Encyclopaedia Britannica Educational Corp.
310 South Michigan Avenue
Chicago, IL 60604
(800) 554-9862 • www.eb.com

ESI/Educational Software
4213 S. 94th Street
Omaha, NE 68127
(800) 955-5570 • www.edsoft.com

GPN/Reading Rainbow
University of Nebraska-Lincoln
P.O. Box 80669
Lincoln, NE 68501-0669
(800) 228-4630 • www.gpn.unl.edu

Hasbro Interactive
(800) 683-5847 • www.hasbro.com

Humongous
13110 NE 177th Pl., Suite B101, Box 180
Woodenville, WA 98072
(800) 499-8386 • www.humongous.com

IBM Corp.
1133 Westchester Ave.
White Plains, NY 10604
(770) 863-1234 • Fax (770) 863-3030 •
(888) 411-1932 •
www.pc.ibm.com/multimedia/crayola

ICE, Inc.
(Distributed by Arch Publishing)
12B W. Main St.
Elmsford, NY 10523
(914) 347-2464 • (800) 843-9497 •
www.educorp.com

Knowledge Adventure
19840 Pioneer Avenue
Torrence, CA 90503
(800) 542-4240 • (800) 545-7677 •
www.knowledgeadventure.com

The Learning Company
6160 Summit Drive North
Minneapolis, MN 55430
(800) 685-6322 • www.learningco.com

Listening Library
One Park Avenue
Greenwich, CT 06870-1727
(800) 243-4504 • www.listeninglib.com

Macmillan/McGraw-Hill
(see SRA/McGraw-Hill)

Maxis
2121 N. California Blvd
Walnut Creek, CA 94596-3572
(925) 933-5630 • Fax (925) 927-3736 •
(800) 245-4525 • www.maxis.com

MECC
(see the Learning Company)

Microsoft
One Microsoft Way
Redmond, WA 98052-6399
(800) 426-9400 • www.microsoft.com/kids

**National Geographic Society
Educational Services**
P.O. Box 10597
Des Moines, IA 50340-0597
(800) 368-2728 •
www.nationalgeographic.com

National School Products
101 East Broadway
Maryville, TN 37804
(800) 251-9124 • www.ierc.com

PBS Video
1320 Braddock Place
Alexandria, VA 22314
(800) 344-3337 • www.pbs.org

Phoenix Films
(see Phoenix Learning Group)

The Phoenix Learning Group
2348 Chaffee Drive
St. Louis, MO 63146
(800) 221-1274 • e-mail:
phoenixfilms@worldnet.att.net

Pied Piper (see AIMS Multimedia)

Scholastic New Media
555 Broadway
New York, NY 10003
(800) 724-6527 • www.scholastic.com

Simon & Schuster Interactive
(see Knowledge Adventure)

SRA/McGraw-Hill
220 Daniel Dale Road
De Soto, TX 75115
(800) 843-8855 • www.sra4kids.com

SVE/Churchill Media
6677 North Northwest Highway
Chicago, IL 60631
(800) 829-1900 •www.svemedia.com

Tom Snyder Productions (also see ESI)
80 Coolidge Hill Rd.
Watertown, MA 02472
(800) 342-0236 • www.teachtsp.com

Troll Associates
100 Corporate Drive
Mahwah, NJ 07430
(800) 929-8765 • Fax (800) 979-8765 •
www.troll.com

Voyager (see ESI)

Weston Woods
12 Oakwood Avenue
Norwalk, CT 06850
(800) 243-5020 • Fax (203) 845-0498

Zenger Media
10200 Jefferson Blvd., Room 94,
P.O. Box 802
Culver City, CA 90232-0802
(800) 421-4246 • (800) 944-5432 •
www.Zengermedia.com

UNIT 1

	Decodable Words				Vocabulary
THE HOUSE					High-Frequency Words the
A PRESENT					High-Frequency Words a
MY SCHOOL					High-Frequency Words my
NAN	an	**Nan**			High-Frequency Words that
THAT NAN!	Review				High-Frequency Words Review

UNIT 2

	Decodable Words				Vocabulary
DAN AND DAD	**Dad**	**Dan**			High-Frequency Words and
DAD, DAN, AND I	**sad**				High-Frequency Words I
I AM SAM!	**am** dam	mad	man	**Sam**	High-Frequency Words is
SID SAID	did dim	in	**Min**	**Sid**	High-Frequency Words said
IS SAM MAD?	Review				High-Frequency Words Review

Boldfaced words appear in the selection.

UNIT 3

	Decodable Words				Vocabulary
THAT TAM!					**High-Frequency Words**
	at	Nat	**Tam**	**Tim**	we
	it	**sat**	tan	tin	
	mat	**sit**			
NAT IS MY CAT					**High-Frequency Words**
	can	**cat**			are
ON THE DOT					**High-Frequency Words**
	cot	**dot**	**not**	**Tom**	you
	Dom	**Mom**	**on**	tot	
	Don				
WE FIT!					**High-Frequency Words**
	fan	fat	fin	**fit**	have
THE TAN CAT					**High-Frequency Words**
	Review				Review

UNIT 4

	Decodable Words				Vocabulary
YOU ARE IT!					**High-Frequency Words**
	ran	rod	**Ron**	rot	**to**
	rat				
TAP THE SAP					**High-Frequency Words**
	cap	pad	pod	**sip**	me
	dip	**Pam**	**pot**	**tap**	
	map	**pan**	rip	tip	
	mop	pat	**sap**	**top**	
	nap				
NAP IN A LAP					**High-Frequency Words**
	lad	lid	lit	lot	go
	lap	lip			
MUD FUN					**High-Frequency Words**
	cup	**mud**	run	sun	do
	cut	nut	rut	up	
	fun	pup			
FUN IN THE SUN					**High-Frequency Words**
	Review				Review

UNIT 5

	Decodable Words				Vocabulary

TOM IS SICK

				High-Frequency Words
dock	lock	**pick**	**sock**	**for**
duck	luck	rack	tack	
kid	Mack	rock	tick	
Kim	Mick	sack	tock	
kit	muck	**sick**	tuck	
lick	pack			

PUG

				High-Frequency Words
dug	gum	**Pug**	tag	**he**
fog	log	rag	tug	
got	**mug**	rug		

A PET FOR KEN

				High-Frequency Words
den	leg	Ned	**red**	**she**
fed	**let**	net	set	
get	Meg	pen	Ted	
Ken	men	**pet**	ten	
led	met			

A BIG BUG

				High-Frequency Words
bad	bet	bog	cub	**has**
bag	**big**	bud	Rob	
bat	bin	**bug**	rub	
bed	bit	but	tub	
Ben				

A PUP AND A CAT

	High-Frequency Words
Review	Review

UNIT 6

	Decodable Words			Vocabulary

HOP WITH A HOG

				High-Frequency Words
had	him	**hog**	**hug**	with
ham	hip	**hop**	**hum**	
hat	**hit**	hot	hut	
hen				

WE WIN!

				High-Frequency Words
wag	wed	wig	**win**	was
web	wet			

THE VET VAN

				High-Frequency Words
ax	fox	ox	**van**	not
box	**Max**	**Rex**	**vet**	
fix	mix	six	wax	

JEN AND YIP

				High-Frequency Words
jam	job	quit	yum	of
Jan	**jog**	yam	Zack	
Jen	jot	yet	Zeb	
jet	jug	**Yip**	**zigzag**	
jig	**quack**	yuck	zip	
Jim	**quick**			

ZACK AND JAN

	High-Frequency Words
Review	Review

Listening, Speaking, Viewing, Representing

☑ Tested Skill

☐ Tinted panels show skills, strategies, and other teaching opportunities

LISTENING

	K	1	2	3	4	5	6
Learn the vocabulary of school (numbers, shapes, colors, directions, and categories)							
Identify the musical elements of literary language, such as rhymes, repeated sounds, onomatopoeia							
Determine purposes for listening (get information, solve problems, enjoy and appreciate)							
Listen critically and responsively							
Ask and answer relevant questions							
Listen critically to interpret and evaluate							
Listen responsively to stories and other texts read aloud, including selections from classic and contemporary works							
Connect own experiences, ideas, and traditions with those of others							
Apply comprehension strategies in listening activities							
Understand the major ideas and supporting evidence in spoken messages							
Participate in listening activities related to reading and writing (such as discussions, group activities, conferences)							
Listen to learn by taking notes, organizing, and summarizing spoken ideas							

SPEAKING

	K	1	2	3	4	5	6
Learn the vocabulary of school (numbers, shapes, colors, directions, and categories)							
Use appropriate language and vocabulary learned to describe ideas, feelings, and experiences							
Ask and answer relevant questions							
Communicate effectively in everyday situations (such as discussions, group activities, conferences)							
Demonstrate speaking skills (audience, purpose, occasion, volume, pitch, tone, rate, fluency)							
Clarify and support spoken messages and ideas with objects, charts, evidence, elaboration, examples							
Use verbal and nonverbal communication in effective ways when, for example, making announcements, giving directions, or making introductions							
Retell a spoken message by summarizing or clarifying							
Connect own experiences, ideas, and traditions with those of others							
Determine purposes for speaking (inform, entertain, give directions, persuade, express personal feelings and opinions)							
Demonstrate skills of reporting and providing information							
Demonstrate skills of interviewing, requesting and providing information							
Apply composition strategies in speaking activities							
Monitor own understanding of spoken message and seek clarification as needed							

VIEWING

	K	1	2	3	4	5	6
Demonstrate viewing skills (focus attention, organize information)							
Respond to audiovisual media in a variety of ways							
Participate in viewing activities related to reading and writing							
Apply comprehension strategies in viewing activities							
Recognize artists' craft and techniques for conveying meaning							
Interpret information from various formats such as maps, charts, graphics, video segments, technology							
Evaluate purposes of various media (information, appreciation, entertainment, directions, persuasion)							
Use media to compare ideas and points of view							

REPRESENTING

	K	1	2	3	4	5	6
Select, organize, or produce visuals to complement or extend meanings							
Produce communication using appropriate media to develop a class paper, multimedia or video reports							
Show how language, medium, and presentation contribute to the message							

Reading: Alphabetic Principle, Sounds/Symbols

☑ Tested Skill

Tinted panels show skills, strategies, and other teaching opportunities

	K	1	2	3	4	5	6
PRINT AWARENESS							
Know the order of the alphabet							
Recognize that print represents spoken language and conveys meaning							
Understand directionality (tracking print from left to right; return sweep)							
Understand that written words are separated by spaces							
Know the difference between individual letters and printed words							
Understand that spoken words are represented in written language by specific sequence of letters							
Recognize that there are correct spellings for words							
Know the difference between capital and lowercase letters							
Recognize how readers use capitalization and punctuation to comprehend							
Recognize the distinguishing features of a paragraph							
Recognize that parts of a book (such as cover/title page and table of contents) offer information							
PHONOLOGICAL AWARENESS							
Identify letters, words, sentences							
Divide spoken sentence into individual words							
Produce rhyming words and distinguish rhyming words from nonrhyming words							
Identify, segment, and combine syllables within spoken words							
Identify and isolate the initial and final sound of a spoken word							
Add, delete, or change sounds to change words (such as *cow* to *how*, *pan* to *fan*)							
Blend sounds to make spoken words							
Segment one-syllable spoken words into individual phonemes							
PHONICS AND DECODING							
Alphabetic principle: Letter/sound correspondence	☑	☑	☑				
Blending CVC words	☑						
Segmenting CVC words	☑						
Blending CVC, CVCe, CCVC, CVCC, CVVC words	☑	☑	☑				
Segmenting CVC, CVCe, CCVC, CVCC, CVVC words	☑	☑	☑				
Initial and final consonants: /n/n, /d/d, /s/s, /m/m, /t/t, /k/c, /f/f, /r/r, /p/p, /l/l, /k/k, /g/g, /b/b, /h/h, /w/w, /v/v, /ks/x, /kw/qu, /j/j, /y/y, /z/z	☑	☑					
Initial and medial short vowels: *a, i, u, o, e*	☑	☑	☑				
Long vowels: *a-e, i-e, o-e, u-e* (vowel-consonant-e)		☑	☑				
Long vowels, including *ay, ai; e, ee, ie, ea, o, oa, oe, ow; i, y, igh*		☑	☑				
Consonant Digraphs: *sh, th, ch, wh*		☑					
Consonant Blends: continuant/continuant, including *sl, sm, sn, fl, fr, ll, ss, ff*		☑					
Consonant Blends: continuant/stop, including *st, sk, sp, ng, nt, nd, mp, ft*		☑					
Consonant Blends: stop/continuant, including *tr, pr, pl, cr, tw*		☑					
Variant vowels: including /u/*oo*; /ô/*a, aw, au*; /ü/*ue, ew*		☑	☑				
Diphthongs, including /ou/*ou*, *ow*; /oi/*oi, oy*		☑	☑				
r-controlled vowels, including /âr/*are*; /ôr/*or, ore*; /îr/*ear*			☑				
Soft *c* and soft *g*			☑				
nk		☑	☑				
Consonant Digraphs: *ck*	☑	☑					
Consonant Digraphs: *ph, tch, ch*			☑				
Short *e: ea*			☑				
Long *e: y, ey*			☑				
/ü/*oo*			☑				
/är/*ar*; /ûr/*ir, ur, er*		☑	☑				
Silent letters: including *l, b, k, w, g, h, gh*			☑				
Schwa: /ər/*er*; /ən/*en*; /əl/*le*;			☑				
Reading/identifying multisyllabic words		☑	☑				

Reading: Vocabulary/Word Identification

☑ Tested Skill

Tinted panels show skills, strategies, and other teaching opportunities

WORD STRUCTURE	K	1	2	3	4	5	6
Common spelling patterns							
Syllable patterns							
Plurals							
Possessives							
Contractions							
Root, or base, words and inflectional endings (-s, -es, -ed, -ing)							
Compound Words							
Prefixes and suffixes (such as un-, re-, dis-, non-; -ly, -y, -ful, -able, -tion)							
Root words and derivational endings							

WORD MEANING	K	1	2	3	4	5	6
Develop vocabulary through concrete experiences							
Develop vocabulary through selections read aloud							
Develop vocabulary through reading							
Cueing systems: syntactic, semantic, phonetic							
Context clues, including semantic clues (word meaning), syntactical clues (word order), and phonetic clues	☑	☑	☑	☑	☑	☑	☑
High-frequency words (such as the, a, an, and, said, was, where, is)							
Identify words that name persons, places, things, and actions							
Automatic reading of regular and irregular words							
Use resources and references dictionary, glossary, thesaurus, synonym finder, technology and software, and context)							
Synonyms and antonyms							
Multiple-meaning words							
Figurative language							
Decode derivatives (root words, such as like, pay, happy with affixes, such as dis-, pre-, -un)							
Systematic study of words across content areas and in current events							
Locate meanings, pronunciations, and derivations (including dictionaries, glossaries, and other sources)							
Denotation and connotation							
Word origins as aid to understanding historical influences on English word meanings							
Homophones, homographs							
Analogies							
Idioms							

Reading: Comprehension

PREREADING STRATEGIES	K	1	2	3	4	5	6
Preview and Predict							
Use prior knowledge							
Establish and adjust purposes for reading							
Build background							

MONITORING STRATEGIES	K	1	2	3	4	5	6
Adjust reading rate							
Reread, search for clues, ask questions, ask for help							
Visualize							
Read a portion aloud, use reference aids							
Use decoding and vocabulary strategies							
Paraphrase							
Create story maps, diagrams, charts, story props to help comprehend, analyze, synthesize and evaluate texts							

(continued on next page)

☑ Tested Skill

☐ Tinted panels show skills, strategies, and other teaching opportunities

SKILLS AND STRATEGIES	K	1	2	3	4	5	6
Story details	☑						
Use illustrations	☑	☑					
Reality and fantasy	☑	☑	☑	☑			
Classify and categorize	☑						
Make predictions	☑	☑	☑	☑	☑	☑	☑
Sequence of events (tell or act out)	☑	☑	☑	☑	☑	☑	☑
Cause and effect			☑	☑	☑	☑	☑
Compare and contrast	☑	☑	☑	☑	☑	☑	☑
Summarize	☑	☑	☑	☑	☑	☑	☑
Make and explain inferences			☑	☑	☑	☑	☑
Draw conclusions			☑	☑	☑	☑	☑
Important and unimportant information				☑	☑	☑	☑
Main idea and supporting details	☑	☑	☑	☑	☑	☑	☑
Form conclusions or generalizations and support with evidence from text			☑	☑	☑	☑	☑
Fact and opinion (including news stories and advertisements)			☑	☑	☑	☑	☑
Problem and solution			☑	☑	☑	☑	☑
Steps in a process		☑	☑	☑	☑	☑	☑
Make judgments and decisions					☑	☑	☑
Fact and nonfact					☑	☑	☑
Recognize techniques of persuasion and propaganda					☑	☑	☑
Evaluate evidence and sources of information					☑	☑	☑
Identify similarities and differences across texts (including topics, characters, problems, themes, treatment, scope, or organization)							
Practice various questions and tasks (test-like comprehension questions)							
Paraphrase and summarize to recall, inform, and organize							
Answer various types of questions (open-ended, literal, interpretive, test-like such as true-false, multiple choice, short-answer)							
Use study strategies to learn and recall (preview, question, reread, and record)							
LITERARY RESPONSE							
Listen to stories being read aloud							
React, speculate, join in, read along when predictable and patterned selections are read aloud							
Respond through talk, movement, music, art, drama, and writing to a variety of stories and poems							
Show understanding through writing, illustrating, developing demonstrations, and using technology							
Connect ideas and themes across texts							
Support responses by referring to relevant aspects of text and own experiences							
Offer observations, make connections, speculate, interpret, and raise questions in response to texts							
Interpret text ideas through journal writing, discussion, enactment, and media							
TEXT STRUCTURE/LITERARY CONCEPTS							
Distinguish forms of texts and the functions they serve (lists, newsletters, signs)							
Understand story structure							
Identify narrative (for entertainment) and expository (for information)							
Distinguish fiction from nonfiction, including fact and fantasy							
Understand literary forms (stories, poems, plays, and informational books)							
Understand literary terms by distinguishing between roles of author and illustrator							
Understand title, author, and illustrator across a variety of texts							
Analyze character, character's point of view, plot, setting, style, tone, mood		☑	☑	☑	☑	☑	☑
Compare communication in different forms							
Understand terms such as *title, author, illustrator, playwright, theater, stage, act, dialogue,* and *scene*							
Recognize stories, poems, myths, folktales, fables, tall tales, limericks, plays, biographies, and autobiographies							
Judge internal logic of story text							
Recognize that authors organize information in specific ways							
Identify texts to inform, influence, express, or entertain							
Describe how author's point of view affects text							
Recognize biography, historical fiction, realistic fiction, modern fantasy, informational texts, and poetry							
Analyze ways authors present ideas (cause/effect, compare/contrast, inductively, deductively, chronologically)							
Recognize flashback, foreshadowing, symbolism							

(continued on next page)

(Reading: Comprehension continued)

VARIETY OF TEXT	K	1	2	3	4	5	6
Read a variety of genres							
Use informational texts to acquire information							
Read for a variety of purposes							
Select varied sources when reading for information or pleasure							
FLUENCY							
Read regularly in independent-level and instructional-level materials							
Read orally with fluency from familiar texts							
Self-select independent-level reading							
Read silently for increasing periods of time							
Demonstrate characteristics of fluent and effective reading							
Adjust reading rate to purpose							
Read aloud in selected texts, showing understanding of text and engaging the listener							
CULTURES							
Connect own experience with culture of others							
Compare experiences of characters across cultures							
Articulate and discuss themes and connections that cross cultures							
CRITICAL THINKING							
Experiences (comprehend, apply, analyze, synthesize, evaluate)							
Make connections (comprehend, apply, analyze, synthesize, evaluate)							
Expression (comprehend, apply, analyze, synthesize, evaluate)							
Inquiry (comprehend, apply, analyze, synthesize, evaluate)							
Problem solving (comprehend, apply, analyze, synthesize, evaluate)							
Making decisions (comprehend, apply, analyze, synthesize, evaluate)							

Study Skills

INQUIRY/RESEARCH	K	1	2	3	4	5	6
Follow directions							
Use alphabetical order							
Identify/frame questions for research							
Obtain, organize, and summarize information: classify, take notes, outline							
Evaluate research and raise new questions							
Use technology to present information in various formats							
Follow accepted formats for writing research, including documenting sources							
Use test-taking strategies							
Use text organizers (book cover; title page—title, author, illustrator; contents; headings; glossary; index)		☑	☑	☑	☑	☑	☑
Use graphic aids, including maps, diagrams, charts, graphs		☑	☑	☑	☑	☑	☑
Read and interpret varied texts including environmental print, signs, lists, encyclopedia, dictionary, glossary, newspaper, advertisement, magazine, calendar, directions, floor plans		☑	☑	☑	☑	☑	☑
Use reference sources, such as glossary, dictionary, encyclopedia, telephone directory, technology resources		☑	☑	☑	☑	☑	☑
Recognize Library/Media center resources, such as computerized references; catalog search—subject, author, title; encyclopedia index		☑	☑	☑	☑	☑	☑

Writing

MODES AND FORMS	K	1	2	3	4	5	6
Interactive writing							
Personal narrative (Expressive narrative)			☑	☑	☑	☑	☑
Writing that compares (Informative classificatory)			☑	☑	☑	☑	☑
Explanatory writing (Informative narrative)		☑	☑	☑	☑	☑	☑
Persuasive writing (Persuasive descriptive)			☑	☑	☑	☑	☑
Writing a story		☑	☑	☑	☑	☑	☑
Expository writing		☑	☑	☑	☑	☑	☑
Write using a variety of formats, such as advertisement, autobiography, biography, book report/report, comparison-contrast, critique/review/editorial, description, essay, how-to, interview, invitation, journal/log/notes, message/list, paragraph/multi-paragraph composition, picture book, play (scene), poem/rhyme, story, summary, note, letter							

PURPOSES/AUDIENCES	K	1	2	3	4	5	6
Dictate messages such as news and stories for others to write							
Write labels, notes, and captions for illustrations, possessions, charts, and centers							
Write to record, to discover and develop ideas, to inform, to influence, to entertain							
Exhibit an identifiable voice in personal narratives and stories							
Use literary devices (suspense, dialogue, and figurative language)							
Produce written texts by organizing ideas, using effective transitions, and choosing precise wording							

PROCESSES	K	1	2	3	4	5	6
Generate ideas for self-selected and assigned topics using prewriting strategies							
Develop drafts							
Revise drafts for varied purposes							
Edit for appropriate grammar, spelling, punctuation, and features of polished writings							
Proofread own writing and that of others							
Bring pieces to final form and "publish" them for audiences							
Use technology to compose text							
Select and use reference materials and resources for writing, revising, and editing final drafts							

SPELLING	K	1	2	3	4	5	6
Spell own name and write high-frequency words							
Words with short vowels (including CVC and one-syllable words with blends CCVC, CVCC, CCVCC)							
Words with long vowels (including CVCe)							
Words with digraphs, blends, consonant clusters, double consonants							
Words with diphthongs							
Words with variant vowels							
Words with r-controlled vowels							
Words with /ər/, /əl/, and /ən/							
Words with silent letters							
Words with soft c and soft g							
Inflectional endings (including plurals and past tense and words that drop the final e when adding -ing, -ed)							
Compound words							
Contractions							
Homonyms							
Suffixes including -able, -ly, or -less, and prefixes including dis-, re-, pre-, or un-							
Spell words ending in -tion and -sion, such as station and procession							
Accurate spelling of root or base words							
Orthographic patterns and rules such as keep/can; sack/book; out/now; oil/toy; match/speech; ledge/cage; consonant doubling, dropping e, changing y to i							
Multisyllabic words using regularly spelled phonogram patterns							
Syllable patterns (including closed, open, syllable boundary patterns)							
Synonyms and antonyms							
Words from Social Studies, Science, Math, and Physical Education							
Words derived from other languages and cultures							
Use resources to find correct spellings, synonyms, and replacement words							
Use conventional spelling of familiar words in writing assignments							
Spell accurately in final drafts							

(continued on next page)

(Writing continued)

GRAMMAR AND USAGE

	K	1	2	3	4	5	6
Understand sentence concepts (word order, statements, questions, exclamations, commands)							
Recognize complete and incomplete sentences							
Nouns (common; proper; singular; plural; irregular plural; possessives)							
Verbs (action; helping; linking; irregular)							
Verb tense (present, past, future, perfect, and progressive)							
Pronouns (possessive, subject and object, pronoun-verb agreement)							
Use objective case pronouns accurately							
Adjectives							
Adverbs that tell how, when, where							
Subjects, predicates							
Subject-verb agreement							
Sentence combining							
Recognize sentence structure (simple, compound, complex)							
Synonyms and antonyms							
Contractions							
Conjunctions							
Prepositions and prepositional phrases							

PENMANSHIP

	K	1	2	3	4	5	6
Write each letter of alphabet (capital and lowercase) using correct formation, appropriate size and spacing							
Write own name and other important words							
Use phonological knowledge to map sounds to letters to write messages							
Write messages that move left to right, top to bottom							
Gain increasing control of penmanship, pencil grip, paper position, beginning stroke							
Use word and letter spacing and margins to make messages readable							
Write legibly by selecting cursive or manuscript as appropriate							

MECHANICS

	K	1	2	3	4	5	6
Use capitalization in sentences, proper nouns, titles, abbreviations and the pronoun *I*							
Use end marks correctly (period, question mark, exclamation point)							
Use commas (in dates, in addresses, in a series, in letters, in direct address)							
Use apostrophes in contractions and possessives							
Use quotation marks							
Use hyphens, semicolons, colons							

EVALUATION

	K	1	2	3	4	5	6
Identify the most effective features of a piece of writing using class/teacher generated criteria							
Respond constructively to others' writing							
Determine how his/her own writing achieves its purpose							
Use published pieces as models for writing							
Review own written work to monitor growth as writer							

For more detailed scope and sequence including page numbers and additional phonics information, see McGraw-Hill Reading Program scope and sequence (K-6)

Scoring Chart

The Scoring Chart is provided for your convenience in grading your students' work.

- Find the column that shows the total number of items.
- Find the row that matches the number of items answered correctly.
- The intersection of the two rows provides the percentage score.

TOTAL NUMBER OF ITEMS

NUMBER CORRECT	1	2	3	4	5	6	7	8	9	10	11	12	13	14	15	16	17	18	19	20	21	22	23	24	25	26	27	28	29	30
1	100	50	33	25	20	17	14	13	11	10	9	8	8	7	7	6	6	6	5	5	5	5	4	4	4	4	4	4	3	3
2		100	66	50	40	33	29	25	22	20	18	17	15	14	13	13	12	11	11	10	10	9	9	8	8	8	7	7	7	7
3			100	75	60	50	43	38	33	30	27	25	23	21	20	19	18	17	16	15	14	14	13	13	12	12	11	11	10	10
4				100	80	67	57	50	44	40	36	33	31	29	27	25	24	22	21	20	19	18	17	17	16	15	15	14	14	13
5					100	83	71	63	56	50	45	42	38	36	33	31	29	28	26	25	24	23	22	21	20	19	19	18	17	17
6						100	86	75	67	60	55	50	46	43	40	38	35	33	32	30	29	27	26	25	24	23	22	21	21	20
7							100	88	78	70	64	58	54	50	47	44	41	39	37	35	33	32	30	29	28	27	26	25	24	23
8								100	89	80	73	67	62	57	53	50	47	44	42	40	38	36	35	33	32	31	30	29	28	27
9									100	90	82	75	69	64	60	56	53	50	47	45	43	41	39	38	36	35	33	32	31	30
10										100	91	83	77	71	67	63	59	56	53	50	48	45	43	42	40	38	37	36	34	33
11											100	92	85	79	73	69	65	61	58	55	52	50	48	46	44	42	41	39	38	37
12												100	92	86	80	75	71	67	63	60	57	55	52	50	48	46	44	43	41	40
13													100	93	87	81	76	72	68	65	62	59	57	54	52	50	48	46	45	43
14														100	93	88	82	78	74	70	67	64	61	58	56	54	52	50	48	47
15															100	94	88	83	79	75	71	68	65	63	60	58	56	54	52	50
16																100	94	89	84	80	76	73	70	67	64	62	59	57	55	53
17																	100	94	89	85	81	77	74	71	68	65	63	61	59	57
18																		100	95	90	86	82	78	75	72	69	67	64	62	60
19																			100	95	90	86	83	79	76	73	70	68	66	63
20																				100	95	91	87	83	80	77	74	71	69	67
21																					100	95	91	88	84	81	78	75	72	70
22																						100	96	92	88	85	81	79	76	73
23																							100	96	92	88	85	82	79	77
24																								100	96	92	89	86	83	80
25																									100	96	93	89	86	83
26																										100	96	93	90	87
27																											100	96	93	90
28																												100	97	93
29																													100	97
30																														100

Notes

Notes

Notes

Notes